HARE

&

HOUNDS

The Aldenham Harriers

by

ERIC EDWARDS

First published November 2002 by
The Book Castle
12 Church Street
Dunstable
Bedfordshire LU5 4RU

ISBN 1 903747 32 5

Typeset by The Yellow Yoyo Company Ltd, The Studio, Barn Cottage,
Brownlow Avenue, Edlesborough, Bedfordshire, LU6 2JE. amanda@yoyo.co.uk
Printed by Antony Rowe Ltd, Bumper's Farm, Chippenham, Wiltshire

Cover artwork incorporates a watercolour specially commissioned
from Elizabeth Ansell

CONTENTS

"I believe I may say that neither precision nor perspicuity is deficient and I offer my volume to the public under the fullest confidence that the few instances which may subject it to criticism will be treated with that liberality and candour which an enlightened nation ever evinces towards works, not of fancy, but intended to diffuse knowledge amongst the numerous and respectable individuals."

Captain Thomas Williamson
'Wild Sports of the East' -1807

Sponsors

Publication of this book would not have been possible without generous assistance from

The Lord Aldenham

The Lady Aldenham - Trustee & Past Master

Mary Arikoglu MH - Master

Valerie Barr - Past Master

Amanda Bishop - Hon. Secretary

Martyn Bishop - Hon. Treasurer

Patrick Burgin - Past Master

Derek Christopher - Trustee & Past Master

Basil Hall - Trustee & Past Master

Andrew Love MH - Master

Ian Pearse MFH - Past Master & Huntsman

Jeremy Quin MH - Master & Huntsman

Roger & Maggie Smith

Nigel, Giles & Laura Tully

"Tell me, in what context do you see the picture?"
"Well, I suppose the hare could be somewhere about Stags End and she
has just heard hounds." "Just how I intended it to be."
From an original watercolour painted by Gordon Beningfield for
Derek Christopher (Facing page 1)

INTRODUCTION

by

Admiral Sir James Eberle GCB., MH.
(Chairman of the Association of Masters
of Harriers & Beagles)

At the very time that this excellent and entertaining book is being completed, the hunting community of Britain is locked in a struggle to preserve a cultural tradition of the countryside whose history goes back for many centuries. We are engaged with the Government in a 'consultation' on the hunting issues of 'cruelty' and 'utility' - more properly described as 'animal welfare' and 'value'. On the 'cruelty' issue, we are in a position to note that neither of the two Government independent enquiries of recent years, Scott Henderson and Burns, has found any grounds for banning hunting on the basis of animal welfare. The interpretation of the positive and negative welfare aspects for both domestic and wild animals is a complex process. Nevertheless, there is ample evidence to indicate that a hunting ban would result in an increase of suffering - and not only amongst the wild and quarry species.

The issue of 'value' is similarly complex, involving the economic, social and cultural aspects of rural life. For an understanding of these latter issues in respect of the future, it is necessary to be familiar with what has gone before. This book provides an outstanding account of the last one hundred and twenty five years of a community living in an important part of England near London. It is a very detailed account, involving a very great deal of painstaking research, and is thus important, because such detail is the 'stuff' of which history is made. It is also thoroughly readable, because it contains many contemporary descriptions and illustrations of what was going on in the social life of the countryside; as well as in the thrills and spills of the hunting field.

The book is the more important because it is written by someone who has "never hunted, killed or shot any living thing". Yet the author shows a remarkably clear understanding of the 'weft and warp' of the fascination of hunting, which so passionately fills the lives of so many people from all walks of life. His first chapter, "Setting the Scene" deserves to be very widely read, not only by those whose primary interest lies with the Aldenham Harriers and the Hertfordshire area, but also by those living elsewhere in the kingdom who wish to understand better what the 'great hunting debate' is all about. The book might very well be sub-titled '(A case study for an understanding of the values of hunting)'.

[Note: *Admiral Sir James Eberle has for 45 seasons been continuously and closely connected, as whipper-in, Huntsman and Master, with the Britannia Beagles, a pack that was founded by officers of the Royal Naval College at Dartmouth in the same year that saw the founding of the Aldenham Harriers.*]

SETTING THE SCENE

"Did I ever tell you the story of the man who tied
a pink ribbon round a lion's neck with a little bow
on top, read it poetry, and fed it on vegiburgers?"
"No grandpa, what did the lion do?"
"It ate him!"

I like hare.

I like it in all its manifestations.

I like it as one of God's more cuddly creatures; one that has few vices on the face of it, apart that is from an unfortunate habit of eating its own droppings and a tendency to box with its mate at courting time. It also tends to be a touch promiscuous and to nurture a fixed opinion that farmers grow crops specifically for its benefit.

I enjoy watching the hare going about its daily business and I am not best pleased if anything, or anybody, interferes with it. It is a simple creature that does not interfere with any other species and it seems indecent to molest it, but life, anybody's life, is not as simple as that.

For instance I also like it jugged or braised in a casserole with plenty of herbs and vegetables, and I particularly like it in sizeable chunks in a game pie. The hare is good eating, though a little 'strong' perhaps to the modern palate (weakened as it is with an intake of fast food), but a great delicacy to those who remember happier times!

I claim never to have hunted, killed or shot any living thing. Admittedly I have fished, once I think, when the fly was selected for me, I was shown where to dangle my hook, and when, after a while, I got a bite, I was helped to reel in my trout, so it suits me to believe that, proud as I was, that does not really count. Also I do a lot of gardening where occasionally, just occasionally, and entirely by accident, I cut a worm in half when digging and I always regret doing it, though I am told both ends survive. On the other hand I have to admit that I object when wild things interfere with my crops. I jump on slugs and snails, I spray blackfly, I happily crush lily beetles between finger and thumb whenever I come across one.

Ah! I sense a reader cry, but what about the twelve bore. Well, the truth of it is that when I was doing my National Service in Northern Ireland I invested the money I had put aside for the fare home in a one third share of a shot gun, fully intending to kill things in wild places. In the event, strained circumstances overtook me and I sold out my interest to the Flight Sergeant before I had a chance to fire a shot. And yet, I regard myself as a nature lover. In my calmer moments I am a birdwatcher, a member of RSPB since God knows when.

I have never owned a dog - nothing whatever against them, in fact I like and admire them enormously, but my wife is allergic to their fur and between them and her there is no contest. Neither do I ride a horse, though I did once ride an enormous, albeit good tempered one for six miles in Ireland in my youth. I had missed the last bus back to Killarney from Macgillycuddys Reeks and a local, believe it or not with one cycle clip on and sucking a straw, offered me a ride on one of the two horses he held by a rope for £1. I accepted with enthusiasm because the alternative was to walk. The friendly owner followed on his bicycle to keep an eye on me, and the horse, and to persuade the animal into being sensible about the route, but my nether regions suffered agonies for two days afterwards and sitting down was out of the question. Perhaps I may be forgiven for being reluctant to repeat the experience, though I have had invitations which I have successfully resisted. Presumably the bottoms of the followers of the Aldenham Harriers are made of sterner stuff!

In hunting circles I am an outsider; I do not speak or think as one who rides to hounds. My vocabulary on hunting matters will prove the point in the pages that follow, but that does not impede my understanding of what motivates them. In some ways I wish that I was motivated in that way because of the very obvious enjoyment that they get out of it.

Having made these points, I can sense the reader asking *"then how on earth can he be so presumptuous as to attempt to write a book about the Aldenham Harriers?"* Admittedly that is something of a paradox and I cannot really explain it except that I was invited to do it and accepted with enthusiasm on the grounds that I had already written A *New History of Flamstead* (where the hounds are kennelled) and *Friars Wash Point-to-Point Races* so had a little background knowledge of the subject. Also I was intrigued by the passionate anti-hunting propaganda then being put about and puzzled as to why I could not understand what all the fuss was about. Here was a way to find out. In any case I was keen to put on record detail about the activities of the Aldenham that could not be found anywhere else and would otherwise be lost forever. Then there is the point that matters connected with hunting in one form or another figure large in country life and although I am not, strictly speaking, a countryman, I was born and spent my first twenty years on the edge of the country, I have lived for the past thirty years in it and my father was the last Hemel Hempstead saddler (W.D.Edwards, King's Arms Yard), so perhaps I may qualify. If further credentials are needed, I have to admit that I find watching a hunt in full cry exhilarating, indeed it is a very pleasing spectacle to me even when it is at rest. It is picturesque, it appeals to my romantic notion of 'Old England'.

Still endeavouring to justify my temerity in writing about a subject that I am something of a stranger to, (journalists do it all the time after all) there is also the little matter of objectivity; I have no place in the hunting circle, I do not share their passions, I do not see things the way they do. I am an outsider; I am not biased for or against what they do, but I seek to record the situation as it is and has been, in a truthful and logical way. Indeed it could be argued that I am the ideal person to do it. However, I have never witnessed the end of of a hunt and perhaps if I did it would change my opinion.

If there is any way of justifying hunting hare with hounds it has to be on the grounds that hare eat considerable quantities of what farmers grow in their fields, but it has to be admitted that nobody knows how many hare there are for certain, though informed guesses are often made about it, and nobody knows for sure how much damage they do to farm crops, nor how much they cost the farmer. An indication might be taken from an old farmers' saying that ten hares eat as much as a sheep. Whatever the figures might be, however, hare have to be controlled somehow because their breeding activities, as explained elsewhere, have the potential to create a pest of plague proportions. The other point is that horse-riding is a very popular sport best undertaken cross-country, and there is no way farmers would let horsemen ride across their land in the ordinary way of things.

Having tried to analyse my own complex and sometimes contradictory thoughts on protecting and encouraging wildlife, versus enjoying eating game, versus justifying hunting, and recording them on paper, it strikes me forcibly that the timing for writing a history of the Aldenham Harriers could not be more opportune. Political pressures suggest that hunting with hounds could soon be outlawed, and if it is, future generations might well ask:

What was this hare hunting business all about?

Why did some respectable, decent people like it so much?

Why did other respectable, decent people hate it so much?

Why did landowners allow it?

How much did it cost?

Did it do anything overmuch to control hare numbers?

Were hare really ever that much of a pest to farmers?

How long had it been going on?

Was it really as ghoulish at the kill as some people would have us believe?

Did anybody stop to think what would happen to all the horses and hounds, hunt servants and vets, farriers and saddlers, when it was outlawed?

Fortunately there are people with long memories about, who have spent a lifetime hunting, and one of the main aims of this book is to put their recollections and thoughts on record before it is too late. At the same time reference will be made to archive material and other sources so that, by the end, the answers to most of those questions will become apparent, partly for future generations, but also for those who demand a ban on hunting on principle, yet do not really understand what it is all about. It may be that they are too entrenched in their urban views to consider the possibility that hunting with hounds is not as barbaric as some people seem to think. I hope not. I would like to think that the more intelligent ones will take the trouble to find out more about the thing they profess to hate so much and maybe some will change their views, but it has to be said that the degree of ignorance, blind prejudice and class hatred amongst them is remarkable and will probably triumph. A reasoned hatred is not nice, but it is understandable; a blind hatred is not; it is barbaric. Now there is an odd thing; we appear to be faced with one supposed set of barbaric types being barbaric to another set of supposed barbaric types. I am only a simple onlooker, but it seems to me that in these matters it is unwise to take sides, best to leave it to the police to keep the camps apart and not get involved in the ethics of weighing one sort of barbarity against another. On the other hand, a work of this sort that does not offend somebody is a pretty weak sort of a thing that will probably not please anybody either, but my aim is to endeavour not to be partisan, or entrenched, or bigoted, or blinkered, on any aspect of the subject.

At this point I would like to make something very clear. If hunting with hounds is banned there is no way that the hounds will survive. They are entirely unsuitable as domestic pets. They have been interbred as pack hunters and have very specific needs that are entirely incompatible with modern urban lifestyles. They will be put down en masse. One of God's cuddly creatures will be killed off to save another of God's cuddly creatures. Can that be right? Surely that is what a lot of well meaning people are trying to stop. The hound will be sacrificed to save the hare. Is that the way it is to be? Surely not, but that is not the end of it. A good many hunters, a type of horse specifically bred for their cross country abilities, will be redundant and will be shot. Anybody who has seen one of these fine animals at close quarters must be appalled at that prospect. Surely everybody must think again.

It might be worth mentioning here, for the uninitiated, that the hare is hunted on horseback with harriers and on foot with beagles, which are a smaller, slower type of hound, easier to keep pace with on foot. The standards are under twenty-one inches at the shoulder for harriers and under sixteen inches for beagles. The legal sort of hare coursing is a contest of speed, usually a competitive sport, though sometimes enjoyed just for the spectacle. Here the hare, having been given an eighty yard start, is chased with greyhounds or lurchers which use sight rather than smell to locate their quarry. Sometimes these are called 'gaze hounds' or 'sight hounds'. 'Lurchers', usually a greyhound cross, are often used in this 'sport', but the term is a grouping rather than a type of hound. The hounds are awarded points by a judge who follows the hounds on horseback. Such meets always have the prior approval of the landowner. However, there is another sort of coursing, an illegal sort, where the object of the exercise is to kill the quarry and the landowner has given no permission. There are frequent prosecutions for it.'

We must not overlook Basset hounds, but what is their function? They are really a badger hound, sometimes used to hunt hare because they have a particularly efficient nose and fine voice, but they tend to be slow and are not much good in hilly country. There are something less than a dozen active packs of them in England and Wales today whereas there are twenty packs of harriers and sixty-nine packs of beagles. All three, together with the coursers, pursue the common brown hare for sport. To put the whole thing into perspective, there are in addition 183 packs of foxhounds, 3 packs of staghounds, 17 packs of mink hounds, 6 packs of bloodhounds and 11 packs of draghounds.

'Taken in the round' there are said to be a quarter of a million people in this country who 'hunt'.

The origins of hunting hare are lost in the mists of time, but the hare is good to eat and would have been the quarry of early man, hunter-gatherers, wherever the two came into contact with each other. There is no doubt that hare hunting on foot was being undertaken in quite a sophisticated manner as early as immediate pre-Christian times and even at that stage the types of dog best suited to the sport were being selected and kept for that purpose. There are early writings about it such as those of the fourth century *BC* Greek historian Xenophon who describes the way that it was done, and his comments have parallels with beagling practice today. On display in the Verulamium Museum at St Albans is a pot, 1900 years old, decorated with a hare hunting scene; indeed, it is believed that the Romans introduced the brown hare (*Lepus Europaeus*) to the British Isles and it is possible that the motive was sport.

Hare hunting on horseback with hounds goes back quite a long way too. It will surprise many to learn that it is older even than fox hunting which has its origins after 1700, and whilst some people say that it is cruel and should be banned, the fact is that hare do considerable damage to farm crops and hunting them with hounds is an effective and exhilarating way of controlling the numbers.

The sport was so popular in Henry VIII's time that concern was expressed about rapidly declining numbers and orders were issued that they should not be tracked in the snow because of the large numbers being caught that way.

There is a reference appearing in J.B.Black's *The Reign of Elizabeth* which suggests that by the late sixteenth century hunting hare with horses and hounds was already well established and recognised as the best of sports:

"The queen [Elizabeth] *too, was an ardent follower of the chase, riding so hard on one occasion that she had to keep to her bed for several days, and could not interview the French Ambassador. But when the Elizabethan sportsman wanted a real thrill, it was the hare that he hunted, not the deer. The hare was the 'king of venerie', the 'most marvellous beast there is'. Shakespeare's stanzas on 'poor Wat', the hare in Venus and Adonis contain, without doubt, the most memorable literary portrait of animal life in the period."*

Thirty years or so later James I is said to have become besotted with hunting hare, though he sometimes cheated by having them released from captivity in front of him.

The way that harrier packs are organised and go about their business, and the lore that goes with it all, has been evolving for centuries; there is no starting point, but it would be an interesting pastime to search for the first mention. Quite an early one is embodied in a drawing kept at the Ashmolean Museum at Oxford of a hare hunt in progress by Francis Barlow (1626-1702) which was made about 1671. There was, and maybe still is, a painting of a similar scene at Nomansland Farm at Wheathampstead which could have been done at about the same time and may suggest that the sport was well established in this part of Hertfordshire by this date. Certainly it was commonplace two or three hundred years ago for larger landowners to keep a pack of hounds for their private enjoyment, such as those of the Earls of Berkeley, which can be traced back to the seventeenth century.

It would seem that at this early stage hare were hunted with what were called 'Southern Hounds', described as 'mottled blue' in colour which was presumably black or grey with a bluish tinge. There is said to have been a remnant of them still with the Hailsham Pack in Sussex into the 1920s. The present day harrier is descended from a breed of West Country stag hounds, with a goodly proportion of fox hound bred in which some say renders them too fast to produce the sport at its best. The modern harrier stands about twenty inches high at the shoulder and tends to be faster than in days gone by. Some consider that the harrier could be improved by cross breeding with bassets to produce a slower hound with enhanced nose.

Although the oldest form of the sport is coursing, many harrier conventions have been inherited from the beagles, some go back two thousand years or more; one that seems to have dropped by the wayside is the dawn start. Not only does the modern hunter of hare need a horse to carry him about, but he has to have had his breakfast and read his Times before he can think about more energetic pursuits! Perhaps this is why so few hare are caught. Certainly the best time for hunting hare is when it is damp and mild in early morning or evening. Beckford's view is that *"You don't draw for a hare after two o'clock"*. In spite of my earlier unkind remarks, the Aldenham Harriers do occasionally meet at dawn, usually at the beginning of the season in September and October, but that appears to be often enough to satisfy their need to pander to ancient tradition.

Many people do not realise how disciplined it all is
Derek Christopher

There are clear rules to hunting hare, conscientiously applied by the Association of Masters of Harriers & Beagles for well over a hundred years. At a meet, however, the way that a field of harriers conducts itself is largely influenced by the activities of the huntsman. He controls the hounds by voice and horn and whip and there are ancient conventions for all three which it is up to him to decide whether to conform to or not. It has to be said however that those who conform tend to be those who provide the better sport. For instance some will do a deal of shouting when the hounds are better left alone, some will tolerate noise from the field which will tend to distract the hounds, some will be unnecessarily harsh with the whip. No, your best huntsman will be moderate in all things, he will be a quiet man and apart from a little encouragement, he will let the hounds do what they do best without interference. He will follow them and not attempt to do their work for them. He will not push them, but will stay behind, flanked either side by his whippers-in, so that when the scent of the hare doubles back on its own tracks, as it often does, hounds will have room to manoeuvre without getting under the hooves of the horses, and he will only use the whip for control, not to chastise.

Whippers-in have an important function on the flanks, controlling hounds that have been distracted and taking care of hazards such as main roads or railway lines. Particular problem Meets in this respect were those at Flamsteadbury because of the M1 and at Robert Dickinson's Cross Farm at Harpenden because of the railway. The Aldenham Harriers caused consternation on one occasion when they got onto the Midland Main Line at Harpenden, but fortunately there were no casualties. Traditional sound advice to a whip, is *"respect the farmers' crops and always keep a couple of half crowns in your waistcoat pocket for crossing keepers"*.

Sometimes the huntsman, from his elevated position, will spy the hare a way off, out of sight of the hounds. If he knows his business he will, nevertheless, be patient while the hounds figure out the trail, even if that means them temporarily turning their backs on their quarry while they follow a doubling back scent. To direct them to the hare that he can see or to try to head it off would be bad sportsmanship; not only would it be unfair to the hare, it would tend to destroy the hounds' confidence in their own abilities and, to a degree, it would negate the need for hounds at all. Early accounts of hare hunting mention the habit of the hare to run in a general circle and to end up at the place where it was first seen, which would often be its 'squat' or 'form', so that all that a huntsman had to do was to let the hounds chase the hare while he stood at the starting point waiting for it to reappear. It would be starting to tire by this time and could be easily dispatched. How very unsporting!

Sometimes there will be a succession of quite short chases of a quarter of an hour or less, but the ideal hunt should be not too fast and not too slow. Two hours is too long, about an hour is good going. Those more interested in exercising the abilities of the hounds than in the chase itself can take much longer. There are records of hounds following a scent for five or six hours, but your modern follower wants action, good jumps and a bit of a challenge and so something under the hour is nowadays about as much as the field can stomach in the way of scent sophistication. This is the glory of hunting hare and the thing that makes it so different from hunting fox which is essentially a direct line chase. It has to be admitted though that individual subscribers have differing interests; some ride to hunt, some hunt to ride. A good huntsman will try, somehow, to cater for both.

A nice little story, taken from his obituary in the *Daily Telegraph* of 27th May 2000, is told about Loppy Morrison, who hunted the Staffordshire Beagles in the fifties. On one occasion he found a hare near Cannock Chase and hunted it for what seemed like hours. On loading hounds at the end of the day he observed to his kennelman, Maher, *"What a stout hare to stand up before your hounds for so long"*. *"You changed hares fourteen times sir"* came the terse reply.

It is the responsibility of the field master to ensure that permission to hunt on their land is obtained from all the farmers likely to be affected by a meet. If, as sometimes happens, a particular field is designated 'out of bounds', hounds may not be stopped from crossing it during the chase, but the horses will go round and pick up the hounds on the other side. Even farmers often do not realise how disciplined it all is. For instance two people are usually designated to open and shut gates as the hunt passes through. They wear green and yellow armbands, but do not be confused; anyone leading the field may have an armband.

At the turn of the millennium the UK hare population was generally estimated to be about a million (Lucy Higginson of *The Field* quotes 700,000) and there is a move afoot to endeavour to double it within a decade. Opinion overall is that there has been a marked decrease in numbers from indications of a hundred years ago, though this is an impression rather than a proven statistical fact. Paradoxically hare thrive better in areas where hunting with hounds takes place because there is a conscious effort to conserve stocks for the good of the sport. Numbers, however, vary enormously; sometimes hare become rare or non-existent in some areas and at others multiply to become a pest of considerable proportions. Some of the declines can be placed at the door of changing patterns of farming; destruction of cover, incompatible crops, extending the use of farm machinery, herbicides, pesticides, etc. etc., then there is inclement weather, hunting of various types, the spread of urbanisation and wider and faster roads. It is estimated that more hares are killed on the roads than by hunting. Dr Stephen Tapper of the Game Conservancy Council said in 1982:

> *"The hare is not a rare species and indeed in some places must still be considered an agricultural and forest pest."*
>
> *"We have good evidence of a gradual decline in numbers of brown hares over the last two decades. This decline we believe is substantial and serious - though it does not put the hare population in danger of extinction. Our evidence is based on the shooting returns each year of between 400-600 estates and shoots across Britain...The government supports through the National Environment Research Council."*

The hare thrives where there are arable crops, particularly cereals, but it also favours diversity including grassed areas and is mainly nocturnal preferring to feed in the daylight hours in hedges or woods or tall grass. It is said that a major cause of premature death is silage cutting. They are usually plentiful where there is a shoot because a keeper will be active to nurture stocks of game, protect it from intruders and encourage a congenial habitat. Conversely, they will be scarce near footpaths, or where people are accustomed to walk their dogs. Nowadays the stretch of country between Lilley and Whitwell is reckoned to be a place where hares are particularly plentiful. There used to be good numbers on Nomansland, Wheathampstead, but there is little wildlife there nowadays because, or so it is said, *"of the urban foxes that are brought out there and dumped"*.

The increases in populations are due to the hare's natural ability to reproduce rapidly; their breeding habits are as peculiar as their characters. They reproduce at any time of year and can have up to four litters, with perhaps four in each, in a twelve-month, the number of litters and the number within a litter appearing to depend as much upon the weather as anything else. The gestation period is only six weeks. The young, called leverets, are born with a coat of fur and with their eyes open; they are born and fed in the open field with nothing more than a 'squat' to call home, usually located in a 'territory'of a couple of square miles or so. A 'squat' or 'form' is the shallow cavity or depression that the hare digs near the middle of its 'territory' as a base point in an open field or amongst scrubland which it tends to return to if disturbed and uses for the purpose of giving birth, and later where it feeds its offspring. It is usually a spot where, when a hare crouches low and keeps perfectly still, its colour enables it to blend with its surroundings so that it is very difficult to spot unless you know where to look. The leverets will have their own squat apart from feeding time, but they are not weaned until almost a month after birth. A hare will delay flight until the last minute when disturbed in a squat and then shoot off at high speed. As a generalisation they are solitary animals and will tend to stay all their lives in the general area where they are bred. Few seem to reach old age which is hardly surprising considering the numbers killed on the roads or by predators such as man and fox.

Derek Christopher's trophy from the Aldenham Harriers meet at Puddephats on 13th March 1965

Rita Huxley's the Aldenham Harriers trophy - Ayot St Lawrence 4th February 1967

It was perhaps a touch unkind to cast aspersions about the hare's unfortunate habits at the beginning of this chapter. Rather than leave it as a casual hint, a little elaboration seems to be appropriate. The fact is that the hare eats some of its food twice over as a matter of routine, by consuming its own droppings. Just occasionally it will have a third go at it. The belief is that some of the beneficial herbs it grazes are too tough to be digested first time round, but sufficiently essential to necessitate a second go. There is another oddity about the hare that needs explaining; she is capable of conceiving while pregnant so that if the leverets she carries have been conceived at different times, she can give birth to some of the young she carries yet still remain pregnant. Those conceived first will be born with a coat of fur as normal, but those of the second conception are likely to be premature and to be smooth. They may not survive, but they will have a chance in good weather.

An odd thing, when talking about the hare, is that it is always referred to as 'she' and has acquired a number of nicknames down the centuries including 'Puss', 'Jenny' and 'Sue', though quite why this should be is a puzzle.

The hare is a splendid animal to hunt, almost ideal; it is cunning and agile and fast and it seems to sense the motivation and ability of the hounds and to do what it can to thwart their talents. It is often successful. It is quite unpredictable and random in its movements, apart that is from the tendency to progress in the broader sense in a circle. It is highly strung, *"goes on as if it had a flea in its ear"*. It is not good at running downhill because of the disproportion between its front and back legs. Sometimes they roll over and over if the gradient is steep, and that is where a lot of them come unstuck. In theory then, you are most likely to catch your hare when it is going downhill. On the level they can run much faster than hounds; speeds of 35 to 40 mph have been estimated and so it is only the old and sick and the unlucky that get caught. When running full pelt their feet only touch the ground every five feet or so. There is a report from a motorist in 1938, when driving was often an enjoyably leisurely business, and I do not question the detail; he was driving along a straight, open, country road and becoming aware of a hare approaching at right angles, at high speed, destined to cut across his bows with a few yards to spare. It maintained its course and in one leap cleared the margin one side, the road, and the margin on the other side. A prodigious jump of twenty feet or more. Another story is of the hare seen to be running fast and straight up a furrow in a ploughed field and suddenly to fling itself sideways a few furrows over, twice, to destroy the scent! They will often remain hidden until the last minute and then jump up right under the horses, spooking them.

They are at their most erratic in springtime when they seem to be possessed by lunacy and to have hardly any self control; *'Mad as a March Hare'* is strongly founded on fact. The Spring 2001 edition of the *National Trust Magazine* quotes an instance:

"Walking early one summer morning Mike Gaston, Property Manager at Castle Ward in Northern Ireland, saw what looked like a council of hares - seven in all, sitting on their hind legs about two yards apart, facing inwards in an almost perfect circle. Another time he watched a mother hare defend an area the size of a football pitch from a couple of crows. If they landed outside her demilitarised zone she let them be, but if they got to within fifty yards of her safe area then she chased them off by the simple expedient of running at them. Richard Wallace at Danbury Common, in East Anglia, tells how a hare once launched itself over a ditch, ran at his Land Rover full tilt, and smashed straight into the side of the vehicle while five or six other hares watched - as if it was a dare."

Much of the spring madness can be put down to courting; to display and to rivalry. The ludicrous boxing that is such a feature of their odd behaviour had always been put down to males sparring for the female's favours and it is only recently that it has been confirmed that it occurs when the amorous male is rebuffed by the unreceptive female. Incidentally, the male is called a buck and the female a doe as are rabbits. The frenzied chasing often commented upon is usually one male seeing off rivals, but can happen when a number of males vie for the favours of a female.

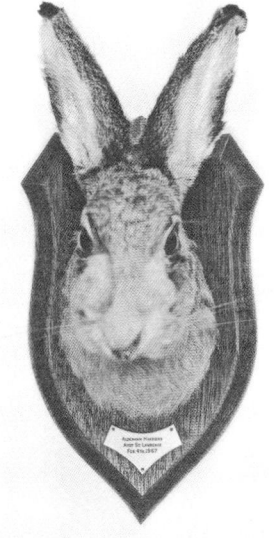

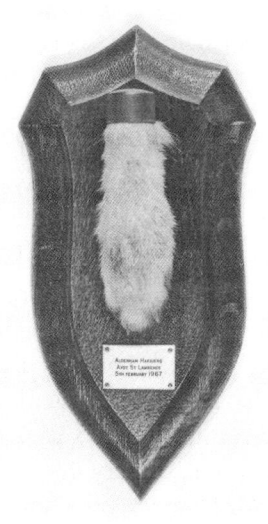

Derek Christopher's trophy from the Aldenham Harriers meet at Ayot St Lawrence on 5th February 1967

Another of Derek Christopher's trophies

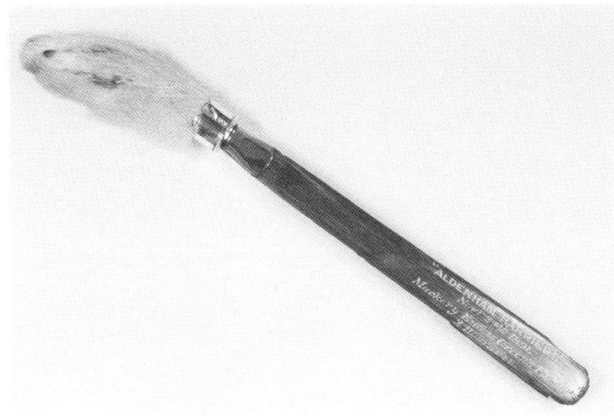

Francis Cory-Wright's trophy from an Aldenham Harriers meet at Mackery End on 24th November 1891 (well before his time!) mounted to serve as a letter opener. The point was from Mackery End to Green's Farm, a two hour run

Sometimes there will be a straight line of a scent up to a hedge, the hounds will go on through, but as often as not the hare will have veered along the line of it. Hare will jump hedges, fences, streams and ditches; they have been known to jump six feet into the air, and they will turn in their tracks at right angles, or double on their own tracks, or perform a manoeuvre somewhere between the two, whereas the following hounds, particularly if pressed from behind, will tend to overrun and will then fan out until they pick up the scent again. This process can appear untidy and random, with hounds milling around in an uncertain manner. It is called a 'check' when they lose the scent and a 'cast' is made when they attempt to regain it. Best defined as akin to an angler when he makes a cast hoping to get a fish interested. When they fan right out there will often be a line of experienced hounds down the centre and that is where the scent is likely to be. Apart from directing the hounds to search in ever widening circles, a good huntsman will be patient at this time and let the hounds get on with their business. He will also discreetly chide any member of the field who makes a noise sufficient to distract the hounds from their task. He will keep a watchful eye on his charges and will know from experience when the scent has been found and encourage the finder by name. He should stand close to the scent when he blows his horn to start the pack off again. Often he will have a fair idea which one will find it; this is where their individual character comes in. Usually the hounds will quickly pick up the scent again, but if they have failed to do so after a couple of minutes the huntsman will direct them to advantage.

As mentioned before, the hare lives (too strong a word really, spends some time in would be better) in a squat or sit and when disturbed will run in an erratic circle back to where it started and when it crouches there, with its ears down, it blends with its surroundings and is very difficult to see. There are other little defences in the hare's arsenal. The weather plays an important part; high winds, or very wet, or very dry conditions tend to reduce the power of the scent for the hounds. Hare are reluctant swimmers, but will take to the water if pressed; they are not even keen to cross a boggy patch and will tend to go round it; even so it is often damp enough at the margins to make the scent there very weak. Also grazing animals in the pasture or amongst kale tend to trample the trail and thus disperse and confuse the scent. A patch where rabbits have been active will do the scent no good at all and hounds are easily distracted by it, as indeed they are by the scent of fox or deer. Sometimes on a moonlight spring night as many as a couple of dozen hare will gather in a circle for what is sometimes called a 'spring conference' or 'parliament'; then the scents become very confusing to a hound, probably not dissimilar to the effect of a knotted hose to you and me. Gorhambury is reckoned to be a difficult place to hunt because the hare are so plentiful. Yes, the hare gets a very sporting chance and a lot of them get away. There is a nice story by Joseph Addison about the hunting exploits of Sir Roger de Coverley that appeared in *The Spectator* in 1711:

> *"... the poor Hare, that was now quite spent, and almost within the reach of her enemies; when the Huntsman, getting forward, threw down his Pole before the Dogs. They were now within eight yards of the Game which they had been pursuing for almost as many Hours; yet on the Signal before mentioned they all made a sudden stand and tho' they continued opening as much as before durst not once attempt to pass beyond the Pole. At the same time Sir Roger rode forward and, alighting, took the Hare in his Arms; which he soon after delivered to one of his Servants with an order if she could be kept alive to let her go in his great Orchard where, it seems, he had several of these Prisoners of War, who live together in a very comfortable captivity..."*

The time has come to consider the least acceptable aspect of the hunt, 'the kill', but after all, that is what the whole business is all about and there is no point in pretending otherwise.

The carnivore pursues, catches, kills and consumes the herbivore. That is nature's way, that is the natural order of things, that is how the world goes on, one living organism consumes another living organism, animal lives off animal or vegetable: it is as God intended, it has been so since the world began. Surely we should not be so presumptuous as to question or criticise God's way? Certainly we should have sympathy and compassion for the victim; we should be distressed at witnessing a living thing being cut down in its prime, and most of us are not keen on blood, anybody's blood, anyway. I have to tell you, believe it or not, that it is much the same for the people who hunt with harriers and all the same principles apply. Most of the witnesses to the kill are not at all keen on it, but it has to be and that is an end of it. So let us not shrink from an unpleasant aspect of hunting, let us consider a 'kill'.

In researching this book I made a point of talking to a lot of people who have ridden, or frequently ride, to hounds and I have asked what motivates them. Most said riding over open country, the jumps, facing the elements in unfamiliar country in all weathers, the open air life and things of that sort; some said *"my family have always hunted"* or *"watching the hounds at work fascinates me"*, some said *"I enjoy the companionship of like minded people"*. Nobody, not one, said *"I like to see one animal kill another"* or *"I hate hare and like to see them killed"* or *"killing things is fun"*. No! No! No! That is not what it is all about at all.

If the hare has been chased for an hour or so it is starting to slow down, it is starting to tire and the hounds are gaining on it. Their excitement is great, both sides know exactly what is going on, but there is still a chance that the unfortunate hare will get away. It still usually has one or two tricks in reserve that may yet win the day. When the hounds catch up with the hare, if the huntsman allows them to, they will dispatch it in a second, the lead hound breaking its neck. There is no pain, no suffering, it is all over as quickly as it would be had the hare been run over on the road, perhaps more so if that is possible. The mask (head) or a pad (foot) will sometimes be donated to one of the followers, but that is all there is to it these days. There used to be something called a 'blooding' which involved a first time follower being marked with the blood of the hare, but this seldom happens nowadays. The 'kill' is rarely witnessed by the field and when it inadvertently happens it gets a very mixed reception; there is not very much to see even then, but it is possible to sense what is going on and most are saddened.

A noble beast indeed
Derek Christopher

Obviously the joy and exhilaration of riding a horse at speed cross country is the major motivation for the followers of harriers, but there are other, more subtle, joys to be had from the sport. One of them is the pleasure of witnessing the way that the hounds go about their business. They will pick up the scent and follow it through all the twists and turns and back doublings of the trail and the tone of their cries will indicate to the trained ear what they are about, for example if they change quarry. Being pack animals, there is a hierarchy amongst them as well; every hound has to know its place and every hound has its own status and character. Sometimes a hound will be so overcome by the excitement of a scent that it will dash off on its own and get lost, but they have a good homing instinct and will usually be back at kennels by the following morning.

Watching how hounds conduct themselves can be a considerable fascination for those who know what to look for and a hound's ability to follow a scent, sometimes an old one, is considered by many to be not far short of miraculous. However, we should not run away with the idea that hound's noses are infallible; hounds are fickle and may switch hares in mid flight where scents converge. In the sixties there was a man called William Allen from Wootton Hall in Warwickshire, who went so far as to maintain a pack of bloodhounds so that he could study their scenting abilities at close quarters. He kept records of all sorts about weather, the state of the countryside and the condition of the hounds, which he contrasted with their performance. He carried out a series of experiments in one of which he put cotton wool up the hounds' nostrils and in another he had one of his men wear Wellington boots and walk into a pond, change them for another pair, which he carried, and walk out on the other side. In neither case were the hounds impeded. He spent twenty five years at this work and at the end of it was forced to admit that he was no nearer understanding the power of the scent, or the hound's ability to follow it, than he was when he started. Now, whether bloodhounds are strictly comparable with harriers in this context is difficult to tell, but there is a strong presumption that they are. Basil Hall, who knows a thing or two about hunting, is of the opinion that if you can get a cold damp day when the soil is warm it is ideal for retaining the scent, and the same principle applies the other way round, warm and dry, especially if there is a strong breeze, the scent just lifts, but he does not know why. The scent does not hang as well on plough as on foliage and it holds best of all on grass, but remember, hares, when at full pelt, can have a five foot stride and that is what gives the hound its biggest challenge.

No matter what you may try to do to prevent it, harriers will sometimes pick up the scent of a fox and follow it. There was such a case at Flamsteadbury when the Aldenham Harriers were religiously hunting hare, but the hounds picked up a fox scent and were in full cry going straight for the M1 motorway. By a miracle they checked within a few hundred yards of it. The trained ear can tell by the 'voice' if they are on the scent of deer or fox or a rabbit (known to the hunting fraternity as a 'long eared one'), but it has to be admitted that this indication is sometimes overlooked and a fox is killed by harriers. Then there is trouble with the fox pack in whose country the evil deed is done and the Harrier Master is called to account. When it occasionally happens nowadays the Master of the Aldenham Harriers has to make a clean breast of it to the Vale of Aylesbury and whilst the whole episode is treated good naturedly the harriers are left in no doubt that they are in the wrong.

Hounds are always counted by the couple, thus twenty five hounds is called twelve and a half couple - why? The reason is very simple once you are told; a young hound starting out in the field is paired with an older one so that it can learn the ropes and the two are counted as one unit - a couple. In earlier times they would be paired on a rope, but the Aldenham Harriers today only couple when exercising and use two collars attached by a chain. The system works this way: a puppy is weaned at eight weeks when it goes out to a puppy walker, as half of a couple, for four to six months. When it is returned, it is introduced to the older hounds and when they are all exercised each day it is attached to one of them using the double collar. That goes on for a month after which two puppies use the double collar for another month and after that they are on their own. All the hounds have names and they all have their individual characters. A good huntsman will know the name and the merits and failings of each.

Anticipation
Derek Christopher

Tanjong Pasir, who was a great one for pontificating about every aspect of the hunt, commented upon the remarkable propensity hounds have for living up to their names:

"I remember a first-season bitch called LONELY. Lonely she was by nature as by name. When the pack were thrown into covert she would make off on some errand of her own; when they were running she was always at least a field or two behind; and when at the end of the day the horn was calling kennelwards the first whipper-in was heard to say 'One hound short Sir - Lonely'. But her really surpassing exploit was when, in company with another bitch named WAKEFUL, she contrived to remain away from kennels for two whole days and nights!

Then there was VAGRANT, a back-yard scrounger of the deepest dye; VAGABOND, another of somewhat similar tastes; and WATCHMAN, who was always the first to come, hackles up and grumbling, to the door when one visited the doghounds' yard at night.... I can close my eyes and see those pied forms fleeting past; flying from the gorses to their well-loved huntsman's cheer; streaming away over the ploughs, the grasses, and the purple hills; or diligently padding beside one's horse, upon the homeward road. A man may love one horse, one woman - but ALL hounds have the power to claim one's heart."

The Aldenham Harriers had a hound called PROWLER who had been walked by Jackie Thrift. This one had a yen for investigating on his own account and if hounds were left standing about for any length of time he could be relied upon to clear off on one of his missions. Occasionally a name produces a character contradiction. At one time the Aldenham had a bitch called POSY, a name that would seem to suggest a placid and endearing nature. Not a bit of it, everybody complained about her; she was often missing and when she produced a litter there was always a completely white pup amongst them.

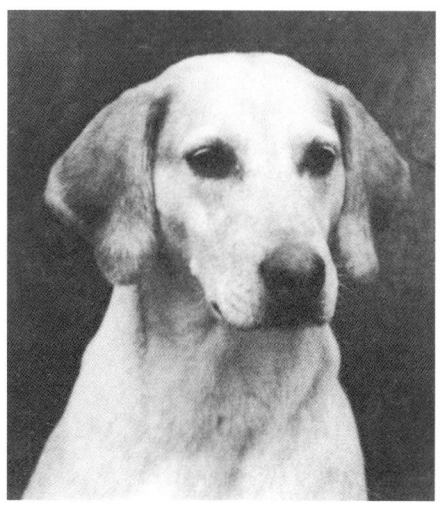

A hound's name can reflect or contradict its temperament
Derek Christopher

For the outsider, the fact that hounds live a Spartan life, mostly outdoors in a pack, with strict discipline imposed by the huntsman and enforced with the crack of a whip, suggests that they are more of a brute and less intelligent than a domestic pet dog. Nothing could be further from the truth. They are just as loyal and loveable and bright as your own canine friend, sometimes more so, but at the same time they are entirely different, they are working dogs and would be miserable left to their own devices with long periods of inactivity indoors.

'Dragon' was another who knew a thing or two about hounds and writing in the *Horse & Hound* in November 1893, he makes a telling point:

> *"Runs with harriers do not look much on paper, but there is often more to do and more to jump with a pack of harriers than either stag or foxhounds."*

The hunting season runs from October to March which enables the hare to utilise the most conducive part of the year for reproduction undisturbed and saves horses trampling maturing crops in the fields. In general farmers welcome the activities of the hunt for the obvious reason that one of their agricultural pests is being controlled, although it has to be admitted that not all that many hares are caught. Indeed some critics have been quite scathing about the harriers lack of success in this regard notably the *Shooting Times and Country Magazine* in 1982:

> *"...and harriers which are an irrelevance to hare populations as they simply do not kill enough hares to make any difference to populations, although the risk to participating human life appears to be quite high."*

That comment is, however, quite a bit 'tongue in cheek'. Individual farms might easily have their populations affected one way or the other depending upon whether harriers have been that way, whereas the national population would not be affected at all. Then there is another, less obvious, more subtle reason why farmers are tolerant to harriers; that of the disposal of old, injured, sick or dead livestock for the purpose of feeding the hounds. It is the job of the kennelman to collect, sometimes humanely to kill animals these days because their value is being outstripped by the cost of their keep, as well as to skin and prepare the material and feed it to the hounds. This mutually beneficial activity ensures that there is always a good supply of fresh meat for them. Whenever possible the farmer will ring up the kennel huntsman to arrange for the carcass to be collected which provides an efficient service for them both. What the hunt actually charges the farmer varies considerably, some hunts charge some farmers nothing; one hunt charges £100 to dispose of a dead horse, £20 for a cow, £5 for a sheep or calf and it is generally reckoned that professional knackers charge double those figures. The charges are to cover hunt costs for the disposal of bones etc.

This is not a joke; hounds are known to have been chosen sometimes for the quality of their voice, regardless of their hunting abilities, to round off the overall musical tone of the pack, it being reckoned that the sound of harriers at work was one of the prime pleasures of the chase. A twenty one inch hound is deemed best for harrier work, smaller than that used for hunting fox, but often nowadays with some fox hound blood. Generally, however, breeding will aim at a good nose, dedication and stamina. Eager, headstrong hounds need too much controlling and unsettle the pack, often heading off on a wild goose chase which does not do anybody any good (except the hare) and means somebody must get them back. In general, it is probably fair to say that the huntsman/kennelman loves and respects his hounds and the feeling is mutual.

Hunting can be a noisy business; the cries of the hounds with the strident tones on the horn superimposed, but to some there is no better music. In earlier times, and particularly in France and Germany, playing tunes on an instrument resembling the modern French horn to enliven the chase, more to let the field know what was going on than to direct the hounds, was very much the fashion. In this country a straight horn about eighteen inches to two feet long was in vogue three hundred years ago, but there has been a tendency for them to get shorter and the modern one measures no more than nine or ten inches. Advertisers tell us that size matters, but apparently not so with harriers. Blowing it in a meaningful way is an art that has to be acquired. Some never master it and have to resort to a reed horn, considered by the purist to be cheating. Its purpose is twofold; to instruct the hounds and to let the field know what is going on. Although the reedless hunting horn only has one note it is possible, with practice, to vary it in such a way as to get a passable tune out of it by timing and volume control. This rudimentary music has a special magic to a follower of hounds, especially when the cries of the hounds are blended in. There are about a dozen standard recognised 'tunes', each with a message to impart.

This calls to mind another story about the eccentric Loppy Morrison ('Loppylugs'), accountant, hunting journalist, extreme extrovert, and one time Master of the Staffordshire Beagles. His second passion, after hunting, was cricket, but his ear-splitting antics with his hunting horn at county matches led to him being banned from the Warwickshire County Cricket Ground. However, he continued to attend matches there, heavily disguised, and part of his act would be to exhibit the correspondence relating to his banning, which he did with great glee.

Jack Molyneux also had a good story about hunting horns which would come from about 1932:

"One of the best horns I have was given me in a strange way. I had an Invitation to the Aldenham Harriers ball from Mr Stevenson, the Master. The ball was held in St Albans Town Hall and when it came to supper time, Mr Fenn, the Huntsman, was blowing a horn to call the guests in. He asked me to give a touch on the horn, a terrible instrument, but I declined. A young man sitting by me pulled a horn out of his pocket and asked me to try it. I did so and finding it a good one went up on the band stage and gave an exhibition blow. The owner asked me to accept the instrument as a present, which I did."

It would be interesting to know who that young man was and what became of him. It might have been Geoff Hartop.

A popular feature in the proceedings of hunt balls has been, and is, a horn blowing contest, usually with a brace of illustrious judges and an appropriate prize. One such, by way of example, was that held at the *Horse & Hound* Annual Ball in the Great Room of Grosvenor House in Park Lane in April 1952 which had 1,300 guests. It was held late in the evening by which time the guests were in high good humour and there were two classes, one for novices, who had never won a prize in such a competition before, and one open to anybody. The Judges were A.W.H.Dalgety, Master of the Southdown and Brigadier Selby-Lowndes, Huntsman to the Hampshire. Competitors could not blow anything they liked, but had to do *"Blowing the Hounds over a Ride"* and *"Gone Away"*.

The hunting horns of famous people such as John Peel sometimes pass through the auction houses where they attract considerable interest and ridiculous prices, providing they have undoubted provenance.

A selection from Lady Lyell's collection of hunting horns. The silver one has a different tone from the others which are of copper and brass. The damaged one is a memento of one of her many hunting accidents.

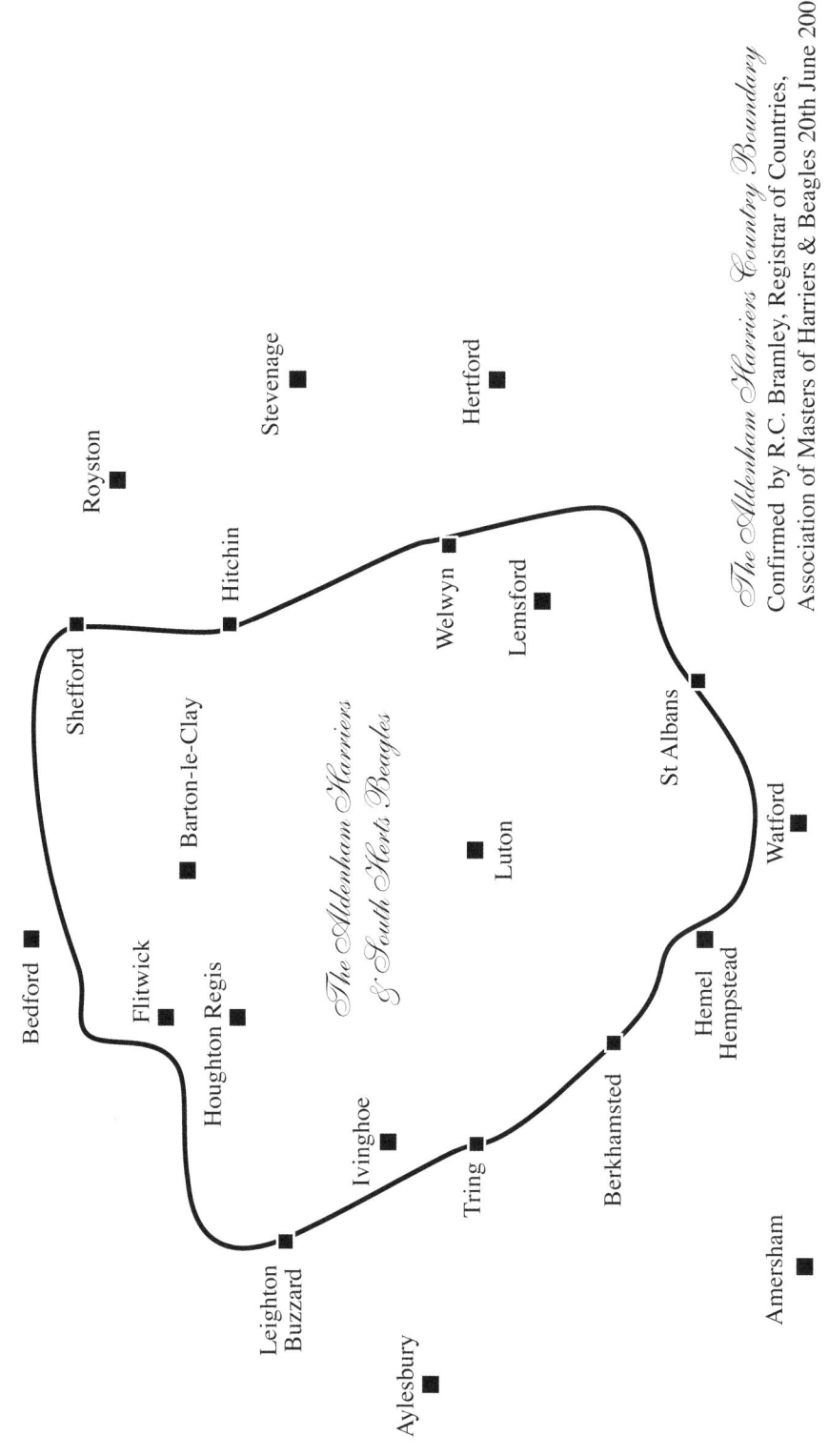

The Aldenham Harriers Country Boundary
Confirmed by R.C. Bramley, Registrar of Countries,
Association of Masters of Harriers & Beagles 20th June 2002

Stevenage

Hertford

Royston

Hitchin

Welwyn

Lemsford

Shefford

Barton-le-Clay

St Albans

*The Aldenham Harriers
& South Herts Beagles*

Watford

Luton

Bedford

Flitwick

Houghton Regis

Hemel
Hempstead

Ivinghoe

Tring

Berkhamsted

Amersham

Leighton
Buzzard

Aylesbury

24

The Aldenham Harriers country is essentially the old Hertfordshire Hunt country, that is parts of Beds., Herts. and Bucks., which it shares with the South Herts Beagles, and contrary to what one might suppose, the two do not compete, but get on well with and support each other. The country is not an ideal one for their purposes having far too much arable land and woodland, too much urban sprawl, too many railways and too much trunk road and motorway which are a particular headache for the huntsman and whippers-in. Nevertheless hare do occur in these parts in considerable numbers in relatively small areas. These areas vary according to the season and to the crop and in general hare prefer fairly open ground with long views, but their preferences vary with the weather; in spring they are partial to fields of winter wheat where they will gorge themselves on the tender young shoots. They are uncomfortable on newly ploughed land and in autumn and winter prefer stubble, or roots, or kale. They avoid rape which upsets the digestion of the young. Modern set aside fields appear to favour them particularly, but there seems to be general agreement that in recent years hare have taken more and more to scrub cover. As mentioned before, when chased in open country hare used habitually to run in a circle to end up where they started, but their behaviour in recent years seems to have become less predictable. The disease, myxomatosis, which decimated the rabbit population years ago, seemed not to affect hare. Today there are large concentrations of hare at King's Walden, Gorhambury and elsewhere.

Let us assume that during the long hot days of summer one has paid one's dues to the Aldenham Harriers and received an acknowledgement. One has acquired a good horse and learned to ride it, taking in the odd fence here and there. One has had it properly shod, and has acquired a set of tack (saddlery) that is comfortable for both. One is ready to go. A card will arrive from the hunt secretary in early autumn detailing the meets that have been arranged. At this stage one should acquire some acceptable clothing so as not to let the side down in the field. Ratcatcher is appropriate for all apart from the Huntsman and Whip before the opening meet then the options would be a black riding hat for either sex and a black or navy coat, although tweed or ratcatcher is more correct. The breeches should be buff or beige. Headgear should be a bowler hat, but velvet caps are now generally acceptable. Riding boots, spurs and crop are correct.

"Of all abominations and sources of discomfort, an ill-fitting pair of riding breeches is perhaps the greatest. For perfect-fitting breeches, in correct style, go for THOMAS & SONS, Sporting Tailors and Breeches Makers, 32 Brook-street, W.
Advertisement in *Horse & Hound* 20th June 1891

Derek Christopher
(Joint MH 1983-1996)
Rita Huxley

The Master, past Masters, the hunt servants wear white breeches, black caps and a 'harrier green' (ladies navy, unless she hunts the hounds) jacket with 'canary' collar and the distinctive Aldenham Harriers brass button. There is a strong tide of opinion against anybody else being allowed to ride thus clad, not only from the point of view that it would be presumptuous, but also to distinguish the responsible people in the field. That word 'responsible' is important. It is the Master and hunt servants who will carry the can if anything goes wrong and they need to be instantly recognisable from the field. There are conventions that must be observed with the buttons; the Master has four of them, the Huntsman has five and the secretary has three. Only those of the masters and huntsman are of brass.

The exceptions to the rules for wearing the Aldenham Harriers buttons and the 'canary' collar are a matter of privilege and honour. For instance the 'canary' collar used to be worn by the lady Master and hunt secretary, but then it was extended to people who had given a lot of time to the hunt and nowadays it is presented to a person who has done some particular service to the hunt. Rita Huxley had hunted for thirty years before she was presented with hers, so it really means something when it arrives. As to the Aldenham Harriers black buttons; they are awarded by the master, or to be more precise the master will 'invite' someone to wear them and that is the point at which a subscriber becomes a member. Both these awards represent an acknowledgement of status, so you proudly display the collar and the buttons to demonstrate in the field that you are a person of some hunting standing.

The corresponding evening wear for male Masters, past Masters and Secretary is harrier green coat with 'canary' collar, white facings, and green lining.

The Trustees are the owners of the hounds. They appoint the Master(s), Secretary and Treasurer of the hunt each season. The Master(s) organise their own committee which consists of:

Master(s)

Chairman

Secretary

Treasurer

Chair of the Aldenham Harriers Supporters Club

Members' representative

One trustee

The Master(s) appoints the hunt servants; the huntsman and the whips. At the moment one of the latter is a paid servant with the title of Kennel Huntsman.

Masters organise the hunting programme on invitation from farmers; it is they who are in contact with the farmers and landowners and the most important aspect of the Master's function is that he/she should be a diplomat. It also helps if they are gregarious by nature because a lot of the detail gets sorted out amongst the farmers socially. It is only by the goodwill of the farmer and landowner that the Aldenham Harriers are able to hunt.

The Hunt was anxious that I should mention by name all the farmers who have been so helpful to them over the years, but this is not an 'official' history and, as I am a rank outsider, it is not entirely appropriate for me to say anything about it. However, there is a debt of gratitude and it needs stressing. It is not reasonable to attempt to mention everybody by name, it would be an impossible task; farms change hands, farmer's attitudes change, farms are built over and their owners move away, but worse, I would be sure to miss somebody out and thus give offence. No, no, much less offence is given if I steer clear of listing individuals, but on behalf of the Aldenham Harriers thank all farmers for their generosity, hospitality, help, encouragement and understanding over many, many years. There would be no such thing as the Aldenham Harriers without their co-operation.

Let it be stressed again here, before we begin the Aldenham Harriers story, and motives will not be queried again in these pages, that hunting on horseback for hare with hounds has nothing whatever to do with blood-lust, nothing whatever to do with an interest in seeing things killed. Nothing could be further from the truth, and members of the hunt were appalled when I put the proposition to them. They are animal lovers first and foremost and the care that is taken with horses and hounds has to be seen to be believed. The joy of it all comes from facing the unknown, from riding over rough country which provides prospects that you would not otherwise be allowed access to, from stretching your horse and yourself, and from watching and hearing the hounds at work. The riders enjoy it, the horses enjoy it, and the hounds enjoy it. Presumably, the hare is not over keen, but the number killed by hunting with hounds each year is greatly exaggerated; it does not amount to much more than 3,000 animals in a good year and most of those are old, injured, or ill, because the hounds would never catch up with fit, healthy ones. It is argued that many are being saved from a long painful death, but then the same claim is made for euthanasia!

Rita Huxley (right) at Upperwood
Derek Christopher

The excitement of anticipation is indeed tangible just before the off as horses and hounds assemble. As mentioned before, there are those who hunt to ride and those who ride to hunt, but that is a comment on motivation; it should make no difference to performance in the field. Rarely is the kill witnessed by the riders at close quarters; it is swift and clean and it has to be admitted that, with a good many hares, if they were not killed this way they would be killed some other way. Few seem to survive to old age.

Shooting is certainly not really a viable alternative to hunting with hounds because hare tend not to be very co-operative; if they are still, they are difficult to see, if they are moving, they are likely to be moving very fast. Wounding rather than killing is more of a probability than a possibility. Those who advocate shooting are being a touch hypocritical; surely a maimed creature crawling away to a slow and painful death is more obscene than one instantaneously dispatched by hounds. Is that not logical, or am I totally missing the point? Yes, I believe I am; this argument does not have very much to do with logic, it has to do with an entrenched dislike that no amount of evidence will alter.

In the pages that follow will be found an abundance of simple stories about the exploits and backgrounds of the people who follow hounds. What is the point of these little anecdotes? What have they got to do with hunting in general and the Aldenham Harriers in particular? Probably very little, but they do demonstrate that people who ride to hounds are 'normal', well, as normal as any of us. They are not disciples of Beelzebub; they do not have horns and a tail, so why are their activities an excuse for badgering them? Is it that they are perceived to be more affluent than the rest of us and they are badgered for that reason under the excuse of concern for animal welfare? The evidence produced to demonstrate their wickedness seems to prove the contrary. Admittedly there are 'toffs' amongst the hunting fraternity, but they are very much in the minority; the majority are very ordinary people existing on ordinary incomes and as a generalisation they are much more concerned about animal welfare, and in a 'hands on' practical way too, than those who profess to champion it in principle. That is not biased easy theory; that is a fact! Look at their horses, look at their hounds, look at the love and care that is lavished upon them. The facts speak for themselves.

Riding to hounds is a dangerous business, there are all sorts of obstacles to be jumped and there are all sorts of unsuspected dangers lurking on the other side. This is especially apparent when a Meet is called for an 'out of the ordinary' location. There are frequent minor accidents, there are frequent minor injuries to horses and riders; mercifully there are few serious injuries and only very rarely is there a fatality. Only one such has been found, so far as the Aldenham Harriers is concerned - may it ever be so. A guest of Monica Shelley's was thrown at Totternhoe when Derek Christopher and Basil Hall were out; he was very badly injured, his tongue was down his throat and he died where he lay. Sometimes hounds are injured; Fiona Kinlock still remembers the horror of seeing one of them with its stomach ripped open by wire, but the worst of it was that she had to hold it while the vet stitched it up.

'The 'Ban Hunting With Dogs Campaign' attracts a lot of media coverage and I have no quarrel with that so long as they are factual about it, but they will go on about a battle between the urban, sub-urban and rural. Now that is not strictly true, although I do not think it reasonable for country people to tell town people how they should conduct their lives any more than I think town people should impose their ideas on country people; they do not really understand each other. Town and country people may have been born and lived all their lives within ten miles of each other, but they are not the same type of person at all, their outlooks, priorities, pleasures and perspectives are quite different. You will hear country people say *"There is no way I could live in a town, all that noise and pollution, I would die of suffocation"*. You will hear town people say, and I have often, *"There is no way I could live in the country, I would be bored to death, all that silence would drive me mad and how on earth does anybody cope with oilseed rape."*

We think that the present anti-hunting campaign, and the endless debate that goes with it, is a modern concept, appropriate to our enlightened times, or at least some of us do. It will come as a surprise to many to learn that very familiar things were being said on the subject seventy five years ago and that appears to have been by no means the beginning of the argument. A debate that took place in public at the Memorial Hall, Letchmore Heath on Tuesday 9th March 1926 posed the question: SHOULD HUNTING BE ABOLISHED? An odd thing about the proceedings was that almost every speaker, for or against, had some connection with the South Herts Beagles, suggesting that the whole thing may have been set up to deal with a local pocket of criticism. In fact it was the president of the South Herts Beagles, Mr Spurgeon Hedges, who proposed the resolution that *'all hunting should be abolished'*, which was very strange coming from him and presumably intended to provoke, though his tone rang true enough. He said that they all agreed that stag hunting was very cruel and some considered that it was no sport at all, but that many considered hunting fox to be justified because of the damage that fox do to poultry and pheasants.

> *"but if I shoot a fox tomorrow, and it gets abroad, I should not be considered an English citizen. Why must we not kill fox? Because gentlemen must have their hunting and we must not deprive them of it."*

He suggested that they should 'drag', but with the aid of aniseed; *"that should be just as good sport"*. He was forgetting, of course, that most farmers would not permit it across their land so that the hunt would be unable to get the variety of terrain that they were used to. He went on:

> *"We claim to be the most civilised nation in the world, but we can't get away from our animal spirit. The opponents of the resolution might say that if hunting were abolished it would do away with a certain amount of labour, but they would employ just as much labour if they hunted after a drag. If Whitechapel, or any other slum*

district in London, were the first to start a pack, the present hunting fraternity would have been the first to turn it down and say it was cruel."

Here seems to be an early acceptance that there is much more to this question than protecting animals. The quote seems to confirm that it is really a class warfare thing. If this is so, and it may well be, then at this stage of the proceedings we ought really to have grown out of it. Why should it be that a man with an impressive car or a man with an impressive boat or an aeroplane or whatever, inspires only a little fleeting jealousy and no animosity whatever, whereas a man wearing a particular style of dress, mounted upon a horse, does, though the value of his turnout is often much less than that of the others. Is it deeper even than that? Does it relate back to earlier resentments when the Master rode and the servant walked? Outlandish perhaps, but some grievances run deep; for example how can a present-day Irishman blame a present-day Englishman for injustices that happened three hundred years ago? But they do, deep down they do, even though most will not admit it.

However, these are the author's thoughts in the modern context and we will return to our meeting. Mr Shepherd, Master of the South Herts Beagles said that the fact that Mr Hedges had said so many things against other people showed that he had no case to put forward. He said that with Mr Woodbridge he had been to Mr Hedges with the idea of starting a pack and Mr Hedges had been given the custody of three hounds, then another six and so on until there were thirty which they then moved to the newly built kennels. Mr Hedges, who had generously turned the cows out of the pigsty to accommodate the hounds, was sorry when they were taken away. *"Mr Hedges and his family have often done us the honour of accompanying the field and now he turns round and tells us this!"*

Mr Shepherd went on to say that he did not like stag hunting and although he had done a good deal of it in his time, he did not approve of it. Fox hunting was a very different matter. With regard to hare hunting; the master said he thought there was no more charming object than these little creatures (the hounds), following their natural instinct and hunting their natural prey. It was one of the marvellous spectacles of nature. To cries of hear! hear! he said *"Long may it last in England."* The kill was the least part of hunting he liked, but there must be a kill; the hounds must have it, although if they could do without it, it would be much better. In beagling there was the absolute minimum of 'the kill'.

Next came Mr Attenborough, Field Master of the South Herts Beagles, who said that he agreed with every word Mr Hedges had said and entirely disagreed with the Master of the South Herts Beagles who had given *"the rottenest lot of excuses for carrying on the South Herts Beagles he could possibly imagine".*

Then Mr Robert Woodbridge, Secretary of the South Herts Beagles, said he would sooner hear the cry of the hounds than the cheers at a football match or applause at the theatre. He admitted that there was a little cruelty in hunting, but a majority of hares and foxes got away.

Mr A.R.Clement said that from the humanitarian side alone hunting was unjustifiable, nobody could deny that. There was cruelty in the running as well as in the killing. The hare was an utterly defenceless animal, except for its legs, which were only for sprinting purposes.

Mr Hedges wound up the proceedings by saying, amid laughter, that he had never been so disgusted, so disappointed, in his life to hear two leading legal men, Mr Shepherd and Mr Woodbridge, put forward such a dreadfully poor case.

These were well aired, presumably 'tongue in cheek', but nevertheless interesting, arguments and although the debate was somewhat incestuous, it was good tempered with occasional laughter and cheers, in sharp contrast to today's sour confrontations. Opponents of hunting are no longer content to argue about it; they become violent, they molest and intimidate and take the law into their own hands. They become in the process much less civilised than the people they oppose, in spite of the high minded principles they profess to have.

I have said that I do not speak the language of the hunting man, but that does not mean that I would cheerfully, knowingly, or even mischievously commit a *faux pas*. Certainly not, but saying the right thing in an enterprise steeped in tradition can be daunting. Where I have erred I trust I may be forgiven. For instance I have had a minor problem with the plural of hare, my inclination is to treat it as one would deer, that is to say that the plural is the same as the singular, but in this case it is not so, the plural is hares. Then there is the problem of the meaning of the Aldenham Harriers. The Aldenham Harriers are hounds and not the people who organise them or hunt with them. It is tempting to use the name to describe the whole set-up, but that is not, strictly speaking, correct. One could, I suppose, omit the word 'Harriers' and refer to 'the Aldenham' indicating the hounds and the people, everything, and maybe I have sometimes. In general I have tried to steer clear of the whole thorny problem. My researches suggest that others are not so circumspect, even those close to the centre of things, and many mean when they say the Aldenham Harriers, the people who organise and follow the hounds, the whole set-up. I also had to come to terms with the traditional hunting pack prefix, the THE; I learned that the correct form must always be THE Aldenham, just as it is for THE Pytchley, THE Old Berkeley and so on. I sometimes erred, and I was corrected!

THE EARLY YEARS

George Gibbs is the man we have to thank for the conception and first three years in the life of, the Aldenham Harriers. Although it was a private pack to begin with and this name was not adopted until later. He built the kennels and acquired hounds in 1878 and we are told that he hunted a country in a five mile circle round Aldenham, which is logical because the kennels were at Elstree, but who was he?

George Louis Monck Gibbs was born on 28th April 1838, the second son (an elder brother died in his infancy) of the Rev'd Mr Joseph Gibbs, who for twenty six years was perpetual curate of Clifton Hampden in Oxfordshire. Joseph had started life working for his father, Antony, in the family business. He lived in the New Parsonage, later the Manor House, which was sold in 2000 by the last Gibbs to live there.

George Gibbs was Henry Hucks Gibbs' (his successor's father, mentioned below) first cousin, but nineteen years his junior. Both were the grandsons of Antony Gibbs, founder of the London merchant banking firm of Antony Gibbs & Sons, by whom they were employed. George was educated at Marlborough, and eventually became a partner in the family business. On 5th January 1864 he married Laura Beatrice, eldest daughter of Sir Arthur Hallam Elton 7th Bart. They made their home at Deacon's Hill in Elstree and there George, a particularly amiable character, acquired an enviable reputation for kindness and liberality.

Amongst his many contributions to the community is the road from Elstree Station to the Barnet Road which he paid for out of his own pocket, but whilst I would in no way wish to diminish his reputation, the truth is that he built it for his own convenience as an access to the newly built railway station. Boreham Wood did not then exist and Elstree was very small. He was a devout and musical man and every Sunday found him in his place in the choir at Elstree Parish Church. Here he donated the funds for the provision of an organ, for building an organ chamber, and for building the parish room which was attached to the rectory.

He was out hunting with his hounds on Saturday 19th November 1881 near Mr Bailey's farm in St Stephen's Parish, St Albans, when he collapsed, as it later transpired from embolism of the brain, and although he was rushed home and appeared to recover, he was dead within a week (26th November 1881). He was aged only 42, had only had the pleasure of hunting his hounds for three years, and left a widow and four young sons aged fourteen, twelve, nine and eight.

George Gibbs was succeeded as Master by Herbert Cockayne Gibbs, the son of Henry Hucks Gibbs mentioned above, then twenty-seven years old. The kennels were moved to Aldenham House, which is in Elstree and should not be confused with Aldenham Abbey, which is some miles away near Radlett and has now been re-named Wall Hall. Herbert's father had inherited Aldenham House from his father, George Henry Gibbs (1785-1842) who had himself inherited it from a distant relative in 1842, the year he died. It was then let out until the time of the Midland Railway's extension to St Pancras in 1868 at which point it was renovated so that it could become his country home.

Henry Hucks Gibbs (1819-1907) had the reputation at that time of being one of the richest men in England. His business, of course, was the family's merchant banking firm, Antony Gibbs & Sons, but in addition, and amongst other appointments, he was a director of the Bank of England from 1853 to 1901 and Governor of the Bank of England from 1875 to 1877. One of his greatest achievements was his prominent association with the restoration of St Albans Abbey, though the present Lord Aldenham (Vicary Tyser Gibbs, 6th Baron), anxious to put the record straight, comments:

> "Mr Beckett, later Lord Grimthorpe should be given most of the credit for restoring the Abbey fabric. He took a very Low Church view and Henry was of the opposing High Church ("bells & smells") approach; Henry got the faculty to restore the Great Screen, much damaged in the Civil War, I believe. I think there was some wonderful church feuding about it all."

Henry Hucks Gibbs was elevated to the peerage as 1st Baron Aldenham in 1896. He had the misfortune to lose his right hand in a shooting accident, but even that brought a degree of fame because of the quality of the artificial hand which he acquired, considered to be something of a technological triumph at the time. After the accident he continued his routine of maintaining a daily diary in longhand with his left hand, until he discovered the typewriter, and fortunately these diaries have been preserved. He was a keen hunting man and the first story in the first of his diaries is about a new horse and a hunt which ran from Slough to Rickmansworth. He also tried to continue illuminating manuscripts, another of his hobbies, but had to give that up.

His third son was Vicary Gibbs, editor and benefactor of the *Complete Peerage* and a noted horticulturalist who made the gardens at Aldenham House some of the most admired in the country. He and his sister Edith lived with their father until his death in 1907; they then rented the house from their elder brother,

Alban, now at the Manor at Clifton Hampden *(see above)*. Vicary, who trained as a Barrister but hardly practised, worked for Antony Gibbs & Sons, was MP for St Albans from 1892 until 1904 when, because his business had accepted an Admiralty contract, he voluntarily vacated his seat, standing again in a by election, but was defeated. He died a bachelor in 1932. Today Aldenham House is occupied by Haberdashers Aske's School which has built extensively in the grounds.

The Chequers, Gaddesdon Row c 1988. At the front is Jean Choake on RUPERT and behind her Carolyn Peterkin on FELLA, both from Upperwood. RUPERT was bred, hunted, raced and shown by Derek Christopher and lived to 2002 by which time he was aged nineteen
Derek Christopher

Portrait of Herbert Cochayne Gibbs (1854-1935) as a young man.
Reproduced by kind permission of Lord Aldenham

Herbert Cockayne Gibbs (1854-1935) served as Master from 1881-1885 and is the great-grandfather of the present Lord Aldenham. He consolidated the pack he had taken over by absorbing the hounds of Mr Chesshyre of Hertford who had hunted to the north of the Aldenham Harriers country since about 1870. Herbert appears mainly to have lived in London until 1908 when he bought Briggens near Ware. He worked for the family firm, becoming chairman in 1921, and was also deeply involved in politics being chairman of the City of London Conservative and Unionist Association from 1912-1932. He went to Russia as part of a delegation to the Duma in 1912/13. He was made a chevalier of the Legion of honour in 1918 for his war work and was elevated to the peerage as 1st Baron Hunsdon of Briggens in 1923 for his work on the Reparations Committee; family legend has it that he tried to tone down French demands for vengeance.

Herbert married on 12th February 1885 Anna Maria Durant, fourth daughter of Richard Durant of High Canons, Shenley and here we ought to pause in the chronology and consider this High Canons connection because it crops up again in the story later in 1912 when William Walker became Master of the Aldenham Harriers (*see page 52*). High Canons, or Canons as it is sometimes called, was formerly the Manor of Holmes and was purchased in 1812 by Enoch Durant. Upon his death in 1848 it passed to his cousin Richard Durant of Sharpenham in Devon and on his death it was inherited by his son Richard, Herbert Cockayne Gibbs' father-in-law.

This Richard (1812-1886) married in 1856 Charlotte, daughter of Lt Col Alexander Dashwood of the Grange, also at Shenley, but she died only seven years after the marriage. They did, however, have five children, a son, another Richard who died when he was only nineteen and four daughters, all of whom married into hunting families viz: Mary Elizabeth, wife of Colonel Frederick Trotter of Dyrham Park, Herts., Louisa Blanche who married John Trotter of Brickendon Grange, Herts., Charlotte Agnes, wife of Charles Parker of Rochetts, Brentwood, Essex, and our Anna Maria mentioned above.

I have dwelt more than is really justified upon the Gibbs family for two reasons. Firstly because, although they were only Masters for seven years, they must be credited with the conception of the Aldenham Harriers and nurturing its infant development to form the nucleus of the thriving institution it became and still is. Secondly, because very little information has been published of these early years, I referred to the present Lord Aldenham who very kindly supplied additional detail and corrected some of the things that have been published elsewhere.

Herbert Gibbs retired as Master in 1885, presenting the hounds to his hunting friends, and it was at this point that the name the Aldenham Harriers was established. He was followed by Mr L.E.Rickards and the hounds were moved to Kemprow. Mr Rickards was an important man in harrier circles partly because of his interest in improving harrier characteristics through selective breeding, but also because he started the Harrier and Beagle Stud Book in 1891 in which were recorded details of the hounds of fifty seven harrier packs existing at that time. Unfortunately he died shortly after publication of the first edition. He was also amongst those who established the annual Harrier and Beagle Show at Peterborough at which Aldenham hounds have often been successful. At this point the hounds, which until then had been essentially privately owned, were presented to the country.

The Hon. Copplestone Bampfylde, took over control of the Aldenham Harriers in 1890. He was then aged thirty, had served in the 1st Life Guards and was married to the Hon. Margaret Harriet Beaumont, daughter of the 1st Lord Allendale. He lived at Hartsbourne Manor, Bushey. He succeeded his father as 3rd Lord Poltimore in 1908 when he inherited the family seat, Poltimore Park near Exeter and 20,000 acres in Devon, where he died on 2nd November 1918. He too had his own ideas about hounds and set about further improvements to the quality, introducing some foxhound blood, and after a few years of his efforts the standard of the pack was said to be second to none. The hounds were kennelled at Hartsbourne Manor. From that time on, apart from the dark days of the two world wars, the high standards of the hounds were maintained and prizes were often won at shows with them.

Reports of activities in the field, contrary to the impression created in this work, were somewhat sparse over the years and in general terms appear in three concentrated blocks: *'Dragon'* in the 1890s, *'Stubbins'* in the 1930s, and *'Ben Adam'* in the 1950s. The earliest piece of *'Dragon'* found is typical of his somewhat quaint style and was published in the *Horse & Hound* on 28th November 1890:

> *"Sharp frost on Tuesday morning made the Common very bad going when we started at ten o'clock to meet the Aldenham Harriers at Harpenden Bury [sic] at 11.15, but hot sun made it all right before noon...this is now as pretty and level a pack of harriers as any huntsman would wish to see, and even on a really bad scenting day their work satisfied the most fastidious of the old talent who mustered in force to welcome the Master, who carries the horn, with his brother and Webb, the kennel huntsman, to turn hounds to him.*
>
> *With them were Mr. Charles Barnett, who used to whip-in or hunt the pack as required, also Mr. J.Reynolds (ex-M.H.) for the famous Bevor [sic] pack, Mr. T.Cox and Miss Cox, Mr. H and Miss Palmer, Messrs. H.Cox, Todhunter, H.Bailey, R.Mather, C.Sibley, G. and C.Nott, Hollingsworth, Archer, E.Arnold, J.Lloyd, Mardall, Dolphin Smith, T.Taylor and Will Smith. Charles Harris with Davis and Gibbons were on foot, also Mrs.T.Cox, when she could get away from dispensing hospitality, and Mrs. H.Cox, Miss Reynolds and the*

Misses Sibley, with a gallant escort.

It was soon after twelve o'clock when they found a strong hare on the hill above Harpenden Bury [sic], *and ran to the railway as if for Knott Wood; but luckily she doubled back, and hounds hunted prettily down to the little covert across the stream, round over the course, where the Hertfordshire Point-to-Point Races were run in the spring, back up hill nearly to Couter's End, round again till she jumped up in view, and they nearly killed her down by the stream; but scent grew colder and colder, while cold showers made it worse, so that hare lives for another day. We were all glad to seek shelter for a few minutes at Harpenden Bury before trying fresh ground by Kinsbourne Green; but fur was scarce, so we turned homeward, hoping to see a good day with them before long."*

The earliest report of the showing successes of the Aldenham Harriers came in the summer of 1891 when they were shown at Peterborough, winning Class 3, for the best couple of working dog hounds above 19 inches, with four year old ALDENHAM PIPER (by CALVERLEY PROCTOR out of their DARLING) and three year old VALIENT (by HINXTON DRIVER out of their PATIENCE). In addition a Champion Cup, given by William Grenfell, later Lord Desborough of Panshanger, for the best single dog hound in Class 3, was also won by VALIENT.

On 24th October 1891 came another report in the *Horse & Hound* of one of the Aldenham Harriers meets:

"...so, when we arrived at Chorley Wood, we saw horsemen and hounds on the common. These were the O.B.H. (East) coming home from cub-hunting, and we heard that they had a good run from the kennels on Monday, also a lot of fun this morning, for several of their followers came on with the harriers. When the Hon. Coplestone Bampfylde arrived with Webb and his second horseman, and twenty-one couples mixed, there were several critical eyes of ex-Masters and ex-whips to look them over, but no one can pick many faults, and hounds from this pack have twice cleared the board at Peterborough. Mr. Harding Cox used to hunt harriers before he took the O.B.H., and Mr. Jaquet and Snaith were his whips, Mr. Ronald Barlow, too, used to help. There, too, were the Hon. L. J. Bathurst, Master of the Exmoor Foxhounds, Mr. and Miss Gilliat, Mr. and Mrs. Burbridge, Mrs. Schreiber, Miss Barnes, Captain Stewart, Messrs. Cowley, A. Clutterbuck, Hounsfield, etc. Drawing the open country down towards West Hyde, a hare was soon found, and hounds ran round to the railway, which they

crossed, and ran through Mr. Gilliat's coverts, back across the railway again with very little scent; but they spread about and cast themselves, showing that they had not forgotten how to hunt, and we saw some real good hound work, but the railway and fear of passing trains saved the life of that hare.

They found another and ran to Loudwater, where Mrs. Panmure Gordon came out on a beautiful chestnut as hounds ran through the pleasure grounds, a pretty bit of hunting till they crossed the river and ran up to Beechen Grove, where a fox was afoot, but their hare escaped. They then drew the open by Goldington's back to Chorley Wood, and found a hare that led them across Mr. Cox's park, over to Chenies Mount, where she, too, saved her scut, and we adjourned to luncheon, after which our host produced his last musical effort, that just filled a gabardine pocket, so we rode home to try experiments on the piano with the 'Days of Yore' gavotte, published by W.J.Elliott of Watford (St. Albans) and now we have heard that gavotte played properly we have come to the conclusion that what Mr. Cockey cannot do is not worth doing, for we have seen him hunt hounds, ride races, lead troops, shoot, row, play games, paint pictures, and now compose music that we did not know before; so for all we know he may be able to play golf and wheel a perambulator, but the line must be drawn somewhere."

James' Hunting Stables in High Street, Berkhamsted, at the start of the 1892/3 season, made an effort to 'sell' their livery services and the merits of the town as a hunting base which they said had excellent rail connections to London making it a first rate starting point for the hunting man. Obviously anticipating rich pickings from their advertising they claimed that Berkhamsted was one of the many hunting centres of England and to prove it listed the packs to be found in the vicinity:

Berkhamsted Staghounds	meets	Wednesdays
Lord Rothschild's Staghounds	"	Mondays & Thursdays
Queen's Staghounds	"	Tuesdays & Fridays
Enfield Chase Staghounds [*sic*]	"	Tuesdays & Saturdays
Hertfordshire Foxhounds	"	Mondays, Wednesdays, Fridays & Saturdays
Old Berkeley East Foxhounds	"	Mondays & Thursdays
Old Berkeley West Foxhounds	"	Wednesdays & Saturdays
Whaddon Chase Foxhounds	"	Tuesdays & Saturdays

Oakley Foxhounds	meets	Mondays, Tuesdays, Thursdays & Saturdays
Bicester Foxhounds	"	Mondays, Tuesdays, Thursdays & Saturdays
Aldenham Harriers	"	Tuesdays & Saturdays

If taken literally, all that leaves one wondering how any stags or foxes managed to survive at all, but James' was being economical with the truth. Whilst undeniably all the packs listed are adjacent, or occasionally visited the Berkhamsted area, outrageously long hacks would be necessary to attend most of their meets. Even so, the number of packs and the number of days they were out in the season is impressive. Even as recently as the 1999/2000 season there was a week when five separate packs of hounds were out at various times on the Gaddesden Estate land and though unusual, that is by no means extraordinary:

Foxhounds

      The Old Berkeley (by invitation)

      The Vale of Aylesbury

Harriers

      The Aldenham Harriers

Beagles

      The South Herts

      The Eaton College

Aldenham hounds had further success at the July 1892 Peterborough Show, which was said to have attracted a record number of entries. It went on for three days; Hunters on Tuesday, large hounds on Wednesday, and harriers and beagles on Thursday. The Aldenham Harriers Master, Hon. C.R.G.W.Bampfylde, retired master, Mr L.E.Rickards and his wife, and future Master, Mr F.C.Swindell and his wife were all there and the hounds made a good account of themselves.

In Class 3 for the best couple exceeding 19in, but not exceeding 21in, five year old Aldenham PIPER (by Mr Beaumont's PROCTOR out of his DARLING) and two year old PILGRIM (by RAVAGER out of POVERTY) made a second.

The Aldenham Harriers then won Class 5 for the best three couples of hounds of any age or any size, but not under 16in nor over 21in from any one kennel, with PIPER, PILGRIM, VALIANT (four years old by HINXTON DRIVER out of their PATIENCE), FINDER (one year old by PIPER out of FESTIVE), WARLOCK & WAVERLEY (one year olds by WAYWARD out of FAIRPLAY).

They also won Class 8 for the best couple of un-entered bitch hounds whelped since 1st December 1890 with ALDENHAM DOROTHY (by VALIANT out of DAFFODIL) and GOVERNESS (by RAVAGER out of GRACIOUS).

To finish off in style they came second in Class 10 for the best couple of bitch hounds whelped since 1st December 1890 with GAIETY & GAUDY, who were sisters of GOVERNESS, joint winner of Class 8.

Standards were high and the competition was great; three firsts and two seconds was a magnificent performance.

Another report came from *Horse & Hound* in February 1893:

"Tuesday was a lovely spring-like day, when quite a large field met the Hon. Coplestone Bampfylde with the famous Aldenham Harriers at Woodside, near Luton, where Mr. Briggs made all welcome.

Squire Crawley of Stockwood, who used to keep harriers, came out on foot to look at them, and his son and daughter were mounted, with several more ladies and the usual followers and supporters of these hounds.

Found a hare at once in the open fields between Crawley's Gorse and the home farm, and ran two rings round the hill near Luton; but a brace, if not a leash, of hares complicated matters, and the scent was none of the best; so after hunting them for about half an hour a move was made to fresh ground near the Hertfordshire Kennels, where Charles Sibley viewed a hare, and they ran well across the road into Luton Hoo, hunting very prettily and sticking to their hunted hare, though several kept crossing the line, past Gibraltar Gate, turning up to the house and pleasure grounds, where they were stopped.

Then drew the Kennels and killed a hare at Charles Sibley's, and found all that was good, and another hare that they ran well for 24 minutes, and killed her. Then in the afternoon they found another near Harpendenbury that kept them busy till hounds and horses had done enough, and we had enjoyed quite a pleasant day."

And again in February 1893:

"On Saturday a nice little field met the Hon. Coplestone Bampfylde with the Aldenham Harriers at Shendish, where Mr. Longman has

*some very strong hares. There were Mr. and Miss. Barnett, Miss
Dugdale, Messrs. H and W.Lloyd, Beaumont, R.Webber, M.F.H.,
Rickards, Van Raalte, Peto, etc. Hounds found at twelve o'clock
near the Home Farm, and ran to the gorse, then back to the farm,
and down to the railway, up again nearly to Felden, and round to
the gorse. Here other hares were on the move, and in the great open
fields near Scatterdells other hares kept moving, so on a bad
scenting day there was not much chance of killing one with two big
woods as sanctuaries..."*

Aldenham hounds were shown at Peterborough in July 1893 and again did
rather well. In Class 4, which was for unregistered pairs of dog hounds, they
managed to win with brothers WAMBA and WARRIOR (by WAYWARD out of
RESTLESS). They were a good pair and had been winners at the Aldenham
Puppy Show. Their sister, RESTLESS, which had been acquired by the
Boddington, was joint winner for pairs of unregistered bitch hounds. In addition
WAMBA won the champion cup given by Colonel Le Gendre Starkie, and the
Bentley Woodbine won the champion cup with ALDENHAM WAYWARD (out
of RESTLESS). To finish off RESTLESS, (by Mr. Lowndes's TARQUIN out of
OAKLEY SARAH) and SPANGLE (by Mr. Taylor's WEATHERGAUGE out of
Mr. Race's SCANDAL) managed a second in Class 10, but the hero of the day
was ALDENHAM RESTLESS which won the champion cup given by
C.Middleton Kemp. Remember these were early days with the Peterborough
show, and an ex-Aldenham Harriers Master, L.E.Rickards, had been prominent
in the move to set them up, so that it was only natural that the Aldenham should
go out of their way to do well and had, from Mr Rickards, the expertise to set
the standards.

In October 1893 the Hertfordshire met at Bricket Wood, *'Dear Old
Bricket'* as *'Dragon'* called it, and it is interesting to note that three future
Masters of the Aldenham were out with them that day; H.Bailey and his son,
H.S.Bailey and Birkbeck Ravenscroft. They adjourned to the Noke for
refreshment, kindly provided by Birkbeck Ravenscroft, whose home it was, and
were able to admire his pack of rabbit beagles which were occupying the kennels
that once housed his bloodhounds. Later that month *'Dragon'* reported:

*"On Tuesday, a small field met the Hon. Coplestone Bampfylde's
Aldenham Harriers at Mr. Briggs's, Woodside, Luton - The Rev.
Douglas Davis, Messrs. Blundell, Carruthers, Batchelor, Carlisle
and Charles Harris. Found a hare near Squire Crawley's Home
Farm, and raced her down in 5 minutes.*

*Found a brace on the same ground, ran well to Runley Wood, and
up hill near the gorse, where she turned back and ran to the open*

fields, then another ring into the gorse, where she was left, as the fox hounds meet here on Friday.

Had a long draw, found a hare near Skimpot, but could not run her far. Found a real good hare near Mr. Batchelor's Kensworth House; ran a good ring round Kensworth, and away into Dunstable, crosed the high road near the Half Moon, and ran over the hill to Skimpot, back again to Stiper's Hill, and into Kensworth near the church, where the Master viewed her, dead beat; but another hare got up in view, and hounds raced to Church Farm, so when they were brought the hunted hare had crawled into a thick shaw [sic], and escaped after a good hunting run of an hour and a half. So to Mr Batchelor's to refresh and home just as the moon rose over the hills."

There was another report in the *Horse & Hound* on 4th November, but it related to the previous month:

"7deg. of frost made the ground hard and dry. A small field met the Aldenham Harriers at Redbourn Common. Grandpapa invalided in his brougham, so we prescribed for grandpapa. Give up good-mannered horses, and buy some rough, wild four year olds, that will shake him into form again. Good-mannered horses and broughams are all very well for millionaires and real invalids; but when a man's eye shows liver disorder, there is nothing like a rough four year old, that does not give anyone time to think about his liver.

These were reflections as we drew for a hare on Flamsteadbury, and when Mr. Hornby found one all these reflections might have been lost, as hounds ran well to the Grove and along Troley [sic] Bottom, where we viewed the hare, and a single hound coursed her to the big rails, where she turned short into the lane, and only the keenest noses could pick it out to the Three Elms, where they began to run on the grass to Newlands. But here they were rabbit-shooting, so hounds were stopped and taken back to Redbourn.

Luncheon at Tom Connor's, and a stout hare at Redbourn Bury [sic], took us across the river at a very smart gallop to Hammond's End, where a fresh hare led them in view to Sir Blundell Maple's Stud Farm at Childwickbury, and there hounds were stopped, as several hares were afoot and horses had done enough."

A week later came a report from more or less the same area:

"...we sent a hunter to Annables, and drove there, knowing we

should get a hearty welcome from Mr. and Mrs. Charles Sibley. At their hospitable board, to meet the Hon. Coplestone Bampfylde's Aldenham Harriers, were Mr. Sworder, Master of the Hertfordshire, who had scored a good run from Ippolitts the previous day. There too, was Charles Harris (his late huntsman), Messrs. Beaumont, H. Bailey, H.Cox, Dolphin and Will Smith, E.Arnold, Knott, Tom Taylor, Hollingsworth, Stewart, Carlisle, Drayson, etc.

Found the first hare close to the Hertfordshire Kennels, and, ran across the Luton Road into the Home Farm at Luton Hoo, so hounds had a merry time; hares were plentiful, but no execution was done, and a hare viewed back across the road waited for us, for when hounds put her up on Mrs. Taylor's farm they ran in view, Whipster leading, and it took the very fastest blood ones to keep them in sight till they ran her down in the brook, and then the leading horseman was too late even to secure a trophy.

Found another near Annables, and ran a ring by Carter's End [sic] *round to Kennesbourn* [sic] *Green, and down to the brook by the steeple-chase course, into the little covert near Harpenden Bury* [sic] *and nearly into Redbourn, but they turned short back to the Osier-bed, and ran up to the railway, where they were stopped, as she had crossed into the Knott Wood, and here was a party rabbit-shooting, so that hare lives with a run of 35 minutes to her credit.*

Then drew Harpenden Bury [sic], *and found another, but the gale and blizzard now commenced, and we were lucky to get home in safety."*

In March 1897 Dragon was again writing in the *Horse & Hound*:

"...Webb [the kennel huntsman] *had orders not to wait when they met at Harpendenbury, where a large field partook of Mr & Mrs Taylor's usual hospitality. A lovely day and quite a red-letter day, though hares were too good for hounds, or rather too lucky in escaping into covers. Found the first near Falconer's* [sic] *End, ran down to Harpendenbury, up again to Falconer's End, where another hare jumped up, and hounds divided. We tried to stop a few couples without success, so followed the body, racing by Thrales End to the Midland Railway at East Hyde, round to Grave Wood, and down to East Hyde again, where Webb stopped them on the railway after a narrow escape from a passing train. This was a real good run, and very fast. Drew back to Kinsbourne Green. Found*

another close to Moreton End Farm, ran round Falconer's [sic] End, out into Kinsbourne Green, where she got up in view, raced to the belt of trees, then into the Hertfordshire kennel-yard, round by Annables, and through the brickfields by Poplars into Gibraltar Wood, where hounds were whipped off after a good run of fifty minutes. Ale and Shrove Tuesday dough-nuts at Annables finished the day..."

The pack was described as 'famous' by the same author writing about it a few months later when they had a meet starting at 12.30 at Chorleywood. He mentioned amongst other things that the pack had just emerged from a narrow escape from blood poisoning; only one hound was lost, FALSTAFF, but the others suffered severely. At this time Mrs Bampfylde rode to hounds beside her husband.

The Hon. Copplestone Bampfylde held the Mastership for ten (1890-1899) very successful seasons, the last two jointly with Henry Bailey who then went on, on his own, for another three seasons.

Henry Bailey, although having been ailing for some time did not expire through illness, but died in April 1901 aged 66 as a result of an accident. He was out in his trap one day when a passing motorist frightened his horse so that he was thrown into the road and although only slightly injured failed to recover. He was a popular man, said to have had the most genial disposition and to have been a true lover of anything of a sporting nature. He was a wine merchant trading as Bailey & Co from 51, Pall Mall, London, and had moved to St Albans thirty years previously when his house, Cuckmans, at Chiswell Green, was built. The same house that was later the home of Bill Corby's family. Henry Bailey's early passion was for coaching, but for thirty years he had been a Hertfordshire Hunt subscriber; no other man was better known in Hertfordshire hunting circles at the time and he was one of their most committed followers.

One of his sporting enterprises was to host an annual meet at Cuckmans for the Berkhamsted Stag Hounds. He was very proud of the length of each chase and runs as far as Barnet, Enfield, Tring, Chesham, Luton and Dunstable were commonplace. One such meet, in December 1893, was reported in the *Horse & Hound* and reveals that the deer was already in a paddock on the premises when the hunt met, which seems a touch unsporting.

In his time Henry had been chairman of St Stephen's Parish Council and a church warden of St Peter's, St Albans. He left a widow, Julia, the same age as himself, a son and two daughters. It seems that a few months later in 1901 his son, Mr Henry S.Bailey, by then aged 36 and a wine merchant in the family business, bought the hounds from the committee and kennelled them on his own land. Will Turk was the kennel huntsman at that time.

By 1905 the Aldenham Harriers were hunting three days a fortnight, there were twenty in the stud book, Henry S.Bailey remained Master and also the huntsman and the whippers-in were Will Turk and R.Dollamore. The kennels remained at Cuckmans.

When Mr Henry S.Bailey retired as Master it was keenly regretted by followers of the hunt and they honoured him in style. Supporters, followers and farmers assembled in large numbers in St Albans Town Hall on the evening of Wednesday 23rd May 1906 to take part in a public presentation to him of a portrait of himself in oils, the work of artist Frank Salisbury from Harpenden. For the purposes of the presentation a banquet consisting of a goodly number of courses was arranged and served in admirable style by Mr T. Slater of St Albans in the council chamber, which had been kindly placed at the disposal of the committee by the Mayor, Councillor Mr S. Ryder. Mr C.T.Part, MFH the Hertfordshire Hunt, took the chair with the support of Alderman Jacob Reynolds and Mr C.F.Sibley as vice-chairmen. At the start of the proceedings the chairman expressed regret at a telegram he had received from Mr F.Swindell, the new Master, announcing that on his way to St Pancras Station he had met with a cab accident and was therefore unable to be present.

The toast of the evening was of course the retiring master and in proposing it Mr Part, who claimed to be nearly the oldest follower of hounds in the room, said that it was now nearly fifty years since he had been sent for schooling to a neighbouring clergyman, on a pony, by himself, twice a week, to learn Latin. He did not learn much Latin, but he learned to ride and he felt sure that it had given him a lot more pleasure over the years than Latin. He had hunted with the Aldenham Harriers under the Mastership of Mr George Gibbs of Elstree in 1878. In those days they hunted all over the beautiful grassland from Mill Hill to Radlett *"long before the days of the infernal wire* [barbed wire] *of which we have so much nowadays"*. Although they had had several Masters since that time, he could say without fear of contradiction that no more popular Masters had ever had the hounds than Mr H.S.Bailey and his late father who was always a keen supporter of anything to do with either the Hertfordshire Hunt or the Aldenham Harriers. There were loud cries of *"hear, hear"* to that and he went on to say that harriers were by far the oldest kind of hounds kept in Hertfordshire. The number of packs, he supposed, ran into hundreds. They had been kept at Hatfield House ever since the time of James I and up to 1797 when Lady Salisbury turned them into fox hounds. Sir John Sebright of Beechwood also kept a celebrated pack which were all black and tan and he sold them to the Duke of Brunswick, nephew of King George III, for a large price. I am open to contradiction, but it seems likely that Sir John sold this private pack when he took over the Mastership of the Hertfordshire Hunt, by which name Lady Salisbury's pack had become known, and that would put the date of the sale at 1828. Sir Peter Swan at Royston had a pack which was very well known in those days and there was also a most celebrated pack of harriers by then belonging to Mr George Race whose father had kept them for forty years. Mr George Race was now nearly ninety years of age and had had control of the pack for sixty three or sixty four years, so that for considerably more than a hundred years they had been in the hands of father and son. The pack had been sold that year, but he was told that Mr Race, in spite of his age, had just bought a new pack and was going to start them that season. Mr Part then presented the portrait to Mr Bailey with expressions of goodwill.

Mr Bailey then got to his feet and said that it was impossible for him under the trying circumstances in which he found himself to say all that he would wish by way of acknowledgment. This is presumed to refer to some unfortunate incapacity, the nature of which is not recorded.

Mr F.C.Swindell duly took over the Aldenham in 1906 when it was darkly hinted that his career had recently been under something of a cloud, but it was not true. Admittedly he came with something of a reputation having, through no fault of his own, been Master of the Puckeridge through eleven turbulent years of civil war when factions split the country in half. He was a man of private means, having been left a fortune by his bookmaker father on the condition that he never gambled, and in monetary terms he never did. At the time of his move to the Puckeridge in 1885 he was in his late twenties and because of his private income was able to accept the mastership with a guarantee of only £500. In the summer months of 1888 he had hunted grizzly bear in America and presumably the switch later on from fox to hare was child's play by comparison. He had been living at Chesterfield Lodge in Lichfield and had been hunting hare and deer with his own hounds in the South Staffordshire country. He also had a property in Brighton and to begin with took Layston House at Buntingford where he built temporary kennels and began drafting in hounds to form a new pack, but it was quickly decimated by a severe attack of rabies. The Puckeridge had started building permanent kennels at Hay Street, Braughing before his arrival and he soon set about building a house for himself alongside, Hay Lodge. His arrival was not the cause of the civil war however, rather it was one of the factors of it. The civil war came about because the Gosling faction who hunted the eastern side of the country on Mondays and Wednesdays could not agree with the Sworder faction, who hunted the western side of the country on Saturdays, about the way the hunt was run and commandeered the hounds to create the Herts and Essex Hunt in the western half of the country.

As the years went on the rift seemed to widen; there were some ugly clashes between the factions, there was intimidation, interference, court proceedings and two referrals to the MFH Association. The second brought forth an edict that both packs should be abandoned, that the Puckeridge should be re-formed to hunt the whole country and that none of the people involved in the two previous packs should be allowed to stand for office for the new one. This is what duly happened and Mr Swindell moved to the Old Berkshire. Perhaps he had not been entirely blameless in this messy and very public dispute, and indeed it was whispered that he manipulated foxes so that they were found where and when they were wanted by the Sworder faction and were not found when they were wanted by the Gosling faction, but this might have been an ugly rumour put about by the Goslings as part of their strategy to smear the reputation of their rival. Nevertheless he inherited a quarrel, but in spite of it is said to have been a popular Master with his own faction and to have shown good sport.

No doubt it was his experiences with the Puckeridge that led him to take the Aldenham 'by the scruff of the neck' and initiate moves to put things on a firm footing at the outset:

Abbey Mills,
St Albans.
April 1906

Dear Sir,

As the new Master, Mr F.Swindell, asks for a Subscription of £120, I give you on the other side a list of those who have hunted for years with the pack, and who are now invited to subscribe £10 each towards the Fund, and most of them have already consented.

It is the general wish that the required amount should come from those who have hunted in the past, and that no one else be asked to subscribe or further subscriptions taken without the consent of the Subscribers' Committee, as by these means the Field can be kept - as they were before- small, and the Hunt continued on the old lines.

Mr Bailey has given the Hounds to the Country, and suggests that a small Committee should be formed to accept them, and only stipulates that if the pack is given up, they are to be sold and the proceeds handed to some deserving Charities. I suggest that Mr C.T.Part, Mr A.Hodgson, and Mr H.F.Reynolds be asked to form this Committee. Mr Bailey's name does not appear amongst the Subscribers as he is assisting the Hunt with Kennels, etc., and has promised to help and assist in every way he can.

Mr Swindell will hunt the hounds, but Mr Reynolds will assist him in the working of the country as he did the late Master, and I ask your assistance to keep the meets private and thus avoid large fields, so that the good feeling which now exists may continue in the

future between those whose land we ride over - many of these do not
hunt - and the Aldenham Harriers.

> *Chas. Woollam*
> *Chairman of the Subscribers' Committee Meeting.*

> *C.E.Barnett, Esq*
> *A.Collings-Wells, Esq*
> *F.W.Dearbergh, Esq*
> *A.T.Hodgson, Esq*
> *John Lloyd, Esq*
> *C.Morris, Esq*
> *C.T.Part, Esq*
> *B.Ravenscroft, Esq*
> *H.F.Reynolds, Esq*
> *G.L.Whateley, Esq*
> *C.Woollam, Esq*
> *H.C.Wright, Esq*
> *Mrs Yule*

This seemed to indicate a promising start, but Mr Swindell only stayed for one season; the reason why his stay was so short does not seem to have been recorded. He was succeeded by Kenneth Walker who retained his Mastership until he retired in 1910. Then followed another brief encounter; Mr Birkbeck Ravenscroft of the Noke, St Albans, who also lasted for only one season. David Sheppard was Kennel Huntsman and whipper-in at this time.

Little seems to have been recorded about Kenneth Walker, but we have two reports of meets while Birkbeck Ravenscroft was Master. Both are from the *Herts Advertiser* and the first is from their issue of 25th March 1911:

> *"...met at Oster Hills, St Albans* [near the City Hospital] *on Tuesday on the occasion of the last meet but one of the season, when a good field turned out, although the morning was none too promising for the first day of spring. The Master (Mr Birkbeck Ravenscroft) the Huntsman (Mr H.F.Reynolds) and Mr H.S.Bailey (the late Master) were there and the company also included Mr A.Marnham, Mrs Marnham, Mr C.H.Watson, Mr Jacob Reynolds, Mr A.J.Reynolds, Mr Oscar Phillips, Mr R.Bricker, Mr G.Elmes, Mr H.T.Smith, Mr A.J.Dixon, Mr W.B.Nott, Mr R.W.Bourne, Mr R.Smith, Mr W.Dickinson, and Mr J.Lyon, Master Dearbergh, Miss Worsnam* [Worssam?] *and Mrs Moir were also mounted, and among those who were present to witness the meet were Mr and Mrs Dearbergh,*

Mrs Ernest Gape, the Misses Glossop, Miss Violet Worsnam, and Mrs A.J.Reynolds.

In connection with the meet a 'cap' was at the suggestion of Mr A.J.Reynolds who is hon. secretary for the St Albans district taken on behalf of the Royal Agricultural Benevolent Institution, and a sum of £12.17.3d or 17.3d over the record collection at last year's meet at Oster Hills, was subscribed.

Shortly afterwards a start was made. Within five minutes of the start a hare was put up on Mr Smith's land, and there was the excited music of the hounds and the merry tootle of the horn. But the run was short-lived, for the hare, evading its pursuers, doubled back and made direct for Townsend Farm, thence across the clover field adjacent to Oster Hills. People watching the sport from the lane turned her and after meandering about for a time in the same field, she found her way through the fence in the dell and made for Batchwood. Meanwhile the hounds pressed forward in the direction of Cheapside Farm, thence round towards Harpenden and Hammond's End, and crossing the river through to Beaumont Hall..."

Not such an entertaining style as *'Stubbins'* later produced, but it is an interesting piece for a number of reasons; much of where they hunted has subsequently been built on, twenty two riders are named and it is the first mention of an Aldenham 'cap' found. However, it is known that the Quorn had tried it experimentally fourteen years earlier, having copied the idea from Ireland. Remember that is ninety years ago. A record of the last meeting of that season was published in the same way on 1st April 1911:

"Ideal conditions favoured the concluding run of the Aldenham Harriers on Tuesday, when the meet was at Heath Farm [St Albans] where a large company of followers and friends were hospitably welcomed by Mr and Mrs Jacob Reynolds whose house was truly 'Liberty Hall' for all who gathered there. These included ...[Master, ex-Master and Huntsman as in the previous piece then]...Dr Hartzhorne, Mr F.W.Dearbergh, Mr C.H.Watson, Mr and Mrs C.Arnold, Mr W.Slimmon, Mr and Mrs A.J.Reynolds, Mr H.R.Stott, Mr S.Welch, Mrs and Miss Worsnam, Mr J. Mousley, Mr A.Scott Moreton, Mrs H.F.Reynolds, Master Jack Reynolds, Mrs H.Mardall, Mrs W.Mardall, Mrs Cecil Scott, Miss Reynolds, Mr T.Smith, Mr D.Smith, Mr H.T.Smith, Mr W.Dickinson, Mr J.Lyon, Mr J.Sibley, Mr A.Martin, Mr A.J.Dixon jun., and Mrs Herring.

The weather was fine and the scent good, and a considerable concourse of people gathered to watch the meet. A start was made down Sandridge Road and a hare was found directly on Heath Farm, and ran by the Midland Railway round by Cheapside just skirting Hawkswick, then back through Beech Bottom and the old Brickyard , which forms part of Messrs. Wiles and Lewis's property on Bernard's Heath. The Hare then got upon the Harpenden Road and was seen to pass the Riding School, making for St Peter's Street, down which thoroughfare the hounds proceeded and there lost scent.

Returning to Sandridge Road, the hounds were taken over Dead Woman's Hill Bridge and found a little hare, which gave them a run round through Beech Bottom, by Sandridgebury and the Rifle Butts over Evans's Farm to Oaklands where the hounds re-found her, and she then came back through Marshal's wick [sic] *and Beech Bottom right on to Sandridgebury again and on to the Sandridge Road where the hounds ran into her. The run was very fast from start to finish...”*

Now that is a very curious circumstance; the hunt in full cry down St Peter's Street, surely we must have here the only record of it ever happening.

Mr. William Walker of High Canons, Shenley, another of the Aldenham's sporting heroes, had his origins in the Manchester district where he hunted with the Cheshire. Once established at High Canons he drove his own coach and four, which he was very good at and which he particularly enjoyed. He was also regarded as a great judge of horses and owned some first class point-to-pointers. He became Master of the Enfield Chace Staghounds in 1903 and stayed with them until 1907 after which he took over the Aldenham Harriers in 1912 and lasted for ten very successful seasons, moving on to become Master of the Hertfordshire Hunt in 1923, where he served for three seasons. Thus he had the unusual experience of having been Master of foxhounds, staghounds and harriers in his time and all three packs were kennelled at High Canons near Shenley for the duration of his Mastership. His huntsman at the Hertfordshire remarked that the reason for his outstanding success was that he never interfered with the huntsman nor the whippers-in at home or in the field, but gave them the credit for knowing their job which gave them confidence. Further, all three hunts went from strength to strength under his leadership. The harriers were duly moved to his kennels at High Canons under the control of the honorary huntsman, Mr H.F.Reynolds, but it was William Walker who took on in 1914, as huntsman, Rick (Patrick James) Fenn, regarded by many as the greatest of all harrier huntsmen; he remained with the hunt for thirty three seasons. Previously he had been with the North Bucks Harriers.

William Walker (MH 1912-1922) of High Canons, Shenley in about 1890
Julian Watson

William Walker was popular with his hunt servants; he always mounted them well and was regarded as generous and fair. When out hunting he was placid and even tempered, never grumbled, or shouted, or swore, in marked contrast to some of the Masters who were to come later. He was a man of few words and on one occasion, at the end of a particularly good day in the saddle his huntsman remarked *"splendid day's sport that sir"*, the response was *"I've known better"*. Thereafter no comment was ever made about the day's hunting, but he never ever found fault. Certainly he was a taciturn man, but there is another story about him that shows that he was not coldly taciturn, but showed kindness and understanding to his staff. The hunt was out one day and finding an iron hurdle in their way the second whipper-in got off his mare to attend to it, but instead of hooking his arm through the reins or giving them to a colleague to hold, he just let them drop and the mare stood on her own. The iron hurdle rattled, and away went the mare at a great pace down onto the main road, where she tried to jump a spiked iron fence and impaled herself, so had to be put down. All the Master said was *"Never mind, she was not an expensive mare"* and that was an end of it. How many Masters would have done that?

William Walker's coach and four at High Canons, Shenley in about 1900
Julian Watson

High Canons was to feature largely in the annals of the Aldenham Harriers for the next decade. It was an elegant house and although the buildings only dated back to the end of the eighteenth century, occupation of the site went back as least as far as 1216 when Henry III granted the manor to the canons of St Bartholomew's Priory. Thomas Fitzherbert who acquired High Canons in 1796 has elsewhere been erroneously confused with the famous Mr & Mrs Fitzherbert, the latter the disputed wife of King George IV, but the dates are wrong and they never lived there. Thomas only held the estate for six years; selling it in 1802 to John Macqueen. Thereafter it changed ownership three times during the next ten years until it was sold in 1812 to Enoch Durant (*see page 37*). William Walker lived here for forty years until his death in 1938. The property was later acquired by the Hertfordshire County Council and has now been demolished.

William Walker (MH 1912-1922) of High Canons, Shenley in about 1910
Julian Watson

Early in William Walker's first season, on 30th November 1912, *Grey Friar* in the *Herts Advertiser* gave a report of an unusual meet:-

"...It came about in this way; after drawing for nearly an hour, the only reward was a stale line which led into Little Pursley Wood. Then the surprising thing occurred. At the far end of the Big Wood a couple of hinds - outliers who had been at liberty for some time - jumped out and went away with hounds in hot pursuit. Before the huntsman realised what was happening, deer and hounds were three or four fields away. Then started a real good hunt of over

seventy-five minutes without a check, with hounds running for blood and a burning scent, the field became somewhat select. The following was some of the country over which we went:- Going away on the far side of Big Pursley Ravenscroft Farm, they turned right handed, leaving Ridge Church on the left, then over Summerswood Farm to Mr Lock's, then right handed towards Dyrham Park into the main road. There they jumped out of the main road and across Mr Mcnamara's farm to Messrs Beale and Bonner's Rowley Farm; then left handed nearly up to Arkley, left handed again over Elm Farm, and left handed again to Mr Mcnamara's spinney where we stopped them. The going was all over the grass, which was strongly fenced, and great credit is due to our Honorary Huntsman (Mr Harry Reynolds) for the way in which we eventually got to hounds and whipped them off just in the nick of time to save a situation which at one time looked like becoming serious. Thus the hinds were enabled to get off none the worse..."

The Aldenham Harriers kennels became somewhat depleted during the First World War and so at the end of hostilities, to bring them up to strength, William Walker bought the Brighton & Brookside pack which was being disbanded. From the start of his Mastership in 1912 William Walker maintained a ledger, *"Record of Sport at High Canons"* (in fact the first entry is dated 6th February 1911) which has survived, being presently in the hands of his grandson, Julian Watson. A selection of a few entries for the period towards the end of his Mastership and beyond are of interest. The ledger records his activities with a number of hunts, but the following are of when he was riding with the Aldenham:

> *"28th February 1922*
>> *Harper Lane Bridge*
>>> *Found at once and ran hare 45 mins. Lost at Wall Hall Covert. After fox found in Munden House Wood ....found near Whitelands Avenue (Lodge). Good hunt.*
>
> *13th November 1923*
>> *Bamville Farm*
>>> *Drew Dickinson & Sibley's then Cox's. Too many hares. Very strong wind. Left 2.30 church side going to Evans Farm.*
>
> *6th December 1923*
>> *High Canons*
>>> *Found hare and ran round by new cottages and*

*left handed nursery to Calterise Bourne &
Brown's. Left handed back to new cottages and
lost. Found twice. Raphaels no scent.*

18th November 1924
> *High Canons*
>> *Found brace of hares on Birch Wood side. Not
>> much scent. Found on Nursery Field. Ran round
>> into Big Pursley. Found on Pond Field. Ran
>> round and found again."*

For the 1920/21 season H.S.Bailey continued as secretary and the hounds continued to be kennelled at High Canons, but in 1922 one of the Aldenham's 'golden eras' came to an end; William Walker retired and a committee took control for the following six seasons. The hounds were then moved to Sportsmen's Hall, which was in Cottonmill Lane, St Albans and the kennels at High Canons later became the home of the Hertfordshire Hunt hounds when William Walker become Master.

The Aldenham Harriers had been essentially a private pack for the first fifty years of its life, but in 1928 another committee was constituted to manage it. The new Master was Mr C.E.Stevenson of Cardy House, Boxmoor; like his predecessor, he was to stay for ten seasons, and he too became immensely popular and respected. Charles Ernest Stevenson was born at Jedburgh in 1871; the fifth son of J.C.Stevenson who was Procurator Fiscal for Roxburghshire. He worked for the Colombo Commercial Co in Ceylon for sixteen years to 1911 when he returned to become a member of the London Stock Exchange, trading as C.E.Stevenson & Co. While in Ceylon he earned a reputation as a keen golfer and first class tennis player.

His early hunting experiences were with the Jedburgh Forest and the Duke of Buccleuch's Hounds, and later he followed not only the Aldenham, but also the Old Berkeley and the Hertfordshire. In 1898 he married Elizabeth Rachel, daughter of Walter Smith of South Hill, Hemel Hempstead. Of his time as Master of the Aldenham Harriers he was to say that he greatly valued his friendship with the farmers; he would often remark that he had never been refused a day's hunting on their land, which was something of a reflection upon his considerable popularity and summed up in a few works what successful 'Mastering' is all about.

It was at this time that 'Stubbins', the second of the Aldenham Harriers' scribes surfaced; he was a neighbour of the new Master at Boxmoor and welcomed him warmly in the *Horse & Hound*:

"This very sporting little pack is lucky in having as a Master one

of the finest type of men one could wish to meet. Big, structurally and in every other way, he is essentially a farmers' man, and that is what is required to-day, especially with harriers. On Saturday, the 24th. Ult., [November 1928] the meet was at his home, Cardy House, Boxmoor, and one realised how very popular he is when one saw the large crowd of followers and great number of farmers who turned up to partake of the hospitality of Mr. and Mrs. Stevenson. It was bitterly cold and a bad-scenting day, but Mr. Fenn, who carries the horn, is a real good fellow to keep on the move, and a really enjoyable day was spent on the farms on the high ground north of Boxmoor. Hares were plentiful, and the last one provided quite a fine little hunt, and was killed on Mr. Howe's farm after a gallop of about twenty minutes."

Eric Goddard was whipper-in at this stage whom Gurney Mercer remembers well because it was he who taught him to ride at the old kennels at Cuckmans. Gurney recalls that his instructor kept the Fox & Hounds (how very appropriate!) pub opposite the railway station at Bricket Wood.

Farmers generally welcomed the activities of the hunt, but an unusual and unnecessary case of trespass and damage was brought against the Aldenham Harriers by the Polar explorer Apsley Cherry-Garrard (member of Scott's Antarctic Expedition) who lived at Lamer Park, Wheathampstead in 1929, during Mr C.E.Stevenson's time as Master. It was heard by Judge H.P.Hargreaves at St Albans County Court; a long rigmarole by counsel about trespass and damage to property went on all morning and part of the afternoon and the upshot was that the Master apologised and undertook to pay for damaged fences. Damage was slight, but compensation of £100 was claimed and the contention arose because the Master was hunting in Lamer Park without obtaining prior permission and when he was stopped adopted a truculent attitude instead of apologising.

The gamekeeper's version of what happened was submitted by Mr Trustram Eve for the plaintiff and in essence was not contested. He said that Aldenham Harriers met at 11am on 4th December 1928 at a place called Pulmore Water. Just before 11.30 Mr Cherry-Garrard's gamekeeper met two horsemen, one of them in hunt livery, upon his master's land. The conversation was opened by the man in livery, who may have been a whipper-in, and who asked whether the gamekeeper had seen his hounds. He replied no, asked whether the horsemen had been given permission to hunt there, and was told he did not know. The gamekeeper then instructed them to leave, which they did.

A quarter of an hour later the gamekeeper saw hounds and the field in full cry going through two woods called Great Norfolk and Little Norfolk, both owned by Mr Cherry-Garrard; some were in the ride and some were in the rough. He did not think that the Master knew that Mr Cherry-Garrard had arranged a shoot in those woods for the following day, but all the game was frightened away.

At lunch time the gamekeeper was in his cottage at Lamer Home Farm when he heard the horn and went outside to find the hunt in full cry coming across the park from north to south towards him. They were stopped by the woodman, East, near the spot where the fences were damaged.

Here were two closes which, with others, plaintiff had planted with small and tender young trees at a cost of about £5,000. From these closes he had eliminated rabbits, which would browse on the young stock, and he had erected a series of three foot high fences around, which were extended one foot underground with the intention of keeping the rabbits out. In spite of East's direct orders, two mounted people, one in hunt livery, jumped the fence around the plantation. East and the gamekeeper told them to go back but they went on. One rider, leading another horse, jumped it with the first then walked back, mounted the second horse and jumped the fence with that.

Later the gamekeeper and East caught up with the field and asked the hunt servant who they were. He was told "*the Waddon Hoo Pack*" which, as there is no such pack, appeared to be a deliberate attempt to implicate the Whaddon Chase. The huntsman then claimed that he had permission to hunt there, which was not true. The Master tried to 'square' the gamekeeper with the price of a drink, which was refused, so he asked to see Mr Cherry-Garrard and was told that he was away. He then asked to see his wife and was told there was not one, at which he was heard to say that he was a lucky man. There was laughter in Court at this and the gamekeeper, who was giving the evidence, said he hoped that Mrs Cherry-Garrard was not in Court; however, Apsley did marry, but not until September 1939 and this may have been a reference to his mother who lived at Lamer Park during the Second World War and died in 1946. The Master then rode away and was heard to remark to a colleague that the grounds were no more than a twopenny-halfpenny birdcage anyway.

Mr Apsley Cherry-Garrard said that his family had been at Lamer Park for approaching five hundred years; he was keen on afforestation and in the past four or five years had planted four hundred acres of young trees. He was not against hunting and had always agreed to it over his land, providing there was no damage and prior permission was obtained. The Hertfordshire Hunt were regular visitors. The Aldenham Harriers had not asked and had not even had the courtesy to send him a printed meets card. He said that no part of the £100 damages he claimed was for his wounded pride, but nevertheless agreed that the fences could be mended for £5, so presumably the remaining £95 was for rabbit damage to young trees.

The parties settled by agreement after the lunch adjournment and an apology plus a nominal sum were accepted.

Trespass by a hunt must have happened thousands of times before, indeed everywhere that hunting is practised, but the case encompasses the very essence of modern day hunting. To be able to ride to hounds over land you do not own is a very great privilege not to be abused, even if the land owner is getting some sort of service by having pests chased off it. It would seem that the Aldenham Harriers had a bad press on this front in 1929, but the lesson was very well learned. They were very careful about all aspects of courtesy to landowners forever afterwards and all the records are full of notes of appreciation to farmers for the use of their lands. Even though it sometimes inadvertently happens, hunts should endeavour never to trespass, but being truculent and untruthful when you are in the wrong is very, very silly.

The new Master took a tough line on discipline after the case and *'Stubbins'* , who was close to him, felt constrained to write about another point of contention:

"on Thursday, December 13th, Mr and Mrs Barratt entertained a large field when these harriers met at their home, Great Westwood, Bucks Hill. The Barratts are rare sporting people, and take interest in our little pack. Among the field was another sport, the parson from Latimer, a jolly good man to hounds, and looks like the picture, hat and all. It was a cold morning, and there was very little scent until the afternoon, when things livened up and we had a most enjoyable day. Three hares were killed after very good runs.

Struth! I would not have been in the shoes of the young man who rode over wheat seeds for anything. Mr. Stevenson, the Master, spoke to him in language the equal of which I have not heard for a long, long time. When I passed the spot where the little ceremony took place I noticed that even the hedge was singed.

The Aldenham Harriers are holding a Hunt ball at St. Albans Town Hall on January 11th 1929, and from what I hear it is likely to be a huge success, thanks largely to Mrs Duncan. [Stubbins is very keen on Mrs Duncan!] I hope she shows us the way to dance as well as she leads us across country."

"A field quite large enough turned up at the meet at Corner Farm, Stags End on 22nd inst. [December 1928] The land around here is mostly under cultivation and it takes a keen eye to see that everyone keeps close in to the hedges round a seed field. During the holidays every sportsman is, of course, delighted to see the kiddies home enjoying themselves, but parents in a country such as ours should give their little ones some instruction as to avoiding seed fields, getting out of the way of hounds etc., before they come out. I felt

sorry for one innocent little culprit who was called over the coals by the Master (who, however, did it very nicely), but the poor little beggar's day was naturally somewhat spoilt. As the father of eight [they did things in style in those days] *who study their HORSE & HOUND more diligently than their Bible and sometimes go out five in a bunch I presume I know what I am talking about where the young entry are (or is) concerned.*

We had quite a lot of fun all round the Stags End district, and hounds were "galloping and barking" most of the time till the fog became too dense to be pleasant. Several people lost hounds in the mist, but it was wonderful how they found us at 'the Cricketers', Redbourn, before closing time. My pal from the North was lucky (or artful) enough to get lost with the best looking gal from St. Albans, [Mrs Duncan again] *and I understand that she impressed on him that all men should wear their Hunt dress coats at the ball at St. Albans on January 11th."*

We can take it that *'Stubbins'* definitely fancies Mrs Duncan; risky coming from a hunting man who admits to having had eight children, but there is no indication that there was anything more than admiration in it, and that is the closest that researches have come to any sort of a scandal with the Aldenham Harriers, leading me to suppose that they are either very virtuous or very discreet. I incline towards the latter. Admitted, later on, there was the husband who rang up to find out whether his wife was out hunting and was plainly relieved to be told that this was indeed the case. Discretion forbade mention that she was hunting with her boyfriend and had been doing so regularly for weeks. The parties must remain nameless and hopefully the secret has been maintained to this day, so the case does not count as a scandal.

An early indication of the new order of things, after the arrival of the new Master the previous year, was a point-to-point race meeting arranged jointly with the Stock Exchange for Saturday 20th April 1929. Stanley White won the first race, the Aldenham Harriers Steeplechase, on Mr T. Mason's NO TRUMP by six lengths. The success of that meeting was such that it was to be repeated each year until racing ceased at Friars Wash in 1964, apart from an interlude over the war years and the aftermath.

The Aldenham Harriers Point-to-Point at Friars Wash 14th March 1931.
Mrs A.S.Beville on her CANDLE (centre) winner of the Nomination Open Ladies
Steeplechase taking the last fence.
Mrs E.Greenall on her TORCHLIGHT TATTOO (left) came second
Joan Cunningham

The Aldenham Harriers Point-to-Point at Friars Wash 23rd April 1932.
he start of the Nomination Open Ladies Steeplechase.
Joan Cunningham

The second point-to-point meeting took place at Friars Wash on 29th March 1930 in excellent weather. That year the hunt secretary, Mr Whitehead retired after eight years in office and his place was taken by Mr W.Stovin Bradford, son of Dick Stovin who had been huntsman to the Bicester and later to the Heythrop. He became well known for his articles in the *Horse & Hound* under the pseudonym '*Stubbins*'. Sadly he was unable to ride in later years following a bad fall. He was to serve as honorary secretary until the end of the 1937/38 season.

The Aldenham Harriers Point-to-Point at Friars Wash on 23rd April 1932. Adjacent Hunts Maiden Heavyweight Steeplechase. Won by Stanley White on SUNBOY
Joan Cunningham

An outstanding feature of the Aldenham Harriers point-to-point meeting at Friars Wash on 23rd April 1932 was the performance of Stanley White who rode three horses to victory. Perfect weather favoured the meeting, but the attendance was not so large as might have been hoped for or expected. *The Herts Advertiser* described Stanley White's three wins thus:

"Mr Stanley White on his horse SUNBOY was favourite for the Heavyweight Steeplechase and led all the way to win by about ten lengths. He was also successful in the Adjacent Hunts Farmers Race, riding Mrs T.H.Merrick's MOSSTOI. He lay third in the first lap, but his mount had sufficient in hand to take the lead three jumps from home to win by six lengths from AL JOLSON. On OAKLAND Mr White won the Aldenham Harriers Point-to-Point Steeplechase easily, with fifty yards to spare. He took it easily for the first lap, being content with third place, and then he swept ahead leaving the rest of the field well behind. During the last lap, at the water, one of Mr White's stirrups became detached and he had to finish the course carrying it on his arm."

Stanley White was a great competitor; he went on to achieve a hundred wins in his long racing career. He had a peculiar style of leaning right back on his horse's hind quarters when taking a jump and it was darkly hinted that he had been known to elbow anyone close enough out of his way. As a nation we have a nasty habit of assuming that success cannot be achieved fairly and this may well be a case in point.

The Aldenham Harriers Point-to-Point at Friars Wash 21st April 1934.
Adjacent hunts steeplechase winner Stanley White on
Lt Col Dalton White's, CHARLIE CHAPLIN (No 3)
Joan Cunningham

The Aldenham Harriers meeting at Friars Wash the following year (1933) was on 25th March and Stanley again had two wins, one of them on SUNBOY. The pair were having a grand run of success, but it was not to last. Three weeks later they were competing at the Hertfordshire Hunt meeting where SUNBOY fell badly, broke his back and had to be shot. Nothing daunted, Stanley raced again at the Aldenham Harriers Friars Wash meeting the following season (21st April 1934) and was his usual prominent self, achieving two wins and a third. He rode in four of the five races, missing out on only the Ladies Race, which was natural enough, and in addition his own horse, LADY GRAY ridden by Mr Tabor managed a second.

That year (1934) was to be the first time for forty years that the Mastership was to become a joint one; Mrs E.Hall of Redcote, Harpenden joined

Mr Stevenson; they were to retire together at the end of the 1937/38 season when Mr Stevenson was presented with a silver hunting horn by members of the hunt as an appreciation for his outstanding service. Mrs Hall was a native of Norwich who, in 1912, married Edward Hall, a hat manufacturer from Leamington. After her husband's death in 1937, she moved to Harpenden where her sister, Mrs A.F.Palmer Phillips lived. She died at her home, Elm Cottage, West Common, Harpenden in 1955 aged 67.

The Aldenham Harriers Point-to-Point at Friars Wash 25th March 1933. Nomination Open Ladies Race. Won by Major J.B.Black's MOHOCK Joan Cunningham

One of the hounds was killed in a road accident on 10th March 1934; it came about this way. The hounds were proceeding along the A5 towards Redbourn when a motor lorry approached from the opposite direction, at speed. As it drew level with the Punchbowl Inn, a man in harrier rig appeared at the door. One hound appeared to recognise him, bounded over in front of the lorry and was killed instantly. There was nothing that huntsman, Rick Fenn, or whip, Edgar Goddard could do to prevent it; it all happened in an instant.

In evidence afterwards at the St Albans Divisional Sessions, the driver, Harry Leonard Hobbs from Cowley said that the Master, Mr Stevenson, was with the party and after the accident became very excited, calling him a cur and a scoundrel and threatening him with his hunting crop.

Mr M.G.Dashwood presiding found the case proved against the

defendant, but dismissed him on payment of £4.2s. costs.

In an ideal world, reports of hunts would appear at regular intervals evenly spaced over the years to provide a valuable comparison with what goes on today. Each would reflect the attitudes, the thinking, and the aspirations of the age. But this is not an ideal world, we have to make do with what there is, and thus our reports come in 'lumps' as each local hunting reporter waxes and wanes. '*Stubbins*' was prominent in the thirties; he had a nice turn of phrase, a quaint way of expressing himself; he was 'one of the lads', but of a bygone age. It must be said, however, that he was invariably entertaining and I am quoting a lot of him for this period in the hope of inspiring modern reporters. For example:

Mrs Duncombe, Huntsman Rick Fenn's sister, and Brenda Gurney near the
Aldenham Harriers Kennels at Sportsman's Hall, St Albans,
while getting fit for a long distance ride to Eastbourne in the thirties
Fiona Kinlock

"Now in the long ago a little baby came from under the gooseberry bush and they called him Harry Green. He is now grown up into quite a big fellow, but nobody knows which New Year's Day was to blame for the event. Some say he has passed the half-way line to a hundred. On January 1st the matter was seriously discussed in the Fox & Hounds after hunting, and Doug Neale accused him of being 'closhe on shicksty'. 'Garn!' says Edgar, the diplomat, 'the lad's

66

shtill growin'. But all they got out of Harry was a smiling enquiry - 'Hic?' and another round, including a couple for absent friends (I say, these pints are mounting up)."

"On New Year's Day the Aldenham Harriers met at the little village from which they take their name, and received a great welcome from Mr Fleming at Church Farm. Unfortunately, the Guvnor is now laid up, and we are really beginning to wonder which is the stronger sex, for Mrs Hall, our popular Joint-Master, blossomed forth as cheery as ever. Mr Fleming's jumping powders were top-hole, and the sausage rolls are top of the league so far this season. There was quite a crowd of kiddies out, and Captain Younghusband brought over a very merry party of youngsters. One of the Wall Hall coverts, Bury Grove, was the first draw, and although there was a whimper occasionally it was apparently stale news. Hounds then jogged on over the Watford by-pass road to High Wood, the long strip of covert which is now isolated on the Watford side of the road. The last time our hounds were here they had several foxes afoot, and had quite a decent run with one. This time it was blank, and, as there was a rumour of a fox in a field of kale at Burnt Farm, Fenn trotted on there, but it WAS only a rumour. Going back towards Aldenham hounds found a hare near the old Red Lion, and ran across to Bury Grove and on down to just above Otterspool, where they lost her. There was no scent whatever. A move was then made across the meadows to Bricket Wood, and although there were foxes about nothing could be done with them. Black Boy Wood (where there is a nudist colony) also disappointed, and so ended a pretty mouldy sort of day."

"The phone beside my bed somehow got connected up to the Fox & Hounds, Bricket Wood. You never heard such a row in your life. 'View holloas', 'hound language', 'Master's language', all mixed up. All my hunting pals seemed to be there, and these are the various packs one or the other had hunted with that day - Oakley, O.B.H., North Hertfordshire, South Hertfordshire, Aldenham Harriers. Harry Green and Doug Neale said they had been out with four packs during the day, but they couldn't remember which they were. 'Nuff said!'

"From Leverstock Green on the 8th [January 1935] the Aldenham enjoyed quite a good day. Finding on Mr Bailey's farm they ran down to Nash Mills, and crossing the Nash road the hare took them along the meadows up to White Gate Farm, gradually coming round right-handed and back towards Nash Mills again. Running

the road for a considerable distance to the plantation close to Nash Mills, she here got the better of matters. Drawing back over the Leverstock Green road, Mr Gale had a real goer waiting on his land, and hounds went away like the wind right up to Corner Farm, swinging right-handed from here over to Gorhambury Park. From close to the keeper's cottage it was a lovely sight to see the old Aldenham running with wonderful music across the park to the spinney near the deer paddock. Puss, however, was not given time to dally here, and away she went on to Kettlewells, where she turned left-handed over Cherry Tree Farm making for Mrs Cook's territory, which was unfortunately out of bounds, and hounds had to be stopped. This was one of the straightest-running hares we have come across for some time, and the pace was good enough for any man....Another good hare was found on the fallow at Mr Hartop's, hounds running again as though they had forgiven everything, straight over to my young pal Reg Booth's father's farm. From here they turned right-handed, the hare going over the St Albans-Redbourn road close to the Punch Bowl. Here an unfortunate accident happened. Old Pistol, our best hound, had outrun the rest of the pack and jumped into this busy main road close behind the hare, and was knocked over by a passing motor car. The poor old fellow was pretty badly hurt, but there are hopes of his recovery."

On 11th January 1935 the hunt ball was held at St Albans Town Hall:

"And what a merry night it was, and what a pace we ran at! Mr and Mrs Stevenson and Mrs Hall welcomed a rare crowd. Miss Margaret Stott, our charming honorary secretary, who runs the show, told me that nearly 300 tickets had been sold, and what's more, nearly 300 paid for. But then, Margaret's one of those girls who's 'got a way wid her' and she and her committee deserve and have, our warmest thanks. The Govnor was a real sport to turn out, for he has been very seedy lately. He stuck it to the bitter end, and we had glimpses of the old fire when the unofficial horn blowing got too thick. All the girls who had backs let us blokes know it, and us blokes liked it. Quite a lot of girls had backs, but didn't let us know it, but us blokes loved 'em just the same....Now our hunt ball is 'different' - if you understand me. We don't encourage cliques, and try to make it all jolly and matey, without overstepping the traces. Above all, we try to get as many farmers there as possible, and you could not wish to meet a nicer crowd than our farmers and their families."

'Stubbins' had a very 'soft spot' for Mrs Hall and he compliments her again and again.

"Once upon a time she used to be known to people in far-off places who read these notes as 'Our lady thruster from the Warwickshire'. Then one summer's day she decided to give up all that sort of thing and come and live among us and become one of us. To-day she is, we are proud to tell you, our popular Joint-Master, and on Thursday 17th [January 1935], *for the first time since she joined the Guvnor, Mrs Hall was thrusting jumping-powders to a very cheery crowd down at Redcote, her home near Harpenden Common. Everybody was delighted to see Mr Stevenson in the saddle again and holding his end up in this centre of gravity business, although the cigar nearly put him down, so it is said, for you can't smoke decently and say what you really think about people riding over other folk's seeds."*

"Of course, if the International Horse Show people adopt your suggestion about a beauty competition you could not have two better judges than Dalesman and myself, but our lady Joint-Master of Aldenham Harriers would sure to be entered and I might be biased, as the saying is."

In the *Horse & Hound* on 25th January 1935 appeared another of his gems:

"Moving off through Hatching Green, there were several hares afoot at once in the first field, hounds settling to one which took them over to Beeson End, crossing the lane, and then on to Childwickbury Stud. From here they turned right-handed and ran as straight as a die down to Redbournbury, swung round towards Shafford and into Low Springs. Round this spinney they bustled a very tired hare till they caught her.... Another hare was found immediately on the plough close by, going away at a rare pace up and over the Beeson End Lane, then up the hill nearly to Hatching Green. She now came round left-handed, and she and 16 couple of screaming hounds had things all to themselves crossing the golf-links till they got to Stanley White's covert at the far side. Stanley's an artful devil, and to get round the links to join hounds again you've got to do a bit of timber-rapping, and we love him for it. Round and round the covert hounds made one's blood tingle with their chorus till away puss skedaddled, and they soon rolled her over in the open. Things had been going very merrily up to now, and most folk had shifted their centres of gravity time after time over the jumps of the said Stanley, backward seats had moved forrard, others had come unstuck, but better was to come.

An exceptional hare from close to the farm down at Redbournbury set a rattling pace and went away absolutely in a straight line right along to Batchwood. With the stud-farm on the right, puss, still going strong, made for Batchwood gardens, where she evidently knew her way about, but there was no denying hounds, and they soon bundled her out of here, and she came away left-handed pointing for Westwood. Running straight through this big covert the hound-music was simply glorious, and going out on the Harpenden side it was a desperate struggle to live with them as they made for Childwickbury, where, after a turn round the park, they rolled over a very gallant hare close to the house. For a hare this was a real good performance, and I make it five miles as hounds run.

Another was quickly killed, making 2 brace for the day, and then everybody, including hounds, made their way back to Hammonds End, where Mr & Mrs Stanley White royally entertained the whole crowd."

Then on 1st March 1935, again in the *Horse & Hound* we get:

"Last season we wrote quite a nice bit of poetry, as we thought, describing how Maggie [his wife?] and I jogged along with hounds all the way down to Kimpton. On Tuesday, the 12th [February 1935], they managed to get there without us. Scenting conditions were very poor, and they could do nothing with the numerous hares they found. Our old pal down there did his best, as usual, and after hunting invited everybody back to his place. Bless his old heart - I wish I'd been there!"

A triviality you may say, but it demonstrates two things: the man's very personal, endearing style and the fact that scent is everything.

The Aldenham Harriers meeting at Cardy House, Boxmoor, home of Alderman C.E.Stevenson (MH 1928-1938), perhaps in 1928
Eve Davis Collection

In the same edition we get the following, spoilt a little because of the 'in house' jokes to which we are not privy, but useful because of the places he mentions which are mostly today underneath Hemel Hempstead New Town :

"Saturday, the 16th [February 1935] *was a cold and windy day, with little prospects, it seemed, of doing any good as far as hunting was concerned, but in the opinion of some of our regulars they enjoyed one of the best runs of the season. Cardy House, Boxmoor, the home of the Guvnor, was the venue, and a large field turned out. Quite a crowd of Old Berkeley people turned up, including Sir Herbert and Lady Wright, Colonel Armstrong, Miss McKenzie, and Miss Middleton. As usual Mr and Mrs Stevenson held open house to all and sundry, and the mince pies are still top of the league. After everybody had had their dues, in a manner of speaking, Mrs Hall, our popular Joint-Master, persuaded the Guvnor to call 'time' and those who could vaulted into the saddle. The mounting block in the stable yard was hard put to it, but George, as ever, had a pair of steps handy for the select few.*

The Master's domains were drawn blank, for a wonder, and, as I've said before, he only jugs Scotch hares. Nothing of note was done at Gravel Hill either, but on going along to Farmer Chalk's a hare was

71

soon away from a ploughed field, making up the hill towards Gadebridge.

Scent was surprisingly good, the hounds ran at great pace right over to the poultry-farm, then with Gadebridge coverts on the right the hare made for the pig farm, and even that didn't seem to interfere with the other scent. Continuing in a wide left-hand circle hounds ran with a wonderful cry all the way back to Northridge Farm, leaving Farmer Chalk's house on the right. Here puss ran the road for a considerable distance, but there was no denying the old Aldenham to-day, and they carried the line nearly down to Green End before going into the fields again right-handed.

Hounds simply flew on the grass down into the dingle beyond Northridge House, and up the other side, leaving Chaulden allotments on the left and so on into the 300 acre field at the back of Chaulden House. It looked as though the hare had crossed the railway line at the far end, but hounds suddenly swung left-handed and gradually made their way back to the spinney below Green End. Without dwelling here they ran on up the hill past Northridge, down into the valley the other side, and so on back to Gadebridge.
Just as hounds reached the Boxmoor - Warner's End Road a tremendous storm suddenly came down and put paid to a wonderful hunt."

On 21st February 1935 the Aldenham were the guests of Colonel Wilfred Wild *"and his two charming daughters"* at Shenley Hill where, to a degree, they broke the rules of the game as '*Stubbins*' reported:

"The Colonel persuaded the Guvnor to take hounds into Coombe Wood and rattle the foxes about a bit. The well-known old dog-fox with the large white tip to his brush was soon away, but although Fenn persisted with a great deal of patience nothing could be done with him a minute after he had gone. Going back into the wood there were several other foxes afoot, but there was not a trace of scent. It was the same out in the field after hares - the hounds could only run with the hare in view. And there is not much fun in hounds coursing."

This was the golden age of the Aldenham Harriers in print; nobody else before or since has done them so proud. At his pinnacle in the mid 1930s, '*Stubbins*' put a piece in the *Horse & Hound* about the Aldenham Harriers almost every week during the season. He set the scene in a way that nobody else had before, nor indeed has since; we could do with a *'Son of Stubbins'*, or perhaps grandson would be more appropriate, today.

The 3rd Lord Cowdray on his MR TRIPLEX winners of the Aldenham Harriers Adjacent Hunts Heavyweight Race at Friars Wash 14th March 1936

There was a crowd of 10,000 at the Aldenham Harriers Point-to-Point Races at Friars Wash on 6th April 1935 and Stanley White had an easy win on SLIDEAWAY.

The 1936 Harriers Hunt Ball was held at St Albans Town Hall on the evening of Friday 6th March when *"it again lived up to its reputation of being one of the most popular social fixtures in hunting circles in the county"*. The Mayfair Band provided the music for the 270 guests and the programme concluded, as usual, with 'John Peel'. Mrs Hall, the Joint Master, provided the flowers which were singled out in the press for particular praise. Hunts represented were the Hertfordshire, the Old Berkeley, the South Herts Beagles and the Pinner Drag.

Jack Molyneux, writing of this period towards the end of Mr Stevenson's mastership said:

"....It turned out to be Dick Stovin, who had a very shrill voice. To finish up my day with 'Stubbins' [Dick Stovin's pseudonym for his

73

writings on hunting matters] *we had dinner with Mr & Mrs Stevenson who lived in the next house.... he and 'Stubbins' are two of the very best. Mrs Stevenson was out with the Old Berkeley the same day."*

At a meeting at the Peahen at St Albans in January 1938 Mr Stevenson and Mrs Hall announced their resignations as joint Masters, the former for health and financial reasons, and the latter because she was not so keen on riding as she had been formerly. Mr H.C.Wright, who presided at the meeting, said joint Masters had worked hard for the Harriers and it was felt that at the end of their time relations with farmers were better than they had been for some time. Mr E.W.Taylor responded on behalf of the farmers. Before considering a successor, a minute was read from a meeting of the committee in 1930 which stated that the new Master then appointed agreed to take over the hounds on condition that when the pack was given up it should be sold and the proceeds should be donated to a deserving charity. Mr Stevenson said that he stood by that commitment and proposed to donate the proceeds to the Farmers Benevolent Fund in recognition of the support that he and the subscribers had received from farmers and landowners during his Mastership.

Herbert Wright of Wright's Coal Tar Soap fame, Mary Allen's father and Fiona Kinlock's great uncle, at his home, Bamville Farm, Harpenden in the thirties. Mary now farms at Chipping Norton and was at school at St George's, Harpenden with Pat Burgin
Fiona Kinlock

The last meet of the season was at Cardy House, Boxmoor in the following March. It was there that Mr Wright presented a silver huntsman's horn to Mr Stevenson and a silver salver to Mrs Hall in recognition of their services. He made a short speech before the large and distinguished gathering in which he expressed regret that Mrs Stevenson could not be there because of her serious illness. In paying tribute to Mrs Hall he made a point of stressing that farmers were anly too pleased to see her wherever she went which only goes to reinforce '*Stubbins*' opinion of her. In reply Mr Stevenson expressed sadness at leaving the Mastership, but said all good things must come to an end someday and he would find a prominent place on his mantle-piece for his hunting horn which would stay there for the rest of his life. By that time he was aged 67 and only survived for another five years; he took a bad fall in February 1942 and died two months later. Amongst the wreaths at his funeral was one from his hunter, AUNTIE.

The secretary, Mr Stovin Bradford, said that he had received a number of enquiries from prospective Masters, one of which had come from Major Sir Jocelyn Lucas, Bart., MC. A sub-committee was formed to consider the matter and report back. At the subsequent meeting a new committee was formed comprising:

Mr Wright

Mrs Hall

Mr E.W.Taylor

Mr W.Franklin

Mr W.E.Lock

Mr H.F.Reynolds

Mr G.Sparrow

and Sir Jocelyn was unanimously elected Master. The choice had not been a difficult one; Sir Jocelyn was, if anything, over-qualified for his new duties. He had succeeded in 1936, his father Sir Edward Lingard Lucas 3rd Bart. Having been born on 27th August 1889 and educated at Eton he had had a distinguished military career in the First World War, being at one time a Major in the Royal Warwickshire Regiment. In the event he was to serve in both world wars. His home was at Michelmersh Court in Romsey, but there is no indication of where he lived while he was Master of the Aldenham and the likelihood is that he journeyed back and forth from his London home. He died on 2nd May 1980. He was a prominent politician, serving as MP for a division of Portsmouth from 1939 until 1966, on top of which he had somehow found time to write extensively on sporting matters, his titles including: *Simple Doggie Remedies, Pedigree Dog Breeding* (1925), *The Sealyham Terrier, The New Book of the Sealyham* (1929) and *Hunt and Working Terriers* (1931). A volume of the latter he presented to his predecessor, William Walker, suitably inscribed, which is now in the possession of his grandson, Julian Watson. Sir Jocelyn experimented with terrier crosses, trying to improve the sealyham and eventually produced a strain which passed his exacting standards. It is called the Sporting Lucas Terrier and although now rare there are still a few about.

Major Sir Jocelyn Lucas (MH 1938-1942) with Huntsman Rick Fenn
passing bomb damage at Letchmore Heath in 1940
Valerie Dickinson

Sir Jocelyn had hunting in his blood, not just for hare or fox, but for anything a dog will chase. Early on he was keen on terriers and bred all sorts of them for the greater part of his life. At times he had up to a hundred of them in kennels. His first pack were smooth haired fox-terriers which he taught to hunt like hounds and he was particularly gratified that they could throw their tongues well. He would train his terriers on rats and had his own system for collecting a sackfull of them live at threshing time, when they were particularly abundant, and releasing them in a controlled manner for training exercises that he devised himself; he claimed terriers never let one get away. He organised meets in his New Forest country which attracted large fields and on one occasion he had a massive two hundred people out, which says much for his talents.

When he became a cadet at Sandhurst in 1909, he was devastated to find that he was not allowed to keep dogs there. Fortunately, his uncle had an estate close by, in fact next door to Field-Marshal Lord Roberts which was very convenient, so he kept his terriers at uncle's and some beagles at the Berystede Hotel, and hunted them twice a week. He said of those days that he was so keen that he would lie awake all night before hunting *"trembling like a terrier outside a rat hole"!*

76

There was still the last meet of the 1938 season to come and here *'Doug'* stole *'Stubbins'* thunder by reporting on it in the *Horse & Hound* on 11th March 1938:

> *"....All a bit quaint he is and so is the Fishery Inn, by the canal at Boxmoor, where from the upper room window, the piscatorial professors of the town dangle their lines into the canal and take the waters, or whatever it is, while they are a-doing of it. Grand, it is, and we passed it on Saturday last on the way up to see the Aldenham Harriers out for the last time this season. It was a glorious day, but no scent at all. It was a sad day too, for the Harriers, because not only was it their closing meet of the season, but also it was the end of the Joint-Mastership of Mr C.E.Stevenson and Mrs E.Hall, and up at Cardy at the end of the day, when Mr Stevenson blew hounds home for the last time on his new silver horn, everyone present stood to watch them go down the drive as they set off for kennels."*

History was repeated as the new Master set about improving the character of the pack by introducing new blood. In fact improving the pack by drafting and breeding appears in sources so often one can be forgiven for wondering why standards declined so rapidly and frequently that they needed improving so often. The answer may be that there was little that could be said about the achievements of a retiring Master when it came to presentation speech time, and as the standards of the hounds seem to have been pretty good over the years, anybody making a speech would be on fairly safe ground by claiming that the outgoing Master had improved the pack. A bit tough on his predecessor perhaps, but people have short memories and in some cases the predecessor had died. In this case fifteen couple were drafted in from the Barnwell Harriers which was then being disbanded and a few couple of fox hounds were introduced. This had a profound effect and in the two seasons prior to the outbreak of the Second World War a record number of hare were dispatched. At this point Eric Goddard, the whipper-in, moved on and his place was taken by Miss Brenda Gurney.

On Friday 21st January 1938 the annual hunt ball was held at St Albans Town Hall to the music of John Tyler's Band. One person who was absent was Geoffrey Hartop, a man who would figure prominently in the annals of the Aldenham Harriers later on; he was on his way to America for his honeymoon, having the previous day married Doris Caroline, daughter of Ernest Stewart Hertz of Manor Farm, Old Knebworth, at Knebworth Parish Church. Both were prominent in hunting and point-to-point circles and Geoffrey, son of William Hartop of Nether Crawley, Luton, was already farming on his own account at Beaumont Hall, Redbourn. He was an enviably vigorous type of man, being a popular figure at Harpenden Rugby Club and Redbourn Cricket Club, and this on top of his farming, racing and hunting activities. It would be nice to know how he managed to maintain his energies, and purse, and enthusiasms, but unfortunately it is too late to ask.

One of Sir Jocelyn Lucas' Christmas cards depicting the Aldenham Harriers at Bamville Farm, Harpenden in the 1938/39 season
Fiona Kinlock

Honorary secretary Mr Stovin Bradford retired in 1938 after eight years in office and the following year his place was taken by Mrs G.Duncan who remained throughout the war years.

Miss Anne Handley Page joined Sir Jocelyn in the Mastership in 1940 and at a meeting at the Peahen Hotel, St Albans that summer the view was expressed that for the duration of the war only foxes should be hunted; it was decided that the Hertfordshire Hunt and the Enfield Chace should be approached to see whether the Aldenham could take over part of their country. In the event the Aldenham did hunt fox, but chiefly in that part of the country given up by the Hertfordshire and Old Berkeley Hunts. This was particularly desirable in view of the necessity of keeping down the number of foxes, but the times were difficult for sporting activity and some doubts were expressed as to whether the Aldenham could carry on. However, farmers offered to keep hunt horses free of charge for the 1940/41 season and it was said that it would cost the hunt £400 to cover the season's expenses if they suspended hunting and very little more if they hunted. In accepting the farmers' generous offer Sir Jocelyn thanked them for the splendid way in which they had supported, and continued to support him and said that he very much regretted that with his Parliamentary and other duties he doubted whether he would be able to hunt that season. He said that at that point the Aldenham Harriers had existed for seventy two years which would give it a starting date in 1868 not 1878 which is the year usually accepted - interesting, but my researches have produced nothing to persuade me to alter the accepted view.

The Boxing Day meet that year was at Aldenham Grange, the home of Mr & Mrs E. Jones whose son, John, was to become joint Master in succession to Miss Handley Page the following year. It was a large field both on foot and mounted; doubtless in war-time such occasions were used for reunions amongst hunting people. Hounds went very well during the day, which was surprising considering their normally restricted activities due to the war. They soon picked a scent which took them across Delrow Lane, behind Church Farm, on to Berry Grove, and so to Otterspool where, refusing to swim the river, the hare doubled back making a line for Aldenham Church, but hounds lost her before the village. Moving over by Wall Hall towards Bricket Wood, they put up their next hare above Mr Macmillan's farm at Little Munden through to Blackbirds Lane where she right-handed down to the River Colne and turned along the water meadows, which normally carry good scent, but hounds lost touch on Four Acres.

The problems were compounded in 1942 when the pack was decimated by a severe attack of distemper, only four and a half couple surviving. Meanwhile Miss Handley Page was only a joint master for one season and in 1941 her place was taken by Mr E.J.M.Jones. In fact at a meeting at the Peahen Hotel, St Albans on 23rd February 1942 Sir Jocelyn and John Jones both tendered their resignations. Some of the farmers present had been connected with the Aldenham since the end of the previous century, the brothers John and Harry Reynolds amongst them, and they felt strongly that a small nucleus of a pack should be kept in kennels so that the old order of things could be restored after the war. Feeding the hounds was the great difficulty. Mrs Duncan agreed to continue as secretary. Accordingly John Jones agreed to continue as Master alone for the time being. The following year Stanley (E.W.?) Taylor became a joint Master with John Jones and they remained in office for the remainder of the war. There is believed to have been only one Taylor involved with the Aldenham Harriers at this time, but he is variously quoted as Stanley or S. or E.W. On the other hand E.W. was usually called Walwyn, so the logic of it could be interpreted as E.W.Taylor being known to his friends as Stanley. More likely, E.W.Taylor, being a contemporary of and close neighbour of Stanley White, has been confused with him in records?

Some time after this Sir Jocelyn kept and hunted his own private pack of sealyhams, a breed to which he had become particularly attached and of which he was something of an authority. He probably hunted ANYTHING with them having purchased Mr Gladdish Hulkes' stoat hunting pack of sealyhams from him and there may have been specialist elements within the same pack. Later on he had a pack of basset hounds and hunted the Old Widford beagle country. He said at one time that although he bred sealyhams he was not prejudiced in their favour and had in his time hunted with, and killed hares with, a pack of pedigree fox terriers and had owned and bred borders, scotties, cairns, highlanders and in fact every sort of sporting terrier

Billy Marsh on MELODY and his daughter Joan (Mrs Cunningham)
on BLACKIE at Bamville Farm, Harpenden in 1929
Joan Cunningham

Joan Cunningham remembers Sir Jocelyn having Bonners Farm in Windmill Lane, Flamstead as his country home in the Second World War, but he also had a home in London. He was seriously injured there in the Blitz of the spring of 1941, but fortunately recovered. Joan confirms that he hunted everything, including the ladies, and had a *"wicked twinkle in his eye"*. She should know because she was in the Wrens in the war and on Saturday evenings took to dancing at the Overseas League in London. Sir Jocelyn would appear on the stage in the evening and if he spied Joan would call her up to join him for dinner. He was a ladies man and a charmer. Earlier she had been thrown when following hounds one day and Sir Jocelyn had called to her *"you flew through the air so beautifully and running down hill afterwards you were even better"*. Later in the war she was stationed at Bletchley Park and rode with the Whaddon Chase.

Today Joan is *'very well preserved'* as they say, a tribute to the merits of a hunting life, and you would hardly believe that her riding days go back to the 1920s. To be fair, the Aldenham has a number of ladies, now 'of a certain age', who demonstrate the therapeutic effects of years in the saddle. Joan was practically born in the saddle which is hardly surprising because her family rode to hounds and she was the daughter of none other than 'Billy' Marsh, one time Secretary of the Hertfordshire (South pack) and Secretary of the Friars Wash Point-to-Point Committee (1920-1961). In his earlier days he had competed at Friars Wash himself and on one occasion won two races on the same horse on the same day. That was on THE SAINT in 1901 and he would have hacked to and from the meeting. In spite of all that, cricket was really his first love and he played for Harpenden Cricket Club for sixty seasons.

Huntsman Rick Fenn and behind him whip Eric Goddard
at Bamville Farm, Harpenden in the thirties
Fiona Kinlock

At the time Joan started riding to hounds the Aldenham's opening meet was always at Bamville Farm, Harpenden, home of Herbert and Mary Wright of Wright's Coal Tar Soap fame and there is a splendid picture of her, when aged five, riding her Shetland pony, BLACKIE there in 1929. She was allowed to ride her father's horse when she was nine and by then was riding every day. Herbert Wright is reputed to have been a MFH at one time, but the pack is not known. He rode with the Aldenham Harriers as did his wife's cousin, Fiona Kinlock, who has provided some of the photographs reproduced here.

On August Bank Holiday Monday in 1936, when she was twelve, Joan decided to take a ride across Harpenden Common, but her horse took fright at a sudden noise and there was nothing she could do but hold on. Straight across the cricket pitch it went, which particularly incensed her father when he heard about it later on, finally coming to a halt at a blackberry patch of the far side of the common. One of Jimmy Joel's stud grooms, out walking his dog, saw what had gone on and said *"what do you think you're doing?"* then he took control of the horse and put it in his stables off Ayres End Lane to calm down, saying *"Come back for it tomorrow"*. *"But how do I get home?"* asked Joan; *"you walk"* came the reply. She did and got little sympathy for it at home.

Although her father was very much a Hertfordshire Hunt man, Joan preferred the Aldenham *"frankly because with Geoff Hartop and Stanley White it was more fun"*.

Joan lived at Mortons Yard, Flamstead, in the 1950s and rented accommodation for her horse from her neighbour, Jack Welch, but she has lived at Kimpton Bottom since 1957.

The Aldenham Harriers had their share of glory, albeit reflected, in the war when Hunt Class Destroyer, Aldenham, was launched on 30th January 1942. It was built by Cammell Laird, had a displacement of 1015 tons, a complement of 170, a top speed of 28 knots and served with distinction for more than two years. HMS Aldenham was part of the 230 ship task force engaged in 'Operation Husky', the Sicily landing on 10th July 1943. Sadly it was sunk by a mine in the north east Adriatic on 14th December 1944 with a loss of 126 officers and men; 63 members of the crew were saved.

On 21st November 1945 a meeting was held at the Peahen Hotel, St Albans, attended by Messrs A.J.Reynolds, J.Hodgson, G.H.Hartop, E.W.Taylor, L.G.Sparrow, D.Lloyd Jones, A.W.Motion, R.J.Booth, W.Noad, M. Goddard, Capt. Younghusband, and Mrs Duncan, the secretary, to decide whether the Aldenham Harriers should continue and whether they should hunt fox or hare. Mr Booth asked how many foxes had been killed during the season and he was told two. Fortunately for us, it was resolved to continue and to restrict their activities to hunting only hare from 1st May 1946

Another meeting was held at the same place three weeks later when one of the joint Masters, Stanley Taylor (E.W.?), tendered his resignation; the reason is not recorded, but it was not accepted; exactly how it was proposed to force him to continue his duties against his will is not recorded either. However at another meeting on 30th January 1946 both joint Masters, Messrs Jones and Taylor, agreed to continue, but only until the end of the hare hunting season. The chairman was not optimistic; for the approaching season they had no Master, no huntsman and no kennels and then the secretary, Mrs Duncan resigned, small wonder. In spite of all that they resolved that a hunt ball would be held in April, that tickets would be 30s., and a subscription list would be opened for the retiring huntsman, Rick Fenn. The hunt ball duly took place on 12th April at St Albans Town Hall to the music of the Lawrence Inns Band who charged a fee of forty guineas. Numbers were limited to 280 and a profit of £640 was made. A silver hunting horn, suitably inscribed was presented to Rick Fenn who was due to retire at the end of the season. Many of his seasons had been very difficult ones and his last was one of his worst. There was a very long hard winter and an outbreak of foot and mouth disease, which severely restricted the activities of the hunt and latterly he was hunting with only seven couple. He had indeed been the backbone of the hunt for thirty three seasons and was very difficult to replace. He did not survive long in retirement and was aged 74 when he died in December 1949.

At another meeting at the Peahen on 8th May 1946 things still looked bleak for the future of the hunt. Advertisements for a new Master had only produced one applicant, a Mr Crowder from Lincolnshire; he was invited to inspect the country, but his conditions for coming to the Aldenham Harriers were that he would be provided with a proper pack of hounds, and kennels, and a house to live in. He was politely refused. The retiring kennel huntsman, Rick Fenn reported that there were only five couple of hounds left and three were of very little use for future hunting. A discussion then took place as to whether the hounds should be disposed of then and there. It was resolved that they should be kept for the time being and Mr Brunt agreed to kennel them until permanent facilities could be arranged. Mr Whitehead was elected secretary in his absence and subsequently declined. Desperate measures indeed!

Geoff Hartop and Stanley White on Hatching Green
Stanley White Collection

Out of that period of uncertainty, when the Aldenham Harriers seemed unlikely to survive, came a period of growth and prosperity which largely revolved around Geoff Hartop of Beaumont Hall, Redbourn and his friend and neighbour, Stanley White, of Hammonds End, Harpenden. These two frequently and publicly congratulated each other and seem to have had a mutual admiration society going. Certainly both were men of considerable ability in horse, and hunting, and racing circles and their mutual admiration was well founded; it was indeed echoed by plenty of others. Geoff Hartop agreed to hunt the hounds for the following season at a meeting at the Peahen on 10th July 1946 and at the same time undertook to go to Peterborough for the impending Hound & Beagle Show and endeavour to purchase four and a half couple of hounds. It was agreed that kennels would remain at St Albans until September and that Rick Fenn would carry on as kennel huntsman on a temporary basis for 50s.a week, and at last a new secretary had been found, John Hodgson, the auctioneer at St Albans Cattle Market. Things were improving. He retained the office until 1952.

At a Management Committee meeting at the Peahen on 11th September 1946 it was confirmed that two and a half couple of hounds, two portable kennels and sundry tackle had been moved from Cottonmill Lane, St Albans to Beaumont Hall and a kennel maid had been engaged. In addition Stanley White had purchased two couples of hounds in Ireland, one hound had been obtained on loan for the season and four couples were on loan through the good offices of Mr Syder. Major Barclay had donated one couple of pups. It was decided for the 1946/47 season to hunt on alternate Wednesdays and Thursdays with by-days on Saturdays. The adult subscription was put at ten guineas with 'caps' at £1 a day (maximum 3). In addition 2s.6d a day field money would be charged which would be donated to the Hertfordshire Hunt wire fund for attention to fences. A hunt ball was planned for Friday 31st January 1947 at St Albans Town Hall. Tickets to be 30s. each. A Boxing Day meet on Redbourn Common was arranged which was to be the start of a tradition that was to go on for over thirty years, admittedly with occasional lapses.

Geoff Hartop with Ben Wilkinson behind
Stanley White Collection

The 1946/47 season was a disastrous one because of the weather and a severe outbreak of foot and mouth disease. The last hunt of the season was on 15th January at Sandridge. The hounds fared badly; there were losses through pneumonia and several old hounds had to be put down. The survivors amounted to seven and a half couple and it was planned to add another two and a half couple the following May. The pack statistics at this time demonstrate how difficult it can be to build up numbers from a limited base-point short of extensive buying-in, and that costs money.

In spite of the gloom created by an appalling winter and with many farms in quarantine some hunting was nevertheless possible as *'Drifter'* reported in the *Horse & Hound* on 25th January 1947, though it probably relates to the last one of the season mentioned above:

> *"The first hare was found on some plough at Nomansland Farm, and the pack ran her hard over the Coleman Green Road to Symonds Hyde Great Wood, which she entered and was left. The next hare was soon found on the plough near Sandridge School. She went away through the vicarage garden, crossing the Sandridge-Hatfield road and pointing for Jersey Farm before turning sharply left-handed and swinging right round to double back on her line through the gardens. Hounds pushed her out of here, however, and then ran her back to Nomansland Farm, next going right-handed towards Symonds Hyde Great Wood, where they threw up and could make no more of it.*
> *Their third hare was put up on some clover leys, and she also ran towards the vicarage gardens. Scent was excellent at this stage, and hounds ran at a cracking pace, bustling their pilot into the gardens, where they killed her in some cabbages.*
> *The last hunt of the day was on a hare which took them for a fast burst back towards Wheathampstead, where she eventually took refuge in a straw stump and was left. As this had been a hard day for hounds and horses alike the closure was applied at 2.30 pm."*

The first point-to-point meeting at Friars Wash after the war was held on 12th April 1947. There had been a gap of nine years. Brilliant weather resulted in a record crowd estimated at 10,000, though how they were counted is anybody's guess. Geoff Hartop won the Aldenham Harriers Chase on his own horse, JACK SHEPPARD, when there were only three runners and only two finished. Mrs Hartop distributed the prizes.

What were said at the time to be the first ever Aldenham Harriers hunter trials were held at Beaumont Hall, Redbourn on 27th September when there was an entry of 139 in five classes. Miss Rosemary Barratt won the Champion Cup which was presented by former Master, Stanley Taylor.

Geoff Hartop at Cross Farm in 1954
Valerie Dickinson

The opening meet of the 1947/48 season was on 25th October at Bamville Farm, Harpenden with sixty mounted followers and about the same again on foot. '*Drifte*r' reported in the *Horse & Hound*:

> "*Mr Geoffrey Hartop had 14 couple out and they put up their first hare on Mr Dickinson's clover ley, running nearly to Amwell before losing her on some plough land which carried no scent. Although several hares were moving on Piper's Farm (Mr Hill's) hounds could do little with them, but it was an enjoyable day with several nice hunts and hounds worked well on little scent. Amongst the new draft hounds, those who hunted well were the Bicester Gossip and Hanover; the Puckeridge Saucy and Delia and the Clonmel Rattler & Beauty, while most of the new entry showed up in capital style.*
> *We were given a great welcome by Mr Sam Blowey at Pulmer Water, Codicote on November 4, where hounds had not been for 15 seasons. They soon found a hare on some stubble and hunted her nicely over the road through Rye Field Farm and on to Lynches before she went left-handed down to the water meadows, again going left handed to re-cross the road to her form. She took them into the small covert by the Ayot St Lawrence road, where they ran into her.*"

A very successful hunt ball was held at St Albans Town Hall on 12th November 1947 when, somewhat predictably, Geoff Hartop won the horn-blowing contest. A fortnight later Mrs Seabrook welcomed the Harriers at the Kings Head, Ivinghoe and '*Drifter*' reported in the *Horse & Hound*:

> "Going first to Mr Leach's at Town Farm, hounds soon put up a hare which they hunted into the vale country, running well to Mr Frank Hartop's farm at the Grove. That good sportsman was no doubt gratified to see puss take them for a big circuit round his farm before she crossed the Whistle Brook to run on to Horton Wharf, where she beat them after a fast 30min, with a two and a half mile point. A hare from Rushy Meadows next gave a good 25min before being bowled over at Horton Wharf. Finding again at once, a fast 30min followed until a fresh hare saved her. The evening hunt on a hare from Mr Mimble's land gave a classic 60min over a grand line of country. From Northall hounds ran their hare nearly to Slapton Mill before crossing the River Ouzel, and going on to the old point-to-point course. Crossing the main Leighton Buzzard road they ran hard and straight to Billington Osiers before going on over the levelcrossing at Stanbridgeford being finally stopped at Stanbridge after a 3-mile point."

In hunting reports that word 'point' is often used, two mile point, five mile point and so on, meaning the distance of the chase. That is alright except that the official definition of the word is *"The distance between the finding of a fox and the finish of the hunt, measured as the crow flies, not as hounds run."* The term is accordingly difficult to apply to harriers, where the quarry often runs in a circle so that the 'point', if taken literally as the crow flies, may be only a few yards. It is a term best avoided as it has provoked much, mostly good humoured, controversy over the years. It did in fact inspire another little battle started by Tanjong Pasir, but as the official definition was left unchanged it would appear that he lost.

For the 1947/48 season Geoff Hartop hunted the hounds himself with Stanley White as joint Master and they took on Ben Wilkinson from the Puckeridge as kennel huntsman and whipper-in. Now Ben was not really Ben; his father was Ben and his elder brother was Ben, but our Ben was born Bernard in 1905. Having been appointed second whip for the South Berks in 1924 and for the Southdown in 1926 our Ben became first whip for the Puckeridge in 1927 and was appointed huntsman in 1937. Although he retained his appointment as huntsman throughout the Second World War it had to be on a part time basis for some of it because he was employed full time at the Royal Observer post at Brent Pelham. Whilst with the Puckeridge he acquired, and later with the Aldenham maintained, a reputation for being invariably cheerful and efficient and for providing excellent sport. At the point when he moved on from the Puckeridge he left behind him a novel situation where the joint Masters were a son, father and grandfather; Edward Barclay had had 69 seasons as Master, 51 of them with the Puckeridge, his son, Major Maurice Barclay had had 37 seasons, and his grandson, Captain Charlie was starting his first season as a joint Master. Thus Ben's first ten years as huntsman were 'Barclay' years and he arrived at the Aldenham very much a fox hunting man and very much a 'Barclay' man, but he very quickly adapted, managing to combine the best of the Rick Fenn tradition with the best of the Barclay tradition and soon proved his worth

Stanley White (left) (Chairman of the Hitchin Branch of the NFU 1926/27) with Alec Wallace and Robert Smith (right) at the NFU Hitchin Branch Golden Jubilee Luncheon at Hitchin Priory on 17th May 1963 Stanley White Collection

The Aldenham Harriers Heavyweights Race, Friars Wash 4th March 1950. First fence, winner, Bill Corby on NIGGER VII 'in the air'

A house in course of erection at Redbourn was purchased by the hunt, on mortgage, for Ben's accommodation. At this time the Aldenham Harriers was very popular; there were fourteen and a half couple of hounds which were hunted three days a fortnight and the fields at times were said to be really too big for a harrier pack. At the AGM held at the Peahen Hotel, St Albans on 21st January 1948 it was reported that the reorganised Aldenham Harriers had had a highly successful first season with the number of subscribers on the increase and large fields turning out to hunt. However, it had also been a very expensive season because they had started out with practically nothing. Temporary kennels had been erected at Beaumont Hall, Redbourn, where the hounds were housed until 1958, and hounds, horses and uniforms had had to be purchased. There were many other expenses, though mostly of the non-recurring variety. The joint Masters were re-elected and the subscription was increased to fifteen guineas. It was decided to hunt on Wednesdays and Saturdays one week and on Thursdays the following week, with occasional by-days on Mondays and Fridays.

At this time, for communication purposes, the country was allocated parish representatives:

St Albans	A.J.Reynolds, R.J.Booth
Harpenden	F.R.Catton, S.White, W.H.Marsh, Miss M.Wright
Wheathampstead	L.G.Sparrow
Sandridge	A.J.Sherriff
Redbourn	G.H.Hartop, E.W.Taylor
London Colney & Colney Heath	W.Franklin
Radlett	R.Woodbridge, Mrs Sparrow
St Stephens & Bricket Wood	D.Neale, C.Morrison, D.Blomfield
St Michaels	D.C.Macqueen
Stevenage & Codicote	E.S.Hertz

The 1951 Aldenham Harriers point-to-point meeting was held at Friars Wash on 21st April with perfect weather and record crowds though the number was not recorded. The Master, Geoff Hartop, managed a second in the Members and Farmers Race on his JACK SHEPPARD, being beaten by five lengths by fellow Aldenham Harriers member Mr J.C.F.Cox on his SLIPSEAL.

For the 1951/52 season, in addition to the usual places, there were meets at Bowmans Green, Kinsbourne Green, Church Farm at Little Gaddesden, the Fox and Hounds at Bricket Wood, Wilton Farm at Shenley, Blackwell Grange and Dagnall.

There was another crisis meeting at the Peahen on 6th February 1952 when Geoff Hartop and Stanley White tendered their resignations. They thanked each other for their services and each elaborated upon the other's skills in the field. After a while Lady Farrer and Geoff Hartop were asked to leave the room while two letters were read; one from Lady Farrer saying that she would be prepared to be a joint Master if Geoff Hartop would partner her, and the other from Geoff Hartop saying that he would agree to stay on providing his expenses were guaranteed to £1,750 per season. This arrangement was accepted except that the guarantee was for £1,000 and Geoff Hartop and Lady Farrer guaranteed £250 each. Later there was a good response to the invitation to prospective guarantors. In the new situation horses, hounds and kennels and the kennel huntsman's house in Ver Road, Redbourn would be owned by the hunt committee and joint Masters would hunt the country three days a fortnight. At that point secretary, John Hodgson tendered his resignation.

Ben Wilkinson, Stanley White & Geoff Hartop (left to right) on Hatching Green
Stanley White Collection

The hunt ball that year was held at Gaddesden Place and was in the grand old tradition of such events. This is the earliest one at a country house for which we have a detailed record and it is worth mentioning how things were done. The tickets cost £1.11.6d each, *The Tatler & Bystander* sent a photographer, Mrs Macqueen did the flowers and decorations, Bill Savill & His Band provided the music and they were expensive, fee - fifty guineas! Messrs Hartridge from Hemel Hempstead moved furniture out of the ballroom beforehand and back again afterwards by arrangement with Mrs Pryor. There was concern about the lack of sitting-out accommodation and it was suggested that part of the conservatory, which led out of the ballroom, might be made available. On the night the fuses blew on a number of occasions and candles had to be resorted to. Naturally enough, six tickets were sent for Sir Thomas Halsey and his party and six for Mrs Pryor and her party and no doubt a good time was had by all, except perhaps by Sir Thomas who was in bed with influenza in a room marked 'do not disturb', while 400 people downstairs danced and blew hunting horns until the small hours. His mother, by then in her eighties, is reported to have attended seated in a wheel-chair wearing a Victorian black velvet gown with white lace trimmings. I am not sure how often the hunt ball was held at Gaddesden Place, nor whether other country houses were used, but indications are that this was an isolated occasion. Mrs Pryor was the sister of Sir Thomas and became the chatelaine of Gaddesden Place, Sir Thomas preferring to live at the Golden Parsonage. She had married in 1925 Capt. Thomas Pryor, but he died four years later and Gaddesden Place was, of course, her home.

John Hodgson, Mrs Hodgson, Lord Farrer and Lady Farrer at the Hunt Ball at Gaddesden Place in March 1952

The 1952 point-to-point meeting was held at Friars Wash on 12th April and attracted a crowd of 15,000. The Aldenham Harriers member Mr J.C.F.Cox won the Adjacent Hunts Heavyweight Race again on his SLIPSEAL. The pair were making a habit of it.

The following month a large number of members and friends met at the Peahen to make a presentation of a silver cigarette case to retiring joint Master Stanley White, who had served for six years, and a silver wine cooler to retiring honorary secretary John Hodgson, who had served for seven years. Reggie Streather was appointed honorary secretary later in the year and served with distinction in that capacity until 1965.

Stanley White of Hammonds End Farm, Harpenden was a renowned horse coper, field sports expert, winner of a hundred point-to-point races, the last when he was aged 67, and now a retired joint Master of the Aldenham Harriers. He was a great character, *"an old style nagsman, somebody you could look up to; he could ride anything and sold horses on the hunting field"*. Sometimes as many as six in a day.

Stanley White
Stanley White Collection

He even had literary skills and combined them with his 'horse magic' to produce the following which appeared in the *Farmer and Stockbreeder* on 2nd April 1934:

"Riding Horses for Profit

Opportunities and Fascinating Pastime for Young Farmers with a Taste for Schooling Light Horses as Hunters
By STANLEY WHITE

In view of the restrictions on the importation of horses from Ireland (our chief source of supply) and the fact that high prices are being paid for really good hunters, it would seem that there will be an increasing demand for home-bred horses. In these difficult times many farmers would help themselves by taking advantage of this demand and breeding each season one or two hunters of the right type.

The most important point in breeding is the choice of the mare. The ideal is a weight-carrying thoroughbred, but one must use the material at hand while keeping that ideal in mind. Whatever her height, the mare should be short-legged, well-ribbed, intelligent, with good hocks and quarters. She must be a true mover. Nothing is more hereditary than faulty action, which is a great drawback when selling.

The sire should have plenty of good bone, good quarters, true action, and be free from hereditary unsoundness. It is usually safest to use a thoroughbred, as one can find out all about him. He should be a stayer, not a sprinter; and if of jumping pedigree, so much the better. In Ireland, however, many good weight-carrying horses are bred by putting a stallion of the roadster type on a smallish, well-bred mare.

The Weaned Foal

The foal should not be weaned until the autumn, after which comes a most important period in its life. If neglected or underfed, it rarely recovers the lost ground. A good warm shelter must be available if running out. Plenty of hay, a few pounds of crushed oats and bran, with the addition of minerals and a tablespoonful of codliver oil per day, will keep it in good growing condition. Our grass does not grow colts as well as the Irish grass, but is counterbalanced by feeding minerals.

At all times, from a week or two old, the colt should be accustomed to the halter and led about whenever possible. At three years old it should start serious work. It is essential that mouthing be properly and painstakingly done, as a great part of a horse's future value lies in his mouth, balance and manners.

If elaborate breaking tackle is available, certainly use it, but it is not necessary. Put on an ordinary headstall, put a straight, thick bit with two large rings gently into the animal's mouth, and attach to the noseband of the headstall so that the bit does not press up the corners of the mouth. Tie securely another bit with large rings to the bit in the colt's mouth.

Put on a roller and crupper. Attach a new chap-rein to the roller on the offside, about six inches from the middle of the back, thread through the rings of the second bit, tie to the near side of the roller, and draw up the colt's head until it is just slightly arched.

It facilitates matters if two rings are strongly sewn on to the roller for this purpose. The colt can now move its head freely from left to right and vice versa. Turn it into a yard and let it move about and play with the bit. After a day or two, arch the head a little more, but do not over-bridle.

Making Progress

When the colt is accustomed to this, two pieces of very strong catapult elastic, quadrupled, may be attached (with rings) to the roller, and the chap-rein attached to these instead of to the roller direct. This allows a little 'give' to the mouth. Judgement must be used here, as one does not wish to encourage the colt to 'rake' at his bit. Remember that everything must be done quietly, firmly and with patience.

After about ten to fourteen days the colt should be ready to drive in long reins. New plough lines are good enough. The animal must learn to answer the bit instantly, as also the words of command. If obstreperous, lunging in circles will help, but always turn equally in right and left-hand circles, so that the mouth does not get one-sided. As soon as the colt appears to be 'coming to hand' it should be driven in figures of eight, alternate ways, and serpentine courses. Do not forget that with long reins and breaking tackle one has complete control. No colt should be backed until his mouth is satisfactory, which is usually about three weeks or a month from first bridling.

Backing

Unless one is a really good horseman, it is safer to tie a sack of sawdust or chaff securely to the saddle before actually backing the colt, and when it goes quietly with this a start can be made. It is best to mount in an enclosed space or yard, with someone to hold the colt's head, both rider and helper being quiet, gentle and patient. A snaffle bridle is best to start with. Ride about quietly, not going faster than a trot for a few days, then only a gentle canter, and keep using its mouth.

As soon as possible, use a light double bridle, with a leather curb if the colt is at all fidgety. It is most important to get it properly balanced. Never hang on to its head; the lightest pressure should be sufficient to ensure obedience. Make the colt stand still while you mount, keep perfectly still, and instantly obey any command.

The colt should now be ready to turn out, or for the collar if required. Unless very valuable there is no objection to its earning its keep if big enough, although it is a mistake to work it too hard. Still, there are many jobs on a farm where it can take the place of a bigger horse. If required for team work, one must be careful not to soil its chief asset - its mouth. Use a strong noseband for coupling to other horses when possible. Most Irish horses work on the farm as well as hunt before coming over to England. Regular work also keeps them fit.

Advanced Stages

At four years the colt is ready to complete its education. Put on the breaking tackle and drive with long reins for two or three days before riding, just to accustom its mouth to the bit. If not at work it should be hacked on the road to get its legs hard and fit enough for hunting. A fixed jump should be available with a strong pole that cannot be knocked down. A few faggots leaning against the pole will make a brush fence, and the addition of another pole (with faggots away) a timber jump. These should be low to start with, not over 2ft. 6ins., but firm.

Put on bandages and kneecaps, and, with a helper, lunge the colt first. As soon as he learns that he must jump or fall he may be ridden over. Put the jumps a little higher every day, staying only a few minutes at a time, so that the colt does not get sickened.

He should be presented at a trot or very slow canter so as to learn to jump from the hocks. A sheet of galvanised iron with dull edges makes a useful imitation ditch for use at this period of his training. The rudiments of jumping should be learned at home, and a short half-day is plenty to start with in the field. Keep out of the crowd, walk and trot about gently, talking and humouring it all the time as it is bound to be excited at first. Get it accustomed to going at your pace willingly; never rush about with the wild ones. After a time or two it should have a small but solid jump or two when necessary, but only at a moderately slow pace.

Always remember that you must be patient but firm. Get the horse to jump both with and away from the crowd, and take his turn quietly at gaps and gateways. He should now be ready to go straight across country if he is a good performer and has a good mouth and balance and you have taught him manners.

Quite a number of people will buy a four-year-old if it is fit and answers the description given. Of course, if one wishes to make a high price the horse must be kept until it shows a six-year-old mouth (when rising six). By then it will have had part of two seasons' hunting and should have a good reputation. A sound, good-looking, well bred 14-stone horse that can gallop and jump a good country is worth anything from £100 to £300.

During the last few years a number of farmers have found light horses a great help to their banking account. Usually, a horse is growing into money. Handling and gentling a colt is a fascinating occupation for summer evenings."

It seems to me that the piece is full of good advice for dealing with horses and I like that last sentence particularly; one can imagine Stanley doing it in the calmer, slower days before the Second World War.

Nubar Gulbenkian, reputed to be one of the richest men in the world in the sixties, was an ardent enthusiast of hunting. He rode with the Whaddon Chase and bought his horses from Stanley White. He was thrown by one of them when out hunting one day which perplexed him, so he resolved to return to the spot to try to determine how it came about. It was a particularly wet season and he arrived in his chauffeur-driven Rolls (not, it would appear in the converted London taxi cab that later became such a favourite with him) wearing his hunting rig, with orchid buttonhole and silk top hat, to find the gate to the field was padlocked and beyond his ability to climb, so the chauffeur went over first and pulled him underneath, through the mud, with the aid of his umbrella. Such is the dedication of your follower of hounds, but perhaps not quite an average follower!

Nubar Gulbenkian and Larry Connell
Stanley White Collection

Stanley White came to the district from his native Cornwall to be agent to Colonel Harrison at King's Walden. He married Mary Edith Dalton at St Paul's Walden in 1922 and to begin with they lived at Offley Grange. After a couple of years they moved to Hammonds End House and before the Second World War, built a new house there. Mary designed the garden which became much admired for her beds of roses. Later they were to sell the land for the Golf Course. They had no children so there was nobody to follow them, but Stanley's brother's wife

Esme had a niece who today is the Aldenham Harriers Joint Master Mary Arikoglu.

Mary White
Stanley White Collection

Mary White died on 18th August 1967 aged 80. She had hunted all her life; she followed the Enfield Chace Staghounds and the Hertfordshire Hounds early on and later, with her husband, followed the Aldenham Harriers, the Whaddon Chase and the Oakley, so that Stanley and Mary between them had ridden over most of Hertfordshire in their long careers. Of all Mary's many accomplishments, and in addition to being an excellent horsewoman, to being very good hearted and a first rate cook, perhaps her most enviable was her ability to swear for half an hour without repeating herself. She would stand in the middle of the road and direct the traffic; nobody ever complained. She would bang on the roofs of the cars that she thought were going too fast, with her crop; nobody ever complained. She got away with it. Stanley would shout *"hold hard!"* to the field which it was his right and sometimes his duty to do, to prevent accidents, but Mary was scornful of such caution and would shout back *"hold hard yourself!"* and carry on. She was a law unto herself.

Mary is remembered affectionately for constantly committing a cardinal sin, the same sin over and over again; she insisted upon calling the hounds "the dogs". That calls to mind another memory; Mary seething with indignation one day when Stanley reversed his car over one of them! Another gem came one day when Stanley was Field Master; that season the then Countess of Dudley hunted with the Aldenham Harriers and contrived always to lead the field. After a good deal of it Mary was provoked to shout *"I see we have a new whip Stanley"*.

Mary White on the far right
Stanley White Collection

She had a horse named CRUISING which Stanley sometimes used for point-to-point racing, but it had a tendency to buck and if it threw you off it was the devil of a job to get back, which made Mary mad. It threw her one day when she was out with the Hertfordshire and she cursed it upside down and backwards in her own inimitable style. After a while it was recaptured and led back to a cattle pen where she, in theory, could climb the rails and remount, but the top rail broke under her weight. She abandoned all pretence of restraint and her performance on that occasion was in a class of its own. She swore in a way that inspired respect, though there were those who had a good laugh behind their hands. It was best not to let her see you do it! Some of the field had their educations completed that day.

Mary's father was William Lisle Dalton of The Holt, Kimpton, and when he died he left instructions that his only daughter, Mary, should follow his coffin in full hunting dress; coat, breeches, boots and spurs, and she did. His favourite dog was led in the procession and a hunting crop was dropped in the grave. Mary's mother lived to be 104.

Stanley was one of the Aldenham Harriers' many 'heroes' and is revered to this day. He died on 10th April 1978 and he and Mary are buried side by side alongside Mary's parents in the little churchyard behind the Strathmore Arms at St Paul's Walden; a small cube of grey granite marks each grave.

Farmer Dalton, Mary White's father, of the Holt, Kimpton in about 1920
Stanley White Collection

Joint Master of the Aldenham Harriers the Hon. Lady Lyell with the hounds passing Valley Lane Cottage, Flamstead in about 1965. Behind her are Whip George Garfoot, Joint Master Sir Maurice Lyell (hidden) and Joint Master Basil Hall on the right.
Derek Christopher

THE LYELL ERA

Some may say, indeed they already have, that there is too much in this book about Lady Lyell and that I have treated her too harshly. I plead guilty on the former count and not guilty on the latter. She deserves a chapter to herself because of the vital part she played in the history of the Aldenham Harriers. Possibly she saved it from sinking without trace - twice, and she was at the helm for nearly thirty years. She put a lot of money and time, and effort, into it and was generous in other ways. Certainly she had first rate support, but she inspired and demanded it. Even today she has vociferous admirers who may think that I have been somewhat uncharitable about her. May I stress that I would not wish to sully her memory in any way; she was kind to me, and to many others, but I must tell it as it was.

She was forceful, she needed to be, she took on a lot of responsibility in the field which makes most Masters a little 'up tight' and she was a good Master. It has been suggested that I have put in too much anecdote that shows her in a poor light. Maybe I have, I leave others to judge, but I hope that I have honestly recorded how it was and in Lady Lyell's time that was how hunt Masters behaved. It was a man's world. A lot of responsibility rests on the Master's shoulders in the field and in consequence the adrenalin is flowing; everything going on has to be controlled and it cannot be done gently. Discipline and respect did not become unfashionable until near the end of her reign.

Continuity of Mastership is regarded as particularly desirable in hunting circles but the best the Aldenham Harriers had been able to achieve in this respect in its first seventy years had been three stints of ten years each. The reasoning is that long service in office presupposes steadily increasing ability, and success, and reliability, and popularity; you would hardly keep a Master in office who lacked these qualities, and these are the very qualities that inspire respect, and confidence, and influence; they are the stuff of leadership, which is what Mastership is all about. For the new man, or woman, these things take time, rather like accumulating one's credits in Heaven; they do not come without hard work and dedication.

At the start of the 1952/53 season Lady Farrer, as Lady Lyell then was, duly became joint Master and later took over as huntsman, carrying the horn until 1971, and remaining as Master until 1983. It was at the beginning of this long period that the kennels moved to her land at Puddephats Farm. Even after

1983 Lady Lyell (as Lady Farrer had by then become) remained a trustee of the hunt for some years, along with Basil Hall, also a former Master, and Pat Turner. In this new situation in 1952 a hunt committee was formed, the first members of which were:

A.J.Reynolds
J.E.Hodgson
S.White
R.J.Booth
W.Franklin
L.M.Legerton
L.G.Sparrow
Miss W.Wright
E.W.Taylor
F.R.Catton
L.Connell
R.J.Dickinson
G.H.Hartop   *ex-officio*
Lady Farrer   *ex-officio*
R.Streather   *ex-officio*

A constitution was drawn up intended to cover all eventualities. It would not be appropriate to quote all its clauses here, but a few selected passages may be of interest:

Each year would start on 1st May

A 'member' was defined as:

> Every person who has subscribed to the hunt funds the amount fixed by the committee as the subscription for the current year and every person who has become an elected member at the invitation of the committee

The committee may hunt the country by appointing a Master or Joint Masters for the current season (1st May to 30th April) or as a committee by appointing a master each time the hunt meets or by any other means

The Master shall have the privilege to invite any member to wear the hunt button in the field

In this first season of the new committee thirty two meets were called, of which six were lost. In addition to the usual places meets were at Chipperfield Common, Gaddesden Row, Flamsteadbury, Colney Heath, Redcoats Green and Latimer and a seventy-fifth anniversary celebratory dinner was held at the Red Lion Hotel in Radlett.

There was a crowd of 14,000 at the Aldenham Harriers 1953 Point-to-Point meeting held at Friars Wash on 18th April when it was pleasing to find Joint Master, Geoff Hartop, winning the Members and Farmers Race on his JURASSIQUE. There were four runners at the start of that race, but three fell out in the country leaving Geoff on his own. The prizes were presented by Joint Master, Lady Farrer. That year the point-to-point meeting made £1,000, as usual the major source of income; subscriptions only produced £480, and this was a pattern that was to apply for the next five years.

An invitation from the Hertfordshire Show Committee for the Aldenham Harriers to be paraded at the annual show on 21st May 1953 was accepted; this was probably the first time that it had happened, but it was the start of a tradition that has continued to the present day.

Huntsman Ben Wilkinson with his terrier pocket
at Cross Farm, Harpenden in 1954.
Valerie Dickinson

The seventy fifth opening meet dinner was held at Radlett on 30th October 1953 when Lady Farrer congratulated Mr and Mrs Reynolds on achieving their Golden Wedding Anniversary and on behalf of the hunt presented them with a pair of silver-gilt sugar sifters to mark the occasion. Mr Reynolds, chairman of the hunt committee in responding said that he had followed the hounds for over seventy years. E.Walwyn Taylor, who had, over the years, been such a benefactor to the Aldenham Harriers by allowing the annual point-to-point meetings to take place on his land was at that time moving away from the district to farm in Gloucestershire; Lady Farrer, at the dinner, expressed her regret that he was leaving, thanked him for his support over many years and presented him with a silver cigarette case as a mark of the point-to-point committee's appreciation.

In their issue of 6th January 1954 the magazine *Sport & Country* featured the Aldenham Harriers - three pages of excellent photographs. They were covering a meet at Hatching Green where good sport was had and a brace of hare was accounted for:

> *"The hunt was entertained by Sir Henry and Lady Wynn Parry and after moving off to Hammonds End Farm, hounds found a strong hare on Stoney Hills and killed after one hour and fifteen minutes, during which they ran several big rings which took the field over many of Mr Stanley White's well-maintained fences. Another hare was killed after a short second hunt, but the afternoon hares unfortunately persisted in running to Mr Harry [Jim] Joel's brood-mare paddocks at his Childwickbury Stud, and hounds were called off."*

The piece is geared to Sir Henry Wynne Parry, a High Court Judge, who lived at Hatching Green, and from an historical viewpoint is more remarkable for what it omits than for what it includes. The point is that on that day Lady Farrer was not out because of her earlier fall and when 'home' was called the hunt was at Childwickbury. Derek Christopher together with his wife Joyce and Groom, Jenny Davidson, who were acting as whips on Joyce's show hacks SWEET SURPRISE & MISS SIXTEEN, hacked with the hounds back to Puddephats along the A6 amid much ribaldry from passing drivers. Imagine the traffic chaos that would ensue if such a thing were to be attempted today, but even in those days it must have been quite a sight and a problem to control. At that time Geoff Hartop was the other Joint Master and the kennel huntsman and whipper-in was Ben Wilkinson, but what had happened to them we are not told; perhaps they were being otherwise entertained.

There was great consternation when Lord Farrer was found dead from gunshot wounds at his home, Puddephats Farm, on Sunday morning 24th January 1954. Lady Farrer was in West Herts Hospital with a broken leg at the time, following a hunting accident on Boxing Day.

At the AGM Mr A.J.Reynolds, who had been hunt chairman for many years, resigned and was elected the first president of the hunt. As it turned out he was also the last - so far.

Miss Lydekker holding her terrier at Cross Farm, Harpenden in 1954
Valerie Dickinson

The Aldenham Harriers point-to-point meeting was held at Friars Wash on 10th April 1954 in brilliant sunshine. Only one horse finished in the Adjacent Hunts Heavyweight Race. Stanley White won the Members and Farmers Race on his SUNBOY III. By this time he was aged 61; he was a remarkable man, and was still competing five years later when he achieved his incredible hundredth win.

Jean Patterson riding sidesaddle with Valerie Dickinson next but
one behind her at Cross Farm in 1954
Valerie Dickinson

Mostly the only existing records of hunting activities are bald statements of dates and places and numbers of people taking part, but every once in a while someone surfaces who is prepared to 'put some meat on the bones'. After a gap of twenty years one of the '*sons of Stubbins*' briefly surfaced, blossomed and faded, only this one called himself '*Ben Adam*'. He was the third and last of the Aldenham scribes; sadly, we have no idea who he was, nor indeed whether his efforts were ever published. The earliest report found is:

> *"These hounds had a most satisfactory opening day from Harpenden Common on October 30th* [1954] *in fine weather. After meeting a large gathering of old friends again, and some new ones, both mounted and on foot, hounds moved off to Cross Farm where our good friends the Dickinsons as usual had hares for us. The first was sent away after a short draw and provided a fast twenty minutes before hounds were beaten on the plough.*
> *Although several other good hares were put up on Cross Farm and on the Salvation Army land, and there were some good bursts, hounds were unable to force a conclusion. However, it was a good day for all and the young entry promised well.*
> *It was indeed good to see the enthusiasm and courtesy of the two young school-girls who followed on foot all day and popped up at all the appropriate moments to shut gates for us and to replace wire. They even helped the aging hon. secretary back to the saddle after an unintended departure from it."*

An idyllic view of a meet, that, but it was not always so pleasant. An example of the sort of thing that can happen if the small matter of obtaining farmers' permission prior to hunting their land is not obtained, came in a letter dated 3rd January 1955 from two farmers at Bowers Heath to the Hertfordshire Hunt, the Aldenham Harriers and South Herts Beagles:

> *"We have already this season received visits from the Herts Hunt and the Beagles and in consequence of the results we feel constrained to write to you and point out that this type of activity is extremely detrimental to our agricultural and horticultural interests.........For your own interest's sake we would point out that the lower two and a half acres of this property have been treated with a systemic phosphorus insecticide which is an anti-cholinesterase and extremely poisonous to man and animals, and having pointed this out to you, disclaim all responsibility for any illness or fatalities amongst your packs."*

On this occasion it would appear that the Aldenham Harriers were blameless, as indeed one would expect, but the message to all packs is clear.

'*Ben Adam*' took up his pen again at the end of the season:

"A combined field of Hertfordshire, Old Berkeley and Harrier followers met these hounds [The Aldenham] *at the Grove, Ivinghoe Aston on March 24th* [1955] *to finish the season.*
Mr Frank Hartop, one of the Hertfordshire masters, and his wife were our host and hostess and welcomed all at their house. Afterwards, they and their neighbour Mr Vaisey provided us with a red letter day with enough galloping and jumping to satisfy even the keenest thruster. Hounds were running all day on a plentiful supply of hares, and managed to effect a kill in spite of the gale force wind that played havoc with scent.
Strange as it may seem, bearing in mind the long hard spell, we have lost no more than the usual number of days and we can record a season probably above the average. Our deepest gratitude is due once again to the land owners and farmers for their never failing generosity and kindness."

The ground was rock hard for the 1955 Aldenham Harriers Point-to-Point meeting at Friars Wash, but the fields were small and there were no casualties. Stanley White managed a second in the Members and Farmers Race on his SANDYLAND.

The puppy show that year was held at Puddephats and was judged by Major M.E.Barclay MFH the Puckeridge and Captain F.Goddard Jackson MFH the Woodland Pytchley. Major Barclay made a big thing of stressing the debt all hunting people owe to puppy walkers everywhere. To emphasize his point, he went on to award first, second and third places for doghounds and first place for bitches to CRUISER, CLINKER, CLASHER and CAUTIOUS; three brothers and a sister, offspring of SPARKFORD VALE VAGABOND and LARTINGTON COUNTESS, all walked by Lady Farrer.

The Hon Lady Lyell
(Joint MH 1952-1956 &
1958-1983)
Rita Huxley

107

On 24th September 1955 Lady Farrer married Mr Maurice Lyell QC at St Leonard's Church, Flamstead; his son, Nicholas, was best man. That autumn she tendered her resignation as a Joint Master explaining, understandably enough, that she had new domestic responsibilities which would not leave her with sufficient time to do the Mastership justice. Unfortunately Geoff Hartop, the other half of the Joint Mastership, resigned as well, both resignations to take effect from the end of the season. Stanley White emphasized the very great contribution made by Geoff Hartop and the enormous amount of trouble he had taken in the interests of the hunt. "*He started with only two and a half couple of hounds and with the help of Ben Wilkinson has now produced a very beautiful first class pack of harriers.*"

As a move to identify a possible new Master or Masters it was decided to advertise in *Horse & Hound* and *The Field*. Then secretary Reggie Streather said that he would resign as well. There seems to have been something of a tradition with the Aldenham Harriers of people resigning and later being persuaded to stay on. In the event Lady Lyell did go, but Geoff Hartop and Reggie Streather stayed on.

The Boxing Day meets on Redbourn Common became a tradition much valued by most of the local community; we are fortunate to have an eye-witness account of one of them before the whole thing turned sour with the activities of the animal rights movement:

> "*Scenting conditions so far this season* [1955] *have been disappointing, but Boxing Day proved the exception, and this very attractive and efficient pack of harriers were able to show themselves to full advantage. All honour to Mr Geoffrey Hartop, who, assisted by Ben Wilkinson, has produced so much from the little he had when he became Huntsman and Master. A large mounted field and an army on foot were not to be deterred by the rain from meeting hounds at Redbourn Common, where Mr and Mrs Larry Webb dispensed generous hospitality. We were pleased to welcome again a strong contingent from the Hertfordshire, including Mr Frank Hartop, a Joint Master, and Mrs Hartop. The latter, by the way, is a sister of Comet III pilot John Cunningham. Their mother was at the meet too, but, unlike son and daughter, was keeping her feet on the ground. A hare was soon found on Fish Street Farm but, taking sanctuary in the marshy field behind the busy A5 road, she was left. A second hare went away as we drew towards Beaumont Hall and was hunted in a wide right angled circle past Bohemia Farm and Dane End Farm to Flowers Farm where she was accounted for.*
> *Returning to Bohemia and finding again, we ran straight to Gorhambury and right handed into Windmill Wood but, with*

shooting ahead, hounds were withdrawn to Jeromes when our last hare was sent away and hunted well until hail wiped out scent and the Masters decided to call it a day."

The piece has all the hallmarks of *'Ben Adam'*, but is unsigned.

At the end of 1955 the Mastership vacancy was advertised in *Horse & Hound*. A Mr A.R.L.Escombe expressed interest, but later backed down on the grounds that he could not find a suitable local property where he could live and kennel the hounds and in any case he considered that the country was rapidly becoming unworkable because of urban encroachment. Thus the Mastership question remained in the balance.

At the hunt ball at the Public Hall, Harpenden on 10th February 1956 the Hon. Mrs Lyell was presented with an inscribed hunting horn in appreciation of her four seasons as Master - presented by Geoff Hartop who announced that he was prepared to carry on for the following season. This was a great relief all round , but particularly so to the lady followers of the hunt; he had a reputation for being something of a womaniser and it can be said with authority that even today there are ladies, now 'of a certain age', who are apt to go starry eyed at the mention of his name.

The Aldenham Harriers Point-to-Point meting at Friars Wash on 14th April 1956 was blighted by continuous rain and the crowd was down to 4,500. This threw the finances out completely, but a special fund was created to retrieve the situation which resulted in a net contribution of £800 to funds. Although the going was heavy the Ladies Open Race produced the only accident of the day when Miss K.Sellar fell heavily and sustained head injuries and concussion. She was taken to St Albans City Hospital.

Finances were very tight with both the Hertfordshire Hunt and the Aldenham Harriers following poor returns from their point-to-point meetings in both 1955 and 1956. William Cooper from the former expressed the view, in the friendliest way, that there was insufficient room for both of them if expenses continued to rise, which turned out to be prophetic, but premature. He thought the practical answer would be a pack of non-charge hounds, similar to those used in the south of France where the same pack hunt boar, fox, hare or partridge depending upon what they find.

That summer the Robarts family raised £130 for hunt funds at the Barnet Horse Show and Monica Robarts and Eric Shelley were married; they were presented with a cheque from the hunt as a wedding present. The family had been running their annual show for eleven years by that time and each year the profit was donated to some worthy cause.

Followers of the hunt were honoured to learn that their Master, Geoffrey Hartop, had been elected President of the Masters of Harriers and Beagles Association.

The Aldenham Harriers at Cross Farm in 1956
Valerie Dickinson

For the 1956/7 season 31 meets were called, of which only one was lost. There were 74 subscribers that season which produced a total income of £642. The range of subscriptions was considerable; £41 for the highest and two guineas for the lowest. Hardly had the season started when exception was taken to the way some people were appearing in the field which led to the following circular:

"The Master wishes it to be understood that the privilege of wearing hunting caps should be confined to farmers, their wives, sons and daughters and to other children up to their seventeenth birthday. A bowler hat is the proper headwear for others"

Reginald Streather
Secretary

Perhaps a particular person was being 'got at', perhaps it was a lapse through ignorance; either way protective headgear became the norm in later years on safety grounds.

As soon as the season got under way *'Ben Adam'* put pen to paper again:

"These hounds gave a great display from their opening meet at Harpenden Common on Saturday November 3rd [1956]. *Mr*

Geoffrey Hartop is now sole Master and continues as huntsman, with Ben Wilkinson as kennel huntsman and to turn hounds.

A hare was found at once on Mr Robert Dickinson's Farm [Cross Farm], but as she ran straight for the railway, hounds were stopped. Shortly afterwards however, a strong hare was sent away from some kale by Thames Wood, giving us a fast, ringing hunt of some 35 minutes through Clappers and Stockings and on to Aldwickbury. Here hounds were drawing up to her on the plough when, fortunately a fresh hare got up and hounds raced her to kill in the kale behind Stockings after 10 minutes.

Scent weakened somewhat for the next hour or so, but improved for our afternoon run which was from the plough below Puddlers then past Roundwood and Hill Farm. After returning nearly to Puddlers she turned again and running the full length of Nomansland Common, and crossing the Sandridge Road, she took us almost to Coleman Green where with both scent and light failing, hounds were stopped and a highly successful day was ended."

One more of *'Ben Adam's'* reports appeared towards the end of the season and then they stopped as abruptly as they had begun:

"On February 16th [1957], these hounds had a somewhat unusual day. After being generously entertained by Mr Kennedy at De Havilland's Astwick Manor, hounds found almost immediately in Symondshyde, to provide nearly two hours of good woodland hunting in and around these covers.

Then, at about one o'clock, with a grand burst of music, they raced from cover as if for the Rifle Butts. Although our Huntsman, Mr Geoffrey Hartop, and Ben Wilkinson were then with hounds they had to make a wide detour to miss two strongly wired up fields, thus losing the line, and neither they nor the Field were ever on terms with hounds again.

From reliable reports subsequently pieced together, it appears that hounds swung right handed across Hammonds Farm, leaving Coleman Green on their right, crossed Samuel's [sic]Farm and Lord Brocket's Chalk Dell Farm, went over the Wheathampstead-Lemsford Road and then over the River Lea and Geoffrey Sherriff's Water End Farm.

Unfortunately, we were misinformed here and directed back to Symondshyde. We believe however, hounds went on into Dowdells as a fox was seen on the move there by Mr Blowey who watched them running hard out of Norfolk Wood, past Hill Farm, in the direction of Shaw's Corner at Ayot St Lawrence at 2 o'clock.

From here they were seen into Brimstones with a fox only a few yards in front of them. Then, heading for Codicote Common they must have crossed the Codicote Road before going into St Paul's Walden Park - the home of the Hon. David Bowes-Lyon at about 3.30pm. Here they remained until eventually collected at about 8 o'clock. Only one hound was left out and she had returned to kennels by the morning.
This was a hunt of some 14 miles as hounds run, with an 8 mile point, nobody being with them."

Now that is a most remarkable and fitting last report for anybody interested in hounds!

At the 1957 Aldenham Harriers Point-to-Point meeting at Friars Wash, Michael Connell won the Members Race on SANDYLAND and only two finished.

Adult subscriptions for the 1957/58 season were fifteen guineas and a visitors 'cap' was £1 a day which produced £525. There were always substantial reductions for young people and the Aldenham Harriers achieved something of a reputation for being particularly encouraging in this respect. 30 meets were called, of which 5 were lost. The average field was 36.

The 1958 point-to-point meeting at Friars Wash was a disaster, but some help again came from the Robarts family whose Barnet Horse show produced £130 for hunt funds.

During the decade of the fifties a rough 'rule of thumb' for the origins of annual average hunt income could be analysed as:

Subscriptions	500
Caps	100
Hunt ball	200
Point-to-Point meeting	1000
Total	£1,800

which amply demonstrates how important a profit at the Friars Wash Point-to-Point Races had become. Alarmingly, for five of those years expenditure exceeded income, but not by much.

On 3rd February 1958 Geoff Hartop resigned again, but this time it did actually happen, at least as far as the Mastership was concerned. He was the last of the sole Masters; those that followed came in twos, threes, even fours, for the next forty years. Even Lady Lyell, who became such an institution later on, was never Master on her own.

At a ceremony at the Red Lion Hotel in St Albans on 1st May 1958 Lord Knutsford presented an inscribed hunting horn, a cigarette case and a cheque to Geoff Hartop who was retiring as Master of the Aldenham Harriers after eleven years. Mr Ben Wilkinson, who had been kennel huntsman to him over all those years, retired on the same day and he too was presented with a cheque. The mood of the occasion was very much that the Aldenham Harriers was being wound up despite the fact that it was to continue as a private pack and the secretary, Reggie Streather, even though he would be continuing in office in the new situation, was presented with an inscribed hunting horn and a picnic basket. The reason for winding up was said to be the new M1 motorway and the urban spread, and Lord Knutsford in his speech said that in his early hunting days, places which are now towns had been open country. Guests included Mr W.O.Case, Editor of *Horse & Hound*, Mr Ellison, Secretary of the Hertfordshire Hunt Club, Dr Wardill, Master of the South Hertfordshire Beagles and Sir Jocelyn Lucas, former Master of the Aldenham Harriers.

Lord Knutsford, the 4th Viscount was prominent in hunting circles, having been MFH the Avon Vale (1924-1933) and MFH the Vale of the White Horse (Cirencester) (1935-1939) and was a good friend of the Aldenham Harriers, living as he did on their 'patch'. He was in the grand old tradition of hunting 'characters' and it is reported that on one occasion he was thrown in the heat of the chase and although in considerable pain, put his practically lifeless hand in his jacket, remounted and carried on. When the excitement was over he was pronounced to have broken his collar bone. The Aldenham had a regular invitation to hunt his land at Munden Park, Otterspool, Bricket Wood and on one occasion Big Harry was hunting the hounds there and his lordship, as was his wont, was directing proceedings on foot near some willow beds where the motorway is now, when he suddenly shouted *"stop!"*, pushed his thumb stick into a hole and a fox jumped out, vertically, (*"probably had it put there beforehand"* said one sceptic!) and dashed off with hounds in hot pursuit. They all had a tremendous run round and round Aldenham School and at the end of it Lord Knutsford, who had watched the whole thing from a distance, said to Basil Hall *"that's a good horse, it should always be with fox hounds"* to which Basil replied *"maybe so, but its owner prefers hare"*. His lordship was popular with engine drivers of the nearby Watford to St Albans Branch railway line; he would give them a fiver if they stopped a train for the hounds. He wrote regularly for *Horse & Hound* and when the M1 motorway was built across his lands stipulated that contractors must erect fox-proof fencing and they agreed. He died in 1976. The story goes that his daughter, Diana, who had been a senior Commander in the ATS in the war, was looking out of her bedroom window one day and was astonished to find a stranger on the lawn shooting rabbits. When she asked him to explain himself he said *"I have to come out here because where I live there is only a window box"* and she let him get away with it.

That year Geoff Hartop was again elected President of the Masters of

Harriers and Beagles Association.

There was great relief in the autumn of 1958 when Mr and the Hon. Mrs Lyell agreed to take over the pack, but it had not been an easy decision for them; the story goes that they were so undecided how best to proceed that they agreed to toss a coin for it *"heads we will, tails we won't"*, no more enthusiastic, forceful or inspired than that, and so much depended upon the outcome. The status of the hunt again became that of a private pack, the responsibility of the Joint Masters, thus reverting to the situation of the first fifty years from the start in 1878. There were to be no subscribers although donations towards the maintenance of the hounds would be gratefully accepted by the Joint Masters. There was some doubt as to whether the usual ten Saturday meets during the season was going to be achievable, but they were confident that the usual mid week meets would be continued.

Sir Maurice and Lady Lyell driving in their trap at Trowley Bottom
Rita Huxley

The huntsman was Geoff Hartop, who had first been appointed to the position in 1946. The whipper-in and kennel huntsman was Harry Smith who, with his son, Terry, who was a groom, had been appointed on 1st May. The pair had moved from Queen Camel Kennels in Somerset where the father's references from his previous employer (H.C.Phillips from the Old Barton) stated amongst other things that he was honest and sober, an excellent kennelman who kept his kennels very clean, that he was fond of his hounds and they were devoted to him, that he was a hard worker and that the discipline of the hounds was excellent. All of this he proved in good measure in his time at Puddephats and he and his son became affectionately known as 'Big Harry and Little Harry'. There were sixteen and a half couple of hounds in the Aldenham Harriers pack, the property of the Joint Masters. This is the point at which kennels were moved to Puddephats Farm. The country was described as Beds, Herts and Bucks, parts of which were shared with the Hertfordshire, Old Berkeley, Enfield Chace Hunts and South Herts Beagles.

However, the move of the kennels to Puddephats was not all plain sailing and doubts were voiced as to whether the premises ought to be registered as a knackers yard under the 'Slaughter of Animals Act' of 1933. Common sense prevailed and the Hemel Hempstead Rural District Council Public Health Inspector confirmed that:

> *"The committee is satisfied that your activities will not constitute a business within the meaning of the Act as the amount of slaughtering is so small."*

The new kennels were only intended to be temporary and Lady Lyell was to say many years later that had she known that hounds would be there so long she would have made a better job of their accommodation.

An early enterprise of the new regime was the start of the Aldenham Harriers Pony Club. Lady Lyell, always keen to encourage the young, started it in about 1958 with the help of Elizabeth Ansell and Joyce Christopher, both of whom owned and ran riding stables, making it a very convenient arrangement. Pony clubs are not just a name, they are a national organisation with many branches and a set of rules and objects. There is still a Flamstead Pony Club, but it is not connected to the Aldenham Harriers nor to the original venture of 1958 which a little later on expanded to became the East Herts Pony Club.

Lady Lyell took the title of district commissioner and Joyce Christopher was the secretary. In those early days Joan Cunningham was also involved.

There was a desire within the East Herts Pony Club to form a Prince Philip Cup team and the first camp was held at Mr Catton's Dove House Farm on Kinsbourne Green. The rules for these camps included no drinking, no taking of prescribed substances and no smoking. However, there were other simple pleasures to be had, the possible occurrence of which was considered to be too remote to put into the rules; the local lads turned up and consternation was caused when the girls decamped and took off with them in a body, but they were all accounted for later on and hopefully were none the worse for the experience.

Hunter trials were held on 27th September 1958 at Rectory Lane, Shenley, by kind permission Mr V.L.Wild. Entry fees on that occasion were 10s. and the prizes were cups and rosettes. There were the usual five classes; Juveniles, Novices, Adjacent Hunts, Open and Open Pairs.

For the 1958/9 season 28 meets were called, of which 3 were lost. The average field was 30. For the first season in the new situation meets were arranged at places that were to become regulars in the years that followed, being at Redbourn Common, Trowley Bottom, Pulmer Water, Studham, Nomansland, Ivinghoe Village, Porters End, Cheverells Green, Potten End, Hatching Green, Ayres End House, Bricket Station, Ashridge Monument, Kensworth House, Leasey Bridge Farm, Streatley, Lea House (Wheathampstead), Long Acre (Harpenden) and Great Wymondley, but, as ever, some were inevitably cancelled. Donations to the Hound Fund totalled £373.18s. The largest single amount was £25, the most frequent sum was £5.5.0d. and there were 42 names on the list. The season was a particularly difficult one because it was so wet. Geoff Hartop continued as honorary huntsman.

The last meeting of the old Aldenham Harriers Hunt Committee took place at the Peahen on 15th January 1959 when people were elected to dispose of the remaining assets to a new Aldenham Harriers Holding Committee, the members of which were Mrs Mary Allen and Messrs. D.D.Bassett, F.R.Catton, G.H.Hartop, R.E.Simons, R.Streather and S.White and at the first meeting of that body, six months later, it was resolved that the net proceeds, £1,383, should be invested in 5% Defence Bonds.

Right to left Lady Lyell,
Basil Hall and Sir Maurice
Basil Hall

Mr and the Hon. Mrs Lyell bought the sixteen and a half couple of hounds for five guineas and there was a formal letter of acknowledgment that they then became their absolute property.

Despite fears expressed the previous year that there would be no more racing at Friars Wash after the M1 motorway had been opened, the Aldenham Harriers staged their point-to-point meeting there on Saturday 28th February 1959. The course was on land owned by Messrs W.C.Blair & Son, E.Lewin and G.H.T.Stovin. The conditions were perfect and the crowd was estimated at 12,000 which the joint course secretary, Billy Marsh, described as average. A profit of £667 was made for hunt funds.

The proceedings started with a Members, Subscribers and Farmers Race at 1.30pm with free entrance and one sovereign to be paid by starters at declaration. First prize was a piece of plate and fifteen sovereigns. The race had a sensational start when one of only four starters, SUPPER TIME, ridden by Mr P. Anderson, refused at the first fence and left the remaining three to battle it out. At 2.15pm there was an Adjacent Hunts Race with an entrance fee of one sovereign and one sovereign extra for starters to be paid on declaration which were standard for the rest of the races that day. First prize was a piece of plate and twenty sovereigns. Then at 3pm came an Open Ladies Race with a first prize of a silver cup, presented by Jim Joel of Childwickbury Stud, and twenty sovereigns. In this race Mrs E. Shelley of the Aldenham Harriers had the misfortune to receive facial injuries when her horse, POPPY DAY, went down at the water jump. At 3.45pm was an Adjacent Hunts Maiden at Entry Race with a first prize of twenty sovereigns. This was the race which caused the most excitement of the day when show jumper Alan Oliver riding HAPPY RETURN was narrowly beaten by Jerry Hartigan on VENLYON II who was the 2-1 favourite. *The Herts Advertiser* did the spectacle justice:

> *"...he opened up a tremendous twelve lengths lead as the field thundered down hill in open country after the seventh fence......Exploiting his advantage Mr Oliver continued to increase his lead as the field went round for the second time, and with only a mile to go he seemed to have the race in his pocket......But then came the surprise. Exactly where Mr Oliver had made his earlier effort, Mr Jerry Hartigan on VENLYON II and Mr H. Harris on GAY ORIENT began to catch up. Making up nearly 75 yards in a superb run, VENLYON II began to challenge strongly two fences from home and came from behind to win by one and a half lengths."*

The afternoon ended with an Adjacent Hunts Heavy-weight Race which had a first prize of a piece of plate and twenty sovereigns.

A hunt ball was held on Friday 3rd April 1959 at the Public Hall, Harpenden. Tickets were two guineas each and the music was provided by Tommy Kinsman and his band. Now this appears to have been the first time that a hunt ball was held in the spring at this place with music provided by this band.

The arrangements were so successful that they were repeated each year for the next thirteen years. The only aspects that varied to any great extent were the dates and the prices of the tickets, both entirely understandable

Hunter trials were due to be held on 26th September 1959 at Grove Farm, Flamstead, but had to be cancelled as lateness of the harvest left insufficient time in which to prepare the course and in any case the ground was *"rock hard"* which would have been dangerous for horses and riders. However, this was only a temporary setback and hunter trials were held regularly each year at Grove Farm for the next four years after which they were moved to Trowley Bottom Farm. Typical entries for this period were fifty or sixty horses representing perhaps a dozen hunts. These trials were the first Aldenham Harriers hunter trials at Grove Farm, indeed they were only the second after a long gap of a good number of years anywhere. However, these two were not necessarily the first ever and trials may have been an annual feature of the hunting scene, as was the hunt ball, prior to the Second World War.

The 1959/60 season was again a particularly wet one; 26 meets were called, of which 6 days hunting were lost through frost and foot and mouth disease. The average field was 36. Subscriptions produced £468. As usual, at the end of the season a point-to-point meeting was held at Friars Wash again (5th March 1960) and produced a profit of £837. For some reason the entries were particularly high and those for the Open Ladies Race in particular were such that it had to be split into two events with seventeen runners in each. Thus there were seven races that day instead of the more usual six and total entries exceeded 80 which was possibly a record for the Aldenham Harriers. In the first race there was a nasty moment when Miss Jane Lindop riding Mr H.H.Lindop's HILL FLAME, half a mile from home and in the lead, was thrown and rolled on. She was taken to St Albans City Hospital. Miss Pat Dawson riding COOL ANSWER also fell and was injured in this race and only five of the eleven runners finished. There was more drama in the second race, the Adjacent Hunts, when FOROUGHONA unseated its owner-rider, Mr R.P.Cooper and made off, eventually being cornered on Redbourn Common. In the event there were only eleven and eight runners respectively in the split Open Ladies Race. Half of them failed to finish, at least two horses fell in each race and four ladies were hurt, one of them sufficiently so to have to be taken to hospital.

Meets in the 1960/61 season included the Cross Keys at Gustard Wood, Caddington Village and Cholesbury, the latter at the invitation of the Old Berkeley Hunt. The season was again a wet one; 29 meets were called of which 7 were lost, 6 of them through an outbreak of foot and mouth disease. The average field was 31. Subscriptions made £496. The point-to-point races were held at Friars Wash on 14th March 1961 which was a particularly cold day. The large number of entries necessitated the ladies' race having to be split again. The crowd was estimated at 14,000 which produced a profit of £1,260 and was possibly a record.

Hunter trials were held on 14th October 1961 when G.F.Martin & Co, the St Albans caterers, provided a marquee at a cost of £10 and lunches for sixty-four at 10s. a head. Shortly afterwards it was announced that Geoff Hartop, who had been so indispensable in his capacity as honorary huntsman and arranger of the Friars Wash point-to-point races, was to move from Beaumont Hall, Redbourn to Priors Marston, which is near Rugby, and this would necessitate him relinquishing his responsibilities. It was a great blow at the time, but none of us is indispensable and the Aldenham Harriers surmounted the crisis.

For the 1961/2 season Sir Maurice and the Hon. Lady Lyell continued in their Joint Mastership and Harry Smith continued as kennel huntsman. The season was a difficult one; 30 meets were called, but 9 were lost including the Christmas holiday ones. The average field was 20. Subscriptions produced £474 but the point-to-point meeting at Friars Wash on 3rd March 1962 only made £25; the going was good, but attendances were down.

By this time Lady Lyell was inspiring a fierce loyalty from those closely involved with her, but at the same time was gaining a reputation for single-mindedness in the field. She was not above shouting her instructions and she had an enviable vocabulary of strong language coupled with a forceful way of delivering it. She did not suffer fools gladly, but people have said of her that although she could have a flaming row with you, it would be quickly forgotten. She was particularly incensed if anybody interfered with the hounds. On one occasion when she had control of them George Garfoot ventured a small item of advice, to be told icily *"When I want your assistance I'll ask for it"*. On another occasion George, having learned nothing from his earlier experience, was behind the pack when Lady Lyell had control of them in a lane coming up to a crossroads. George advised her to keep them back, only to receive a similar response, but he had his moment because a car came through at the same time as hounds bounded over the junction and one of them was bowled over. She laid down the law for the kennels and was particularly insistent that hounds should not be out after dark.

George Garfoot (mounted - right) and Harry Smith (mounted - left) with Dick Turpin holding lady Lyell's horse Derek Christopher

One of her employee favourites was Dick Turpin, a bachelor who lived in one of the Puddephats cottages and acted as a sort of general factotum. Lady Lyell treated him like a son and allowed him all sorts of liberties. At the same time they often raged at each other in an uncontrolled and fearsome way, but no lasting offence was ever taken on either side. When George Garfoot first arrived, Lady Lyell advised him *"Dick likes to be the first to tell me everything"*, such was her concern for his privileged position.

In Harry Smith's time as kennel huntsman the Aldenham Harriers were said to be one of the best packs that you could come across, but hounds were inclined to be unruly and whilst this could be irritating at times it was believed to be the secret of their success. This on the premise that there is a fine balance between initiative and obedience and Harry's way tended towards lenience. Times were good for Maurice Lyell too; the Hunt was prospering and he was Master of it, he had been appointed a Judge of the Queen's Bench Division of the High Court of Justice (1962-1975) and with the appointment came his knighthood.

Lady Lyell & Pat Turner at Stags End
Derek Christopher

Pat Turner, now in his eighties, hunted with the Aldenham for thirty years and in his own words *"got a lot of fun out of it"*. It could hardly be said that he came from a harrier family. Admittedly his father was a member of the Hertfordshire, but they hunted fox, and in the end Pat was the only one of six children who hunted anything. The person who started him with the Aldenham was his daughter, Susan, who had a pony and was keen to follow the chase when the hunt met that year at Nomansland, which was not very far away from their

Kimpton home, so Pat borrowed a horse and went with her. That was in about 1950.

One of his horses later on would never admit to being tired, but late one day she stumbled in a bad patch, put her foot in a hole, threw him, and ran off. He was in considerable pain so his companions decided to take him to Luton and Dunstable Hospital, but he insisted that he must have a scotch first. They found a pub near to the hospital and after a little while in the snug he announced that he had had enough and was ready for anything. In hospital they discovered that he had dislocated his shoulder, but to set it would need an anaesthetic. He smelt like a distillery, but still they had to ask the question, had he had any alcohol? Then no anaesthetic. They tried to set it without, which caused him great pain, but in the event they had to wait four hours for the effect of the drink to wear off. Serious drinkers might like to make a note of that!

Another time Sir Maurice Lyell was in the field; he was an academic, not the best qualification for a great huntsman, although he was a great enthusiast, but that is not at all the same thing. It seems that one day, whilst the hunt was standing, waiting for the off, a hare appeared from nowhere directly in front of them. Hounds and the horses went off at a great pace, but Sir Maurice somehow stayed put and landed flat on his back in a patch of mud, minus spectacles. Pat was one of those who rescued him and in the process laughed so heartily that he felt obliged to apologise afterwards. He was forgiven in good grace. Pat had never heard of a fatal accident with the Aldenham Harriers, but there was one, as revealed later on, and it is, in a way, remarkable, considering what the hunt is all about, that this has been the only fatality the Aldenham Harriers have ever had, though there have been a good many with other hunts and a good many fairly serious accidents to followers and horses alike. In fact on another occasion Pat himself was thrown and ended up breaking a hip.

The 1962/3 season was a disaster because of the weather, said to be the worst within living memory. Hounds were out on only eight occasions when, after a good start to the season with some very pleasant days, the snow came and there was no hunting after 20th December. It was impossible to hunt on Boxing Day, but, in order not to disappoint all those who looked forward to seeing the Aldenham Harriers on Redbourn Common on that day, the Master, very sportingly, took the hounds down to meet on, and indeed over, the doorstep of Mr and Mrs Larry Webb. Their never failing hospitality did much to brighten up the gallant twenty who rode down to make a show, knowing that there was no chance of hunting. Even the point-to-point races at Friars Wash scheduled for 2nd March had to be cancelled, which resulted in a loss of £270. The snow and frozen state of the ground prevented the preparation of the course and the stewards decided that racing should not be allowed to take place. This was the season when Basil Hall joined Sir Maurice and the Hon. Lady Lyell as a Joint Master. Basil at this point was described as a young farmer from Leighton Buzzard who was a past European motor-cycling champion and member of the

121

British team for four years. The report of Basil's appointment got as far as *the Times* who speculated upon whether, with Sir Maurice's pastimes being quoted in *Who's Who* as 'idling', the new Joint Master's might be the same.

Tommy Kinsman provided a six-piece band for the hunt ball on 29th March 1963 and charged £73.10s for five hours of music. 171 suppers were provided by Bell Catering of Aston Clinton for 14s.6d. a head, but 9 suppers for the staff and the band cost only 10s.6d. a head, though they did get through £5.13s.2d. worth of drinks on top.

It was in 1963 that Derek Christopher took over as Field Master, a position that he was to hold with distinction for the next thirty three years. His good friend, Stanley White, had acquired by this time two artificial hips and a lifetime's hunting experience, and after spending a Wednesday in the field he would say to Derek *"Come back home with me and have a Scotch"* and the pair of them would chew over the day's activities into the small hours. Derek acknowledges *"That is the way I learned most of my craft and I particularly remember an early tip - when you go out first thing in the morning be sure to check which way the wind is blowing"*. He said to Derek's wife, Joyce, *"I like the way you ride - I shall buy you a horse to show"* and he did. Another of his comments was *"you'll sell a few horses Derek, but Joyce has these"* and he waggled his little fingers to indicate that Joyce had 'good' hands. When Stanley retired he gave Derek all his tack; he still has most of it.

Joyce Christopher riding side-saddle
Joyce Christopher

Bert England lived at Kensworth House and when World War Two came to an end and the Government started disposing of stocks of war material, Bert bought a mountain of army surplus buttons. Some he was able to turn to a profit fairly quickly, but that left a considerable quantity that did not move and became an embarrassment. The solution was novel; there was, and is, a mile long drive to Kensworth House which was in need of repair, so he had the buttons spread along it as hardcore, bought a steamroller and persuaded Basil Hall to change mounts and roll his drive flat. It worked and the drive is still known as Button Lane today. Now what has that got to do with the Aldenham Harriers? Well, Joyce Christopher was riding nearby with Lady Lyell one day and naturally enough the conversation turned to buttons. *"why do you not wear the hunt buttons?"* asked her ladyship; *"because I have never been asked"* came the reply, but Joyce wore them from that day on.

Meets were reduced for the 1963/4 season and as usual a number of them had to be cancelled. In addition to the usual places there was intended to be a meet at Chipperfield at the invitation of the Old Berkeley Hunt, but it had to be cancelled because of floods. Out of the ordinary meets this season were those at Linces Farm (Welwyn), and Edegrove (Aldenham). Hounds only lost half a dozen days and the season was deemed a success.

Aldenham Harriers Point-to-Point races were held at Friars Wash on 7th March 1964 when the jumps were said to be *"better than ever"*, but that comment was often made. Attendances, however, were not and an estimated 6,000 resulted in a serious financial loss which again induced fears that the meetings might no longer be viable. In the event the Hertfordshire Hunt forced the issue by moving to the Whaddon Chase course. The Aldenham Harriers could not continue alone and so 1964 became the last year that there was point-to-point racing at Friars Wash. The first race that year was won by Bill Shand-Kydd on his horse, NO REWARD, which was 5-1 favourite. The biggest field of the day with twenty runners was the Open, but only seven finished. In the last race, the Members, Subscribers and Farmers Race, only one of the four starters completed the course, Michael Connell on GAY ORIENT. Major V.Smith's (of the Belvoir) MERRYWEATHER, which had a good lead on TWO PINS in the Open Race fell with a broken fetlock while taking a bend and had to be destroyed. The rider, Mr D.Gibson, was unhurt.

Afterwards, and particularly around the time that the 1965 point-to-point meeting might have been expected, there was a lot of speculation and recrimination about why the meetings had ceased. Some unkind things were said, but people were very disappointed. One rumour was that the Hertfordshire Show, which had just bought a permanent site on the opposite side of Watling Street, had created problems. It was not true. Another rumour was that that the farmers upon whose land the races had been run had become impatient about having their farming activities interfered with and had raised their demands to impossible levels. That was not true either. Mr Sandy Blair of Annables Manor, one of those on whose land the races were run, commented:

> *"There is no question of our being unwilling to let them use the land. We shall miss this outing ourselves. It has been held on our land since we came here about twenty years ago and for many years before that."*

The plain fact was that costs had risen at the same time that, because of a couple of very bad years for weather and the fact that watching sport on television was becoming increasingly popular, gates were declining. The point was made that it cost about £1,500 to stage a meeting and it was easy to lose £500 on it, which had to be covered somehow.

The accounts for that last Friars Wash meeting (1964) have survived and it is easy to see why the annual fixture could not go on; remember this is a long time ago and to equate them to today's values you probably ought to multiply them by something like thirty.

INCOME		EXPENDITURE	
Reserved cars	£136	National Car Parks	£47
Cars at Gate		Catering	43
[1961-1174][1962-611][1963-0	470	Herts. Constabulary	104
Race card sales		Hertfordshire Hunt	
[1961-614][1962-356][1963-0]	237	for the course	450
Entry fees	142	Public address system	37
Bookmakers	53	Advertising	94
Tote commission	141	Prize money	215
Other	34	Tent hire	120
Net loss	591	Race cards	101
		Farmer Blair	75
		Farmer Lewin	15
		Insurance	375
		Other	128
	£1804		£1804

There was great relief when Sir Maurice and the Hon. Lady Lyell and Mr Basil Hall agreed to continue as Joint Masters for the 1964/5 season. The opening meet was delayed until late November and in spite of losing eight days through frost and snow, including, unfortunately, Boxing Day and the Pony Club

Meet, it was still a good season. In July 1964, and again in the summer of 1965, Monica Shelley organised a horse show at the Homestead Farm, Barnet, by kind permission of her mother, Mrs Robarts, and from the proceeds made another donation to Aldenham Harriers.

Secretary Reggie Streather's Retirement in 1965. (left to right) Sir Maurice and Lady Lyell, Harry Sewell and Reggie, with Reggie's wife Ba in front with the bouquet.
Basil Hall

Honorary secretary Reggie Streather announced his intention to stand down at the beginning of 1965; he had held the office since 1952. He was said at the time to have been the lynch-pin of the hunt throughout those years, but his days of hunting were over; he had been thrown and fell heavily on a harrow which punctured his lungs - nasty! Field Master Derek Christopher was elected to succeed him.

There had been a long dry summer so that at the start of the season the ground was rock hard in October for the first meet. Lady Lyell would not hear of the horses hunting in such conditions because of the high risk of injury, so Sir Maurice hunted the hounds on foot. The result was described by one of the participants as *"a very undignified rabble with people scuttling about like scalded cats trying to keep up with the hounds"*, though this was contested by others who argued that the Aldenham were never undignified. Whatever the circumstances, it was pronounced not to have been a success, but nevertheless there were other occasions when hunting on foot was resorted to, more usually following long periods of heavy frost.

Redbourn Parish Council was in uproar at their January 1965 meeting when Councillor F.J.Reed accused the Aldenham Harriers of "feudal arrogance":

"We as owners of the common have the right to know that the hunt is meeting there and I suggest that the clerk writes to the Joint Masters and points out that it would be good manners and polite to let us know. We were told nothing about the Boxing Day meet."

Having received the letter the Joint Masters responded:

"Over the past 40 years, with the exception of the war years, Aldenham Harriers have regularly met on the common, and that fact can hardly have been unknown to your council at any time during that long period......May I add a word with regard to the recent Boxing Day meet, which one of your members is reported as having described as a display of feudal arrogance. On that day the ground was frozen and hunting was impossible. Our only reason for bringing horses and hounds four miles to Redbourn was not to disappoint the crowd of several hundred who obviously expected us to turn out whatever the weather."

There the matter was left for the time being, but a number of councillors were far from happy.

Left to right: Derek Christopher, Lady Lyell,
Sir Maurice Lyell, Grizelda Block and Audrey Chambers
the first day Derek was Secretary
Derek Christopher

The future of the Aldenham Harriers was again the subject of discussion in June 1965 when concern was expressed about what would happen when the

Lyells retired from Joint Mastership. In that eventuality the following agreed to act as a hunt committee in their place:

Stanley White	Deirdre Milnes
Robert Dickinson	Nick Lyell
Monica Shelley	Philip Hall
Frank Weinert	Geoffrey Sherriff
Pat Turner	Rita Huxley

The plan was that the kennels and the kennel huntsman's house would be moved to a site at Valley Farm, Flamstead, so as to be under the eye of Basil Hall, the new Master. In the event it quickly became apparent that all this could not be put in hand until the following season and the existing Joint Masters agreed to continue for a further season and to the kennels remaining at Puddephats.

Basil Hall with Frank Weinert
Derek Christopher

Basil Hall has a fund of memories of his time in the field and being a man with a good sense of humour makes the whole hunting exercise sound like a riot. Early on he was riding ROMANY, which was his daughter Rosamund's (Jill) horse, and he hunted with Geoffrey Hartop at a time when Geoffrey had his arm in a sling and a broken collar bone. Basil recalls a time when the meet was at Sharpenhoe where they have some deep and wide ditches. Frank Weinert fell in one of them and so did his horse. Frank was quickly rescued, but the sides of the ditch were too steep for the horse and it had to be led along for almost half a mile before a place was found to pull it out. Frank seems to have been accident prone; he hunted in 'swallow tails' and a top hat and at the first jump at one meet his horse somehow managed, in slow motion, to pitch him between its ears, but that was not the end of it; it then stood on one of his swallow tails and split his jacket up the back, knocking his top hat off, whereupon it put its hoof through the crown. Frank was not to be beaten that way however; he remounted, put the only intact part of his hat, the rim, firmly on his head and with his jacket tails flapping wildly in his wake proceeded to enjoy the rest of his day's hunting. Basil had had an indignity of that sort himself when, on another occasion, in the excitement of the chase at Cross Farm, Harpenden, he split his breeches right round and the hunt looked on with some glee while Robert Dickinson's wife, Valerie, put needle and thread to them; a deft manoeuvre skilfully achieved without the need of removal. The telling of these stories prompted Derek Christopher to top them. He remembered a time when he jumped a ditch to find he was passing over Jim Clark, Master of the Vale of Aylesbury, who was ferreting about in the bottom of the ditch up to his elbows in the mud. Challenged, he said he was looking for his pedals (stirrups) which had somehow come adrift in the heat of the chase.

The kennel huntsman, Harry Smith, 'Big Harry' to his friends, became ill shortly before Christmas 1965 and asked to be relieved from his duties at the end of the season. He had served the Aldenham Harriers well for eight seasons and members were invited to subscribe to a testimonial for him. Lady Lyell organised the collection and the Joint Masters suggested that the maximum per subscriber ought to be two guineas, which seems a trifle unfair. Nevertheless it was possible in this way to present Harry with a cheque for £100, a sizeable sum for those days and no doubt very acceptable.

Hunter trials were held at Trowley Bottom Farm, Flamstead on Saturday 16th October 1965 by kind permission of Denis Huxley and were reckoned to be the best ever, partly because the weather was perfect. This was to be the start of an institution that was to go from strength to strength at Trowley Bottom Farm for the next seven years. Denis, who sadly died some years ago, was quite strict about the arrangements though and his widow, Rita, recalls that they had to plan the milking to accommodate the trials. She competed in the trials herself and on one occasion was thrown in a cow pat; not only that, but she made the mistake of holding on to her horse and so was dragged through some more for good measure - she was a bit of a mess and people kept well clear of her. Staff from the Lyell estate prepared the course and made the jumps. There was a Juvenile Class open to Pony Club members aged sixteen and under with an entry fee of 10s. won by H.Growcott's GOLDEN GUINEA. There was an Open Novice Class for hunters the property of subscribers to, or farmers in, any recognised hunt which had not won a prize before. The first prize was £4 and the entry fee £1. It was won by L.Ensten's GAMBLE. There was an Adjacent Hunts Class for hunters belonging to the Hertfordshire, the Old Berkeley, the Enfield Chace, the

Whaddon Chase, the Puckeridge, the Oakley or the Aldenham Harriers. The first prize was £5 and the entry fee £1. It was won by F.Oliver's BEN ridden by Alan Oliver . Then there was an Open Class with a first prize of £5 and an entry fee of £1, which was won by F.Oliver's JOHNNY also ridden by Alan Oliver. Next, an Open Pairs Class with a first prize of £4 and an entry fee of £1 per horse, won by Basil Hall's HYDEWAY ridden by his daughter, Rosamund (Jill), and Joyce Christopher's THUNDERBALL ridden by Derek Christopher, the Aldenham Harrier's joint secretary. Finally there was a Consolation Class for those who had not won a prize in any other class.

Rita Huxley with Pat Burgin
(Joint MH 1980-1996)
Rita Huxley

Returning to Rita Huxley who has been a staunch supporter of the Aldenham Harriers for many years; she recalls that she came to hunting quite by accident when she was out riding with a friend one day in 1952, got caught up in the hunt as they went by and never looked back. Mostly she hunted with one horse, but when she was also hunting with the Grafton she had two and hunted three times a week. She mentions that early on in her hunting career her horse had to be whipped over one of the jumps, but it paid off for her and her horse. She rode a bay for sixteen seasons which would jump any timber, but was not very keen on hedges. She has many happy memories of her days in the field. There was the time when Lady Lyell was thrown at a fence at Wood End; she landed softly, but the man riding beside her was thrown as well and had an even softer landing; he landed on top of her! In such circumstances Lady Lyell could be relied upon for some very choice language, but what she said on that occasion is not recorded, perhaps it was not that strong at all. There is a suspicion that it was more of the tender sort, drowned by the chortles of those that surrounded the pair lying on the ground! On another occasion Lady Lyell was hunting on Flamsteadbury land and one of George Blair's sons shot the hare in front of her. She was predictably furious and her language on that occasion was certainly of the stronger sort. One of Rita's horses was called DEREK which caused some confusion when the name was shouted and Derek Christopher was Field Master, but whether the horse had been named in honour of the man has yet to be proved. Rita and Basil Hall are the same age and what is more, their birthdays are on consecutive days; surely that says something for astrology!

Rita Huxley

The three Joint Masters continued in office for the 1965/6 season and the opening meet was on 30th October at Redbourn. The subscription by this time had become twenty guineas for a full adult hunting member. A Wire Fund of 2s.6d. was taken from all who hunted each day to enable hunt jumps to be put up to make the country more rideable. Other meets arranged for that season, some more than once, some subsequently cancelled, were at Redbourn, Kensworth, Ayot St Lawrence, Trowley Bottom, Harpenden Common, Gaddesden Row, Caddington, Streatley, Hatching Green, Water End, Coleman Green, Gorhambury, Nomansland and Puddephats. They mostly hunted on

Wednesdays, Thursdays and Saturdays. The maximum field was forty six and the minimum nine. Top of the list for days hunted was Eric Shelley, amateur whip, with twenty two then Rita Huxley and Joyce Christopher with nineteen each.

Kennel Huntsman Graham Hughes at Gorhambury
Rita Huxley

At about this time Monica Robarts, who kept over a hundred horses at her riding school and livery stable at Barnet, rode regularly with the Aldenham Harriers and was very supportive. Robarts was her maiden name and, as mentioned earlier, she married Eric Shelley who sometimes whipped-in for Aldenham Harriers. Sadly she is no longer with us. One of her many acts of generosity was to present a cup for the best child handler (no jokes please) and another for the hunter trials. She provided a horse for the season for Audrey Chambers and Reggie Streather, *ex-officio* as hunt secretaries. For the Boxing Day meet on Redbourn Common she brought three box loads of people and horses, dropping some off half way so that they could hack on and returning to collect subsequent contingents. She would 'suit' horses to people for the Aldenham Harriers' guests and visitors who were without a mount. One day she did this for a French guest riding with Pat Turner who was told later that it had provided the happiest day of his life. She would bring out, and mount for the day, batches of London taxi drivers. Another of her specialities was to mount and take out thirty or forty people for four hours riding with a picnic lunch. She was a good sort, tough, but would always be ready to help anybody. The riding school and livery stables were at the Homestead Farm at Barnet from where the family also operated a milk round. Money raised at the Barnet Show each summer arising from this connection with Monica contributed significantly to hunt funds for a number of years and in 1966 amounted to £90.

For the 1966/7 season Sir Maurice and Lady Lyell and Basil Hall agreed to continue as Joint Masters and the kennels remained at Puddephats. George Garfoot was appointed 1st whip and kennel huntsman. He came to the Aldenham Harriers from the Hertfordshire Hunt where he had been 1st whip. The Masters agreed to hunt on Wednesdays and Saturdays each week. To the already mentioned venues were added Haynes Park (Bedford), Cross Farm (Harpenden), Aldbury, Studham, Long Acre (Harpenden), Lilley, Mantle Green Farm (Amersham) and Sharpenhoe.

Left to right John Hodgson with secretaries Reggie Streather,
Audrey Chambers and Derek Christopher at the Centenary Dinner
Derek Christopher

Someone who had put in a tremendous amount of work for the Harriers, and was well liked, indicated her intention to retire at the end of the 1966/7 season. Audrey Chambers had been joint honorary secretary for nine years and a collection was made for her which produced many letters of appreciation. Audrey was much respected for the tremendous amount of work she put into the Harriers, but in addition she is fondly remembered for being a stickler on etiquette and for a number of waspish witticisms concerning it, including, on one occasion, accosting a young visitor with *"I see you are an otter man"*. His unconscious and innocent choice of colour for the lash of his whip was blue which is, of course, the colour reserved for, and always associated with, otter hounds. For those who had not thought about this point before, the other recognised colours are red for fox, white for stag and green for hare. As secretary, she was often involved in ordering bouquets or wreaths for the

Aldenham Harriers special occasions and always insisted on yellow flowers with a red and green ribbon exactly one and a half inches wide. She often clashed with people who came out improperly dressed and was fearless in pointing out to them the error of their ways. After Audrey's retirement the 'other half', Derek Christopher, who had been joint secretary since 1965, carried on as secretary alone. In spite of the worries of two years earlier the future seemed more secure.

At this point there were eighteen and a half couple in kennels, a number achieved by a young entry of two and a half couple and a litter of three and a half couple. The Joint Masters acknowledged that last season, thanks to help from the Hertfordshire Hunt, there had been meets in new country for harriers which had provided one or two days of first class sport which they hoped to repeat.

For the 1966/67 season 34 meets were called; hunting took place on 29 days and the average field was 26. Lady Lyell was out on all 29 days, Basil Hall on 23 days, Derek Christopher on 29 days and George Garfoot on 28 days. "Little Harry" was out and specially mentioned on 9 days; he was Lady Lyell's stud groom, *'a lovely man, one of the old school'*. (Harry Sewell was called 'Little Harry' to distinguish him from 'Big Harry', the kennel huntsman)

At a meeting on 17th October 1967 it was agreed that the country should be opened up still further by erecting new hunt jumps, particularly at Sandridge (Salvation Army Farm), Harpenden (Grove Farm) and at Streatly, Redbourn and Ayot St Lawrence. Eric Shelley said that he would deal with it and Pat Turner and Robert Dickinson agreed to assist.

Derek Christopher on NOT AN INCH at the Enfield Chace Point-to-Point at Northaw in 1978
Derek Christopher

There was a fence at Puddephats that was called 'the Olympic Fence'; four foot plus, out of the plough, and few had jumped it at any time. Joyce Christopher was one of those that did. Her husband Derek had earlier tried to persuade her over when he was riding one of her horses, to be told in no uncertain terms that he ought to take up beagling! There was one epic day at Puddephats when three fences claimed three falls and Jill Saunders, Monica Shelley and Derek Christopher had to be carted off to hospital. Then Sir Maurice broke a stirrup leather and promptly announced *"I think we have done enough damage for today, I'm taking the hounds home"*. Sir Maurice would jump the biggest rails on Joyce Christopher's KUMMEL which, though only a little horse, he trusted and it trusted him. He had 'good' hands so it was said. Sometime a spate of accidents like this would 'get' to people and in fact it was at about this time Lady Arran from Pimlico, who had been riding regularly with the Aldenham, came to the conclusion that it was too dangerous and took up power boat racing instead. She was good at it too; won the Round Britain Race.

With the 1967/68 season being the 90th of the Aldenham Harriers it was decided to hold a celebratory dinner in the Culpin Room at the Pavilion, Hemel Hempstead on Friday 1st December 1967. Tickets were 50s. a head including wine and invitations to make speeches were extended to Dorian Williams, MFH and Neil McElligott. They accepted and their efforts were well received, but it was a speech from Sir Maurice Lyell that caught the attention of a *Horse & Hound* reporter:

> *"Sir Maurice's contribution, I thought, was a particularly charming one. He claimed for the Aldenham none of the glories one usually hears about a hunt's sporting activities. Instead he emphasized how useful the hunt had been as a 'nursery' in encouraging all classes of people to enjoy a day with hounds and possibly to extend their pleasure to hunting with foxhounds."*

Over one hundred guests and friends attended.

Stanley White and Geoff Hartop at the Aldenham Harriers 90 years celebrations in 1967
Stanley White Collection

1967 was notable for a particularly severe outbreak of foot and mouth disease which affects pigs and sheep and cattle, while horses and some wildlife, which are not affected, can nevertheless help to spread infection. It is spectacularly contagious so hunting activity is prohibited over wide areas. The disease was so widespread that year that virtually all hunting and racing ceased for two months and in some cases for as much as eight months. There were over two thousand confirmed sites and nearly half a million animals were destroyed. The effect on the countryside was so dramatic that people still talk about it today. The enormous bonfires built to burn the carcasses, and the smell that came from them, had a profound effect on country communities and have been dreaded by farmers ever since.

Foot and mouth disease is a scourge to farming communities and has in the past resulted in many suicides and bankruptcies, and much unhappiness to the people in the countryside generally. It used to occur in the British Isles every few years, but after the 1967/68 outbreak, apart from an isolated outbreak in the Isle of Wight in 1981, there was a respite of thirty three years before it struck again and, although the outbreak of 2001 resulted in greater numbers of animals being slaughtered, the main areas of the epidemic and the season of it were different. The outbreak in 1967 was worst in the West Midlands whereas in 2001 it was worst in Devon and Cumbria. Likewise the 1967/68 outbreak was an autumn/winter affair whereas the 2001 one was at its worst in the winter/spring period. In each case there was massive Government assistance for farmers, but it was nowhere near enough to compensate for what, in many cases, was the elimination of a lifetime's work at a stroke. In both cases movement of livestock regulations countrywide eliminated any possibility of hunting activity for the duration. In 2001 that meant no more hunting that season after 14th February. Ironically, that day Aldenham Harriers met at Sam Clark's New Medbury Farm at Elstow in perfect weather and had their best day of the season. One ironic consequence of the 2001 foot and mouth restrictions was the cancellation of the Countryside March, a protest against anti-hunting legislation, which had been planned months before and had been expected to attract a million protesters to the centre of London.

Returning to the 1967/68 season, only 14 meets were called; hunting took place on only 11 days and the average field was 29. It was said that it would be long remembered as the most frustrating season the Aldenham Harriers had ever had. Basil Hall resigned from the Joint Mastership after five seasons, but Sir Maurice and Lady Lyell carried on with George Garfoot as 1st whip and kennel huntsman. There were twenty two couple of hounds in the kennels including three and a half couple of young entry. In previous seasons, when it had not been possible to hunt on Boxing Day because of frost, it had still been possible to meet on Redbourn Common. This year not even that little show was possible.

By this time Aldenham Harriers had become, by degrees, a whole way of life; all kinds of social events were organised to fill the boring period between the end of one hunting season and the start of the next. Typically this interlude started with a hunt ball, and went on with coach outings to such delights as the Cheltenham Gold Cup and Badminton Horse Trials. In high summer there was an 'Aldenham Harriers At Home' at Puddephats or a summer ball and then, once the harvest was in, came the hunter trials. All in all a very full year, a lot of hard work for the organisers and quite an intensive social life if you were involved with everything.

The tradition of a Boxing Day meet on Redbourn Common probably goes back to the time when Geoff Hartop had the hounds kennelled just across the road at Beaumont Hall. The usual assembly point was outside 'The Bee's Nest' and there Larry Webb, year after year, extended generous hospitality, much to the delight of the hunt. It is possible that this particular year (1967) Sir Maurice had met other generous supporters along the way, maybe extending back to the festivities of the previous evening; suffice it to say that, in modern parlance he was 'well tanked up' and leaning heavily on the side of his mount demanded *"Wheresh my horsh!"* Not unnaturally those around him were not over anxious to explain its whereabouts to such an illustrious equestrian, but when its proximity eventually dawned upon him he proceeded to mount the wrong way round, whereupon his groom, 'Little Harry', always attentive, said *"I think you would be more comfortable facing the other way sir"*. Once forward facing in the saddle he was quite alright and the Harriers moved off.

Derek Christopher

Whether Larry Webb's hospitality or laughing at Sir Maurice had anything to do with it is not recorded, but Derek Christopher's mount, VODKA (how very apt) lent to him for the occasion by Joyce's head girl, Jenny Garner, stepped on a patch of ice soon afterwards, came down, and crushed Derek's foot in the stirrup, breaking his ankle. There was nothing for it but to abort the day's sport and make for home. So Derek, accompanied by Basil Hall and with Joyce's father filming the whole proceeding, made his way to Park Stables, riding VODKA and in considerable pain. Incidentally, there are no laws about riding a horse under the influence and in any case Derek was a police officer!. There, fearful of damaging his expensive riding boots, he refused to let them cut one off to ease his rapidly swelling ankle, so they plied him with Scotch until he was past caring (it only took a little over half a bottle, and that with some comradely help from Basil Hall, so he must have been well on the way already) and then Audrey Chambers snipped the boot down the back and they carted him off to Luton & Dunstable Hospital. It seems that there was a considerable gathering at Accident & Emergency and what with it being the festive season and the further imbibing that had gone on it must have been quite a party. When the treatment was started the first job was the removal of Derek's breeches, completed with strict decorum and some ceremony and supervised by Audrey Chambers who, anxious as ever to maintain standards, felt constrained to throw her dog blanket, still covered in dog hairs, over Derek's nether regions, *to keep you decent dear"*. Oh, and a postscript; Joyce's father had forgotten to put a film in his camera so that although there are a number of versions of the story, nobody can prove it one way or the other.

Derek Christopher on THUNDERBALL with Gig Blowers
Derek Christopher

It would seem that Derek has often sacrificed his lower limbs, over and above the call of duty, in the cause of hunting. There was the time, about 1986, when he was at Upperwood holding a 'freshman', PICEA, a three year old stallion in process of covering a mare for the first time. Derek had chosen an old, experienced, mare to make things easier for PICEA, but nevertheless things got a bit out of hand. PICEA trod on his foot and nothing would persuade him off. This was unfortunate because Derek was wearing gumboots; the pain was considerable and the bruising extensive. Derek was rushed to hospital for his crushed foot to be treated. They were incredulous; *"but why didn't you take your foot away?"* His reply was predictable *"I couldn't possibly move it at such a moment"*. Derek is older and wiser now and always wears steel capped boots for these delicate operations. He forgave PICEA and has only just given him away in 2001 aged eighteen.

There was the time when his brother Malcolm had booked him for a midnight matinee in favour of the Police Dependents Trust Fund, at which the cast of 'Z Cars' and Roger Moore, *alias* James Bond, (Roger's and Derek's fathers were police officers together at New Scotland Yard) would be guests of honour. It was an important occasion, but it was late in the day and there was no reason why Derek should not spend the earlier part of the day hunting as usual. He did, but when they were stabling the horses afterwards Old Harry's horse somehow managed to jump on Derek's foot and broke all his toes which. put something of a damper on the evening!

Derek Christopher at the Crooked Chimney, Cromer Hyde
Derek Christopher

For the 1968/69 season 36 meets were called, hunting took place on 27 days and the average field was 26. At the start of the season the Joint Masters reluctantly decided to postpone hunting indefinitely because the ground was so hard. Not only were the horses at risk but the hounds' feet even more so. Later the scenting conditions were excellent, especially in January, and twenty nine and a half brace of hare were killed, which was well above the average. That year the Boxing Day meet on Redbourn Common was cancelled again.

George Garfoot, the kennel huntsman, was given a number of fox hound pups at about this time by hunting friends that he met at shows. In fact he would ask for them, and over the years this meant that the Aldenham Harriers became mostly foxhound blood. There is no basset blood in the pack.

The 1969 hunter trials were held at Trowley Bottom Farm on 27th September. The course was built by Dick Turpin and Jim Snape and produced very satisfactory results. The Open Class was won by Prue Lyell on Lady Lyell's RUMPUS with a clear round and the Pairs was won by Monica Shelley on PERRY IV and Mr N.Maxey on ROYAL TOKEN.

The Aldenham Harriers branch of the Pony Club ceased to exist on 30th September 1969. It had lasted for nine years and Lady Lyell and Joyce Christopher were thanked for all the hard work that they had put into it, as was Valerie Dickinson who, with Joyce Christopher, had taken a major part in instructing the young entry.

Valerie started her involvement with the East Herts Pony Club in 1976 and became their District Commissioner. She has been riding since she was a child and attributes her enthusiasm to being taken, when only six months old, from the train to where she was staying in Norfolk, in a pony and trap, although her memory of that momentous event is understandably somewhat dim. By her own admission she has always been besotted with horses and has nearly always ridden with the Aldenham, though she had brief spells with the West Kent and the Porlock Vale. She makes the point that harriers are more interesting than foxhounds because you can see so much more of what is going on.

Valerie was a Harpenden girl and after school obtained a job at Mr Williams' stables at Long Acre, Pipers Lane, Harpenden. She started hunting in 1954 and had some good days with Geoff Hartop and Stanley White who taught her how to ride to hunt. She met her husband, Robert, in the hunting field. Quite how she came to fall off her horse in front of him has never been properly explained, but it was Robert who picked her up and fetched her horse, and they were married six years later. Robert's family had farmed Cross Farm, Harpenden, for 200 years and the Aldenham Harriers has always enjoyed a friendly welcome there. He was a keen follower of hounds and point-to-pointer, but took a few bad falls which played havoc with his back until one day his horse, IKE, bucked and put his joints back in their proper place.

For the 1969/70 season 33 meets were called, but hunting took place on only 21 days because of the bad weather in February and March. The average field was 32. That season there were 57 subscribers contributing a total of £902. The smallest contribution was £2 and the largest £50. As far as the finances were concerned this represented a very considerable improvement on the 1962/63 season when the corresponding figures had been 38 meets, subscriptions £352 and the contribution range between £2 and £21. At the end of the season it was decided that as the hunt committee had existed for five years it would be appropriate to disband it and appoint a new one. The new committee appointed in June 1970 comprised:

Mrs M.Shelley (Barnet)

Mr R.Dickinson (Harpenden)

Mr C.Park (Offley)

Mr P.Turner (Kimpton)

Mr J.T.G.Withycombe (Studham)

together with, *ex-officio*:

Mr S.White

Mr B.Hall

Mr E.Shelley

Mr D.Christopher

Sir Maurice Lyell

The Hon. Lady Lyell

When they met for the first time they agreed that due to rising costs the annual subscription would become £25 for those who subscribed for the 1969/70 season and £40 for new subscribers. The 'cap' for adults was increased to £3 a day up to a maximum of three days. There was concern about the size of the field to be expected as a result of the proposed Hertfordshire Hunt amalgamation.

The hunter trials held on 26th September 1970 at Denis and Rita Huxley's Trowley Bottom Farm were, as usual, a great success with 120 horses competing in superb weather.

Secretary, Derek Christopher, made a number of important points in his circular to subscribers at the end of the year:

"Once again, the eighth time in nine years, to the great disappointment of the Masters, the weather has thwarted us on Boxing Day. Our Boxing Day meet on Redbourn Common has become something of a local tradition in the years since the war, as is shown by the very large numbers of the general public who come to see the hounds. It is also the traditional occasion upon which we

pass the Cap round for the Hunt Servants. For them each day starts very early, seven days a week, whatever the weather and on hunting days, when hounds and horses have been brought home there is still a lot of work to be done. After the end of the hunting season, there are bitches whelping and puppies to be reared in addition to the every day work of feeding the grown hounds and keeping the Kennels and Stables as spotlessly clean as they always are."

So many things there that everyone takes for granted all the time and it is nice to see recognition of it once in a while. How many followers of hounds one wonders have ever stopped to ponder upon how the whole thing comes about? *"Well, I pay my subscription"* they will say, and so they do, but that cannot buy the dedication, the loyalty, the inconvenient hours and un-quantified hard work that comes from the sheer love of hunting, and horses, and hounds that inspires the effort.

The hunting year (1970) was marked by a couple of important points; the Government announced that it was going to introduce its own bill to abolish live hare coursing and the Old Berkeley, the Hertfordshire and the South Oxfordshire Hunts amalgamated to form the Vale of Aylesbury. This latter development led Aldenham Harriers to enquire from the Masters of Fox Hounds Association how it would affect their country. Following appropriate deliberations between the parties the following resolution was advised:

1.   *"The Vale of Aylesbury to hold all the country."*

2.   *"They allow the Enfield Chace to hunt by permission at LILLEY, PIRTON, HEXTON, KING'S AND PAUL'S WALDEN. The Enfield Chace should apply for permission each time they want to hunt. This permission is in no way automatic. The Vale of Aylesbury should satisfy themselves that hunting is conducted in a proper manner and to the satisfaction of the farmers."*

3.   *"The country around AYOT ST LAWRENCE, KIMPTON, WHEATHAMPSTEAD should be hunted only by the Aldenham Harriers. Apparently no fox hunting has been carried out here in the last few years. The Aldenham Harriers have a keen following and the area is rapidly becoming urbanised ."*

4.   *"The country South of the B652 should be considered as entirely Aldenham Harriers country, but the Harriers should permit the Enfield Chace to have one day a season at BROCKET HALL, if they so wish."*

141

These arrangements worked well to begin with, but after a few years the Enfield Chace, which was hemmed in when the M25 motorway was built, began to stray more and more into Aldenham Harriers territory. To make matters worse they frequently did not advise their meets beforehand, nor seek permission. Further, because the size of their fields tended to be large, they created crop disturbance which alienated farmers in Aldenham Harriers 'country' who until then had been very supportive. The thing festered through the 1970s with the Enfield Chace masters seemingly ignoring the Aldenham Harriers.

Eventually patience ran out and Lady Lyell felt constrained on 11th January 1980 to seek the advice of John Kirkpatrick, Secretary of the Association of Masters of Harriers & Beagles:

> *"We met in the Ayot St Lawrence country on 1st December to discover that the Enfield Chace had been there not very long before, quite unknown to us, as it is only with great difficulty that I can ever get a fixture card from them and in Horse & Hound it frequently just says 'phone kennels'. We were all horrified to see the damage that had been done to the corn...This all sounds like a personal vendetta, which by now it very nearly is on both sides, but the damage which is being done in all senses is very distressing. Knowing as I do, only too well, that even the worst foxhound pack takes precedence over harriers, I feel that I must state our case as strongly as possible. We have not found a fox in this particular country for at least fifteen seasons. It has always been very closely shot over. There are , however, a large number of barking deer which are a pest to us, but we cope as there are plenty of hares."*

Accusations and counter accusations and claims and explanations followed and on 13th May the Masters of Foxhounds Association met at Ashridge House to consider the matter. The minutes included:

> *"It was established that each pack hunts on two days a week. The Enfield Chace on Tuesdays and Saturdays and the Aldenham Harriers on Wednesdays and Saturdays."*

> *"Major Mann emphasised that he wished to ensure that both packs, Enfield Chace and Aldenham Harriers, continue to hunt as a pack of hounds... the Enfield Chace had disobeyed the rules. Clough Park accepted that it was largely his fault through ignorance of what had been arranged. The size of the field on Saturdays for the Enfield Chace was between 90 and 100."*

After this, on 10th June 1980, John Kirkpatrick in a letter to Lady Lyell said:

> "...the Enfield Chace have disregarded the 1970 agreement... although you have sent them a copy each year, and are likely to continue to disregard that or any other agreement made...if all packs disregarded rules concerning countries as the Enfield Chace have done, hunting throughout England would be in a proper mess...how many times a year are you prepared to allow Enfiled Chace to meet in your country?"

Following this and other debates, the 1980 agreement was drawn up intended to supersede that of 1970:

1. *The Vale of Aylesbury to hold all the country.*

2. *The area bounded in the north by roads linking Henlow, Lower Stondon, Shillington, Apsley End, Higher Gobion, Barton-in-the-Clay; the west by the M1; the south by the St Albans to Hatfield Road; and the east by the east by the A1(M) road is loaned to the Enfield Chace on a yearly basis*

3. *The above area will be hunted by the Enfield Chace and the Aldenham Harriers who will each ration themselves to a maximum of twenty meets per year (subject to farming and shooting). These two hunts will draw up a joint outline plan at the beginning of the season until 15th January and subsequently another plan from 15th January to the end of the season. The two agreed plans and the two hunts' fixture cards will be sent to the Senior Master of the Vale of Aylesbury.*

4. *The Cambridgeshire will continue to hunt the Vale of Aylesbury country to the north of the above defined area and to the east of the M1 on a yearly basis.*

That should have been the end of it, but then on 3rd July Lady Lyell wrote again to John Kirkpatrick:

"The suggested arrangements are quite unacceptable to Aldenham Harriers...what appears to have happened is that the Enfield Chace, by flouting the rules laid down in 1970, have succeeded in acquiring the whole of the territory for themselves."

Nevertheless these new arrangements have applied without too much of a problem for the last twenty years, but all of that is to 'jump the gun' somewhat. We will return to the chronology, but before doing so there is an editorial matter that needs mentioning; the Whaddon Chase is spelt with an 's' and the Enfield Chace is spelt with a 'c'. Both spellings are used indiscriminately in quite respected sources and must irritate the respective hunts enormously. Their undying gratitude for this 'plug' will be gratefully accepted.

Lady Lyell
Derek Christopher

There were severe outbreaks of fowl pest in Hertfordshire at the beginning of the 1970/71 season which led to a number of autumn meets having to be cancelled and caused difficulty in fixing meets very much in advance. In spite of this the season was a record on two fronts; firstly, hounds killed a remarkable fifty brace of hare and secondly, the average number of followers that were out over 27 hunting days reached 36. The latter figure caused the Masters some concern, particularly taking into account changes in farming practices, such as greater acreages of wheat being sown in the autumn and in larger blocks. A minor step taken to reduce numbers in the field was to reduce the number of days permissible on a 'cap' to two, the point being that two days ought to be sufficient opportunity for someone to decide whether to become a subscriber and that 'caps' should only be taken as a way of enabling potential subscribers to see what the hunt has to offer. On Sunday 6th June 1971 the Joint Masters held an 'Aldenham Harriers At Home' at Puddephats Farm. By Saturday 25th September 1971 Rita Huxley, who had allowed the hunter trials to take place at Trowley Bottom Farm each autumn, had sold the farm, but the new owners, Mike and Jill Spragg, kindly agreed to the arrangements continuing.

A new pack of harriers, the Avington, had been formed in Hampshire. Their Masters paid a visit to Puddephats and as a result Aldenham hounds, HARRIET and HARMONY, and two young hounds were drafted to this pack, leaving twenty couple at Puddephats. Hounds were paraded at Hertfordshire Show and Hemel Hempstead Show that year.

Fears of encroaching urbanisation were again expressed and efforts were put in hand to find new areas to hunt north of Luton.

George Garfoot and Joyce Christopher at Stags End
Derek Christopher

For the 1971/72 season 38 meets were called; hunting took place on 31 days and the average field was 34. After Lady Lyell's accident, when she broke her shoulder at a meet at Cross Farm, Harpenden, Prue Lyell and George Garfoot carried on ably and showed good sport, but the arrangements drawn up for the 1972/73 season were that George Garfoot would be hunting the hounds with Eric Shelley as amateur whip and Derek Christopher as Field Master. Prue Lyell would act as Master if neither of the Joint Masters was out. The season was one of the most open in living memory. A large number of hare were killed and, thanks to the hard work of George Garfoot in hunting hounds and keeping them fit and well, good sport was enjoyed. Thirty five meets were called and hunting took place on 26 days with an average field of 52. There was as usual an acknowledgement of the hunt's deep indebtedness to farmers and a degree of concern that, with the ever increasing number of people hunting, many of whom were new to the sport, there was a greater risk of damage being done to stock, crops, fences and gates. There were other problems; increasing urbanisation and consequent loss of country made it difficult to arrange meets twice weekly especially with Saturday meets before Christmas because of shooting fixtures. To help ease matters, visitors were only permitted to hunt once of a 'cap' for the season.

One evening in 1972 Sir Maurice, the Hon. Lady Lyell and Prue Lyell, together with Robert Humbert, Basil Hall, Derek Christopher and others, attended a Horse of the Year Ball at the Hilton Hotel in London. It was Derek Christopher's birthday. The band was Nigel Tully's *Dark Blues* and during the evening Nigel asked Derek and Joyce to introduce him to Prue. That was all there was to it at that stage, but in 1976 Nigel was invited to *"come and meet the master's daughter"* and they married two years later.

Quite what provoked it is not recorded, but at this stage [1972] the Joint Masters decided that the field was not looking up to scratch and issued the following:

> *"The correct wear for hunting with Harriers is a tweed jacket, coloured stock or collar and tie, black or brown boots and drab breeches. Members who wear the Hunt button are, of course, entitled to wear it on a black coat, when a white stock must be worn. Bowler hats should be worn by everyone who is NOT a Hunt official, a genuine farmer or a child. To these people alone belongs the privilege of wearing a velvet hunting cap. While many hunts do not welcome ladies who hunt wearing velvet caps, we will not ask those who have been accustomed to doing so for some seasons to change their ways, but we do ask our newer members and certainly all the men members and subscribers to respect the old-established tradition.*
>
> *M.Lyell, K.Lyell"*

January 1973 saw an outbreak of swine vesicular disease in Hertfordshire and meets at Beechwood Park School, Nomansland and Kensworth had to be cancelled.

The hunt ball was held at Harpenden Public Hall on Thursday 15th February 1973. Tickets cost £3.50 and dancing was to the music of the *Dark Blues*. This was the first appearance of the *Dark Blues* at the Aldenham Harriers hunt balls, one of the results of Nigel Tully's (whose band it was) introduction to Prue Lyell the previous year. 281 tickets were sold which produced a profit of

£367.23 for the evening. The arrangements were applauded and were then continued each year through to 1980. In 1973 the summer ball was held at Puddephats on 20th June with dancing to *'The Colours'*. 253 tickets were sold to produce a profit of £782.53. One of the reasons why these events were so profitable was that the ladies of the hunt, or rather some of them, often Prue, Joyce, Rita, Ros and Jill, did the catering themselves.

Monica Shelley raised £200 for hunt funds at the Barnet Show in 1973 which was perhaps her record year. She was always a staunch supporter and had in fact contributed significantly to the hunt's survival from this source with an annual contribution, often in excess of £100, for twenty years.

The 1973 hunter trials were held at Stags End, Gaddesden Row on 29th September by kind permission of Mr W.E.Russell. This was where Derek and Joyce Christopher also lived which is why they were held there and it was the first time that the trials had moved to a new home from Trowley Bottom Farm since 1964.

Around this time Tony Harvey was taking a day with every hunt to provide the material for his forthcoming book *If St Peter Has Hounds - A day with every British mounted pack*. He visited the Aldenham on Wednesday 30th January 1974 when the meet was at the Lilley Arms. George Garfoot carried the horn because Lady Lyell was recovering from a fall. The visitor's sport was spoilt because of a high wind and too many hares, so he did not really describe what went on, but he did comment that hounds were *"a little independent"* which we know to be fair comment. Having little to say about the chase he contented himself with being complimentary about the varieties of correct attire that the Harriers displayed *"a copy-book example of almost every type of dress in the hunting field"*.

The Vale of Aylesbury Hunt kindly agreed to a Joint Members Race at their point-to-point meeting at Kimble on Easter Saturday, 13th April 1974 which allowed members, subscribers and farmers of the Aldenham Harriers the opportunity to take part in a joint hunts race confined to the two hunts. This gesture was particularly valued because the Aldenham Harriers had not been able to stage their own point-to-point meeting since the last one at Friars Wash ten years earlier.

There was an 'Aldenham Harriers At Home' at Puddephats on Saturday 8th June 1974. The following November members were urged to join the British Field Sports Society as there was felt to be a very real threat of the Government introducing a bill to ban hunting *"in the very near future"*. Subscribers were entreated to cause farmers as little trouble as possible. Late-comers would be severely frowned upon as they were apt to go where the hunt was not wanted, or to leave gates open, or slip rails down while looking for the hounds. The following month the Joint Masters announced that because of increasing costs they had been forced to follow the practice of most other hunts by charging field money. It would be £1 a day from the first meet of 1975.

At the start of the 1974/75 season there were twenty one and a half couple of hounds in kennels including a nice young entry. *"Their splendid condition and well-being is due to the devotion, hard work and enthusiasm of George Garfoot who is now in his ninth season with the Aldenham."* At this point Philip Watts was taken on as kennelman and was expected to act as whipper-in from time to time. Hunting days were Wednesdays and Saturdays with the occasional Thursday. Hunting was possible on 31 days and the average field reached an astonishing 48, though even this high figure was to be exceeded later on.

Local Labour MP Robin Corbett, who signed a back-bencher's motion in the House of Commons the previous November calling on the Government to outlaw all field sports, was shown round the Gaddesden Place Estates by Derek Christopher and Gordon Beningfield, the wildlife artist, who were local joint secretaries of the British Field Sports Association, in January 1975. He acknowledged that a lot of good work was done there to encourage wildlife and accepted that numbers of some species had to be controlled, but remained adamant that, in his opinion, hunting hare was cruel.

The Vale of Aylesbury extended their invitation to share the Members' Race at Kimble Point-to-Point meeting again on 29th March 1975, but in addition to the usual prizes there was a Challenge Cup for the first Aldenham Harriers member's, subscriber's or farmer's horse past the post.

Joint Master, Sir Maurice Lyell, who had been a judge at the Queen's Bench Division from 1962 until 1971, died at his home at Puddephats Farm on 27th May 1975.

The point was made at a committee meeting on 13th July 1975 at the Cricketers, Redbourn, that the cost of keeping the hunt running fell mainly upon the Master to a sum in excess of £1,500 a year and to cover increasing costs it was agreed that the adult subscription would be increased to £75 a year plus £1 field money daily. The 'Cap' for occasional visitors up to a maximum of three days was increased to £4 a day plus the £1 field money.

The 1975/76 season made a late start due to the illness of the kennel huntsman, George Garfoot. Forty meets were called and hunting took place on 34 days with an average field of 44.

Many subscribers at this time were contributing considerably more than the standard subscription of £75, including one of £200 and seven of £100 and over, but costs were still rising alarmingly. That season Lady Lyell hunted on 31 occasions, Basil Hall on 29, George Garfoot on 34, Prue Lyell on 32, Derek Christopher on 30 and there were another dozen subscribers who hunted twenty times or more.

The imperative need to maintain farmers' co-operation at all times has been stressed all too often in these pages and a case in point occurred in January 1976. Aldenham Harriers had met on Mr Flint's land at Holwell on 10th January and the usual courtesies had been observed, but the chase had spilled over onto the land of the neighbouring Holwellbury Estate where no advance notice had been given and permission had not been sought. To make matters worse a planned shoot took place at Holwellbury two days later when only five brace of pheasant were bagged against fifty brace on Boxing Day and an estimated twenty five brace seen a couple of days before the Aldenham Harriers meet. Hoof marks across the land proved the point and all the Aldenham Harriers could do was to apologise and promise to do better in future, but the damage was done and no doubt there were strained relations for some time afterwards. The letter of complaint used the words *"very annoyed"* which probably said it all.

Sometimes a potential risk of being black listed by a farmer, maybe for years afterwards, can be turned to advantage and to a lasting friendship. One such happened to Basil Hall when there was a meet at Robert Dickinson's farm hunting back to Wheathampstead. There were some inexperienced pups out who got into a field of sheep and ran amock. The farmer came out with a .410 and threatened to shoot the pair of them, but Basil retrieved the pups, apologised profusely and was told *"come back at six o'clock and we'll sort out the damages"*. Basil duly presented himself at the appointed hour and with some trepidation was shown into the office by the farmer's wife to discover two glasses and a bottle of Scotch on the desk. A very mellow evening followed. Now, that is an example of the civilised way to settle a dispute that comes highly recommended.

It was in 1976 that Lady Lyell took on a new groom, Gillian Haworth, who remembers that somehow she managed to arrive for her interview on time and this so impressed Lady Lyell that she took her on the spot. Gillian lived in, as indeed did the other two girl grooms, and Lady Lyell did the cooking. She was a good cook and even made her own butter in the summer months. Every morning there was bacon and eggs for a nine o'clock breakfast, but when there were guests for dinner the staff had to eat after them and do the washing up afterwards.

Starting wages were £12 a week with no overtime, but there was an annual rise of £2 a year. Gillian eventually replaced Anita Dix as head girl and stayed at Puddephats for eight years. The three girls had twenty horses to look after comprising two brood mares, hunters, eventers and livery. Pat Burgin had his hunter in livery there and liked to help look after it, but that got him into trouble with Lady Lyell. At that time Lady Lyell was riding a massive bay hunter by the name of GAMEBIRD (17.2hh). Gillian mounted it one day without noticing that there was no girth, but GAMEBIRD gave no trouble and she got away with it. Gillian was of slight stature, and still is, and so it is not surprising that she also had difficulty in controlling the horse that was hunted by the whippers-in. The horse, SULTAN, was huge, black, miserable and mean. You had to dope him to clip him and it needed two to load him; he had a habit of just 'taking off' and would drag anybody, man or woman, with him when being led in hand. Gillian was caught in this way one day when she was running the horse up in the yard for the British Olympic Team Vet, Peter Scott Dunn. She was running alongside and looked set for being dragged across the county, but had the sense to jump sideways at the estate petrol pump as they passed, which gave her leverage and brought SULTAN up very sharply. Just to make the whole thing more exciting Gillian had, and has, *"shoulders that come out"* and when she rides has to have her upper arms strapped to her body, which sounds a touch dangerous. However, not so much so as you might think because she is double jointed and on being thrown from her horse when out hunting one day was seen to do a complete somersault and land on her feet. In her early days at Puddephats Lady Lyell served a boiled egg, which although she did not realise it was rather unkind because there was no way that Gillian's shoulders would permit her to eat it, but Gillian had her revenge because shortly after came April Fools' Day and she left a plastic broken splattered egg trick on the kitchen floor. Lady Lyell found it, of course, as she was meant to, and was taken in by it; made a hell of a row about staff carelessness and said there was no way she was going to clear it up, the culprit must do it. Worse, she could not see the funny side of it afterwards.

The Hon. Lady Lyell Joint Master the Aldenham Harriers 1958-1983
Rita Huxley

There was trouble too when Gillian, who usually had a system for making sure that everything was loaded for an eventing trip, somehow or other, on one occasion, accidentally left the tack behind. The air was blue and to be sure, it never happened again. Prue managed to borrow a saddle and did well, but if she hadn't Gillian would have been blamed. She had huge admiration for Lady Lyell and makes the point that there were more good times at Puddephats than bad, though she admits that she and Bill Stirling, the estate manager at that time, devised an *"across the breakfast table code of looks"* each morning to advise whether it was a good day or a bad one.

Now here is something to conjure up the imagination, something unusual and heart warming; Harry Sewell's breeches, hunt coat and showing cane survive; preserved for posterity by Gillian. She keeps them *"for sentimental reasons"* and her husband has never objected! Harry Sewell was Lady Lyell's stud groom for a good number of years from about the time of her second marriage. Gillian was awarded her hunt buttons by Val Barr.

For the 1976/77 season there were 69 subscribers of whom nine contributed more than the standard subscription. 38 meetings were called, 26 days were hunted and the average field was 43. Lady Lyell hunted on 19 occasions, Basil Hall on 22, George Garfoot on 25, Prue Lyell on 22, Derek Christopher on 20 and nine others on 15 or more.

A summer ball was held at Puddephats on Friday 24th June 1977 with dancing to the music of *'The Wallace Collection'* ; 262 people attended and a profit of £565 was made.

The grand old horseman Stanley White died on 10th April 1978 aged 85. His obituary appeared in the *Horse & Hound* on 28th April 1978:

> *"I first met Stanley White almost 50 years ago in Ireland. He was farming and dealing in horses in Herefordshire, with another yard in the Whaddon country.*
>
> *In those days he made frequent trips to Ireland buying horses and, to a fraternity not uncritical of English horse-dealers, he was known as 'a fair and decent class of man' - praise indeed!*
>
> *I met him again before the war when I had an odd day with the Whaddon, but it was not until after the war that I got to know him well.*
>
> *A fine horseman for whom all horses went well, he was in the first flight across country or on the point-to-point course. In the late 40s and early 50s, though years older than most of us riding at that time, round his own Friars Wash course, at Kimble, or at Hemingford Abbotts, he was a hard man to beat.*
>
> *Brave, shrewd, kind and a good friend, he was a really loveable person. He never really got over the death of his wife, Mary, but in the last few years of his life he showed all the qualities of John Bunyan's Mr Standfast.*
>
> *I used to visit him at home at Hammonds End; he was old, deaf and a cripple, but I never heard him complain. His interest in the world of horses never waned; there amongst his photographs and his trophies, he loved to relive the great days of his past. I never visited him without coming away better for the experience.*
>
> *FEDAMORE"*

At this time Lady Lyell and her step-daughter, Prue, were frequently out hunting together and there was a great area of mutual interests between them. Although not related, they were remarkably alike in many ways and in addition to shared outdoor interests both had domestic talents; Lady Lyell was good at butter making, cooking and needle point, Prue was a brilliant cook and a talented seamstress. So far as temperament was concerned there was something of a clash of personalities and the 'fur could fly' at times. Both were strong minded and forceful, both had a robust vocabulary, and both could shout. Groom Gillian Haworth remembers with pleasure the times she was taken by Prue to Harrods to shop or to the Dorchester for lunch or the time when she was asked to be godmother to Prue's son, Giles. Life at Puddephats was not all turmoil for the staff, there were plenty of good times. Sadly Prue was to die about twenty years later, aged only 56, almost exactly a year before her step-mother, but that is to 'jump the gun' again; Prue Lyell married Nigel Tully in 1978.

There was a novice horse show held on 20th August 1978 at Sandridgebury Livery Stables by kind permission of Mr & Mrs Burrows and H.Mortimer. The competitions were Class 1 for a working hunter, Class 2 for working hunter pony and Class 3 for a clear round jumping.

Hunter trials were held at Little Wood End on Sunday 22nd October 1978 by kind permission of Basil Hall, MH., Messrs E.J.Herbert & Sons, Lady Lyell, MH and Nick Lyell. There were three classes:

1.   Martin Wilkinson (saddlers) Novice with a first prize of £10

2.   Kensworth Garage Intermediate with a first prize of £15

3.   Rentokil Open with a first prize of £30

One of those rare accidents that serve to emphasize the dangers of hunting anywhere near a main road occurred on 22nd November 1978; it is a miracle that it does not happen more often. Fortunately the only casualty was one of the hounds and the damage was slight, but it could have been much worse. The Aldenham Harriers had met at the Crooked Chimney at Cromer Hyde, and at about 1.15pm were on Cromer Hyde Farm. Prue Tully was acting as whip that day and she and the hounds were between the farm buildings and the main road to Welwyn Garden City. One of the hounds got into the road and was hit by a passing car. It was nobody's fault and there was nothing anybody could have done to prevent it.

The centenary of the Aldenham Harriers was celebrated with a dinner and ball at Harpenden Public Hall on Friday 16th February 1979 with music provided by the *Dark Blues*. It was almost a social disaster; a thick fog descended upon the district which lasted until well into the following day and the caterers, who were coming from Cheltenham, got lost in it! Fortunately they did arrive eventually, although very late, and in spite of the late start managed to provide a good meal. The guest speaker, Michael Clayton, Editor of *Horse & Hound*, also managed to find his way through the fog, as did, amongst others, Sir Jocelyn Lucas, Geoff Hartop, Chris Todd, Audrey Chambers and John Hodgson. That was the last time that the annual hunt ball was held at Harpenden Public Hall; it had been there since 1959. Tickets on this occasion were £15 each.

Sir Maurice and the Hon Lady Lyell at the Centenary Dinner
Derek Christopher

Monica Shelly and Graham Hughes at Monica's
60th Birthday at Bridens Camp
Rita Huxley

Graham Hughes was taken on at this time as kennelman and whipper-in to George Garfoot. Graham came from the Tanatside, whose country is in

Shropshire; he had been with them for twelve years and felt he needed a change. He was born in Oswestry, and although his father was a farm worker who followed the Royal Artillery Drag Hunt he could hardly claim to have come from a hunting family. He was to serve the Aldenham well for over twenty years.

Lady Lyell was a good horsewoman, particularly good at dressage, achieving a score of ten on at least two occasions. One small problem was her bad leg; it stuck out at an angle as she hunted and necessitated her having to mount on the wrong side, which some horses took exception to. She rode a great deal and so it is hardly surprising that, over the years, she built up a fair record of mishaps; sometimes she broke things, sometimes she bruised things, more often she just got away with it. One such occasion at about this time was when she was out hunting at White Way Bottom, Kimpton for the first time on her new horse, CLAUD, and it had the misfortune to tread on a ploughshare lying partly concealed in the undergrowth, severing a tendon. It was a nasty wound, but it was quickly and expertly tended and CLAUD survived. Later on though he came to a sad end when he developed a heart problem and had to be put down.

The grooms used to get the horses fit by riding them across Dunstable Downs in the very early morning, but one day Gillian Haworth on this duty, riding PERCY, took a wrong turning near the bottom of the downs and had to get off to lead him through tangled undergrowth. Unfortunately she slipped and fell and let go of PERCY who, relishing his newfound freedom, trotted off happily with Gillian in hot pursuit, but losing ground by the minute. It was a foggy morning, and it was in the rush hour, and PERCY was getting nearer and nearer the main road, so Gillian accosted a conveniently placed warden and had an alarm call put through to Lady Lyell who came out with groom Sarah and a bucket of oats. The bucket acted as a magnet to PERCY. Lady Lyell was not cross, or if she was she kept it to herself, and Gillian was unharmed, apart from her pride.

Lady Lyell passed her advanced driving test and was greatly inspired by the experience, so elated indeed that she abandoned all pretence of using the correct lane approaching roundabouts or indicating from that time on. She was as much a force to be reckoned with on the road as she was on the hunting field, but she never had an accident. She often drove the lorry and because of her bad leg developed a fail-safe system of double de-clutching which involved grabbing the back of the seat with her left hand, hoisting herself up so that she could position her bad leg on the clutch pedal, changing gear, then transferring the leg and settling back as before. Sounds a touch unlikely written down, but when it is demonstrated it makes sense. It was she who taught Groom Gillian to drive the horsebox and was with her in the Land Rover when she had to drive on snow and ice for the first time. They came upon considerable drifting near Hill Farm and Gillian's caution was too much for Lady Lyell who shouted *"attack it girl, attack it!"* and her ladyship's tactics somehow got them through.

In the early 1980s the anti-hunting demonstrations at the annual Boxing

Day meet on Redbourn Common became more concentrated. On one occasion Joyce Christopher and Alison Abbey riding two 15.00hh. horses were surrounded by protesters trying to hit them with placards. Police linked arms round the horses who stood like rocks although their hearts were pounding. The Police were marvellous and the horses were very brave; it was an awful experience for them all. On another occasion Lady Lyell was very roughly jostled, almost pulled off her horse and on two occasions TV cameras recorded the confrontation for all to see. One of the problems was that most of the locals cherished the tradition and brought their children along to witness the colourful spectacle. At the peak there could be two hundred mounted and a thousand spectators on foot on these occasions. Redbourn Parish Council took up the cause at the beginning of 1980 and tried to be helpful by suggesting that it would be a good idea if the Aldenham Harriers gave up the hare and substituted a sack drenched in aniseed which could be dragged cross country to provide an artificial trail. This idea was dismissed by the Aldenham Harriers as totally impracticable. Before the First World War there had been a pack of hounds in the area known as the Hemel Hempstead Farmers Draghounds and there is a newspaper report of a meet at the Rose & Crown in Tring in 1911 when their Master was a Mr Cornwall. Later in 1980 Redbourn Parish Council held a referendum on the subject because they were so divided about it amongst themselves and the vote went 747 to 580 in the hunt's favour. In spite of that the campaign against the Aldenham Harriers meeting on Redbourn Common on Boxing Days continued and was led by Redbourn Parish Councillor Colin Hucklesby for a good number of years.

Pat and Elizabeth Burgin in 1982
Rita Huxley

From 1st May 1980 Joint Masters Lady Lyell and Basil Hall were joined by Patrick Burgin, another hunting character with a very interesting background; a man who was to serve as a Joint Master for sixteen years. He was the son of Rt Hon. Edward Leslie Burgin, (Leslie) a solicitor, and MP for Luton from May 1929 until retirement in 1945. He was Minister of Transport, from 1937 - 1939, Minister Without Portfolio, from April to July 1937, later Minister of Supply from July 1939 until May 1940. His son Pat, having been educated at St George's School, Harpenden and Cambridge, joined the army in 1940 as a 2nd Lieutenant in the Beds and Herts Regiment, later becoming an instructor at the Intelligence School in Karachi with the rank of Captain. He was still only 23 when he was promoted to Major in the Security Planning Section in New Delhi. Pat was a modest man, always reluctant to talk about his achievements and he was particularly not keen to talk about his later army service in Burma, but it is known that he and his unit were parachuted into the jungle to conduct a guerrilla style operation destroying communications behind the Japanese front line for which he received a gallantry award. No doubt it was some of these experiences that enabled him later in life to make such a good job of being Master of the Aldenham Harriers. After the war he joined the family firm of solicitors, Denton, Hall & Burgin where his grandfather, great-uncle and father had all been partners. He qualified in 1948 to become a partner in the family firm remaining so for forty six years, ten of them as senior partner. In 1950 he married Elizabeth who later on was to share with him the joys of following the Aldenham, riding her COPPER, and to give him the support a Master of hounds needs.

Pat was a man of many parts; he was a director of the UK subsidiary of the Danish company, Rentokil, for thirty two years, twelve of them as chairman and in 1967 the Danish Government made him a Knight of the Order of Danebrog for services to Anglo-Danish relationships. When he returned from his frequent business trips to Denmark and went hunting some members of the field would be offered his flask for a quick drink; it was always Schnapps so all who partook knew where his travels had recently taken him. His firm also had an office in Paris and Pat was a legal adviser and board member of a number of leading French companies. In 1989 the French Government awarded him the Cross of Chevalier de la Legion d'Honneur. Nearer home, he was a member of Hertfordshire County Council for 10 years and a very generous member of the governing body of hare hunting, the Association of Masters of Harriers and Beagles, of which he was a member during his Mastership and until his death. He was also a Liveryman of the Worshipful Company of Gold and Silver Drawers, a tradition in his family going back to 1830. With such a busy life it is perhaps surprising that Pat found time to hunt at all, but he did and this is how. His hunters were named COLONEL MOSS and SIR PERRY; Wednesday was hunting day when Pat would mark in his office diary *'Out with Colonel Moss'* or *'Out with Sir Perry'*. Certainly that was the truth, and what is more it sounded well on the telephone! He was a fearless rider cross country, his horses always carrying him well as he was always well-mounted.

Pat Burgin on COLONEL MOSS
at Upperwood
Derek Christopher

Graham Hughes was appointed kennel huntsman, which was promotion for him, and it came about because George Garfoot had unfortunately died in the saddle on 15th February 1980. It is rare for anyone to die in the saddle, but maybe the way every follower of hounds would want to go. George was out hunting one day with the harriers in the field to the right of the Chequers public house at Gaddesden Row, when it was thought that he had been thrown, but he had had a heart attack and died shortly afterwards. While the business of getting George to hospital went on, the hounds, of course, had to be returned to kennels and Joyce Christopher remembers someone dashing into the house at Upperwood to borrow Derick's horn as George's had been smashed when he fell from his horse. He was buried at Brigg on Humberside and a goodly number from the Aldenham attended. A nice touch was when Graham Hughes blew the *'gone away'* at the graveside and there was hardly a dry eye present. There was also a memorial service held for him at St Leonard's, Flamstead on 3rd March 1980. A memorial fund was set up for his widow, Hilda, which raised the not insignificant sum of £1,500. David Bartlett was the whipper-in that season.

The 1980 summer hunt ball was at Puddephats on 20th June with dancing to the music of *'Runcible Spoon'*.

For the 1980/81 season 38 meets were called; 29 days were hunted and the average field was 38. Individual attendances included:

Lady Lyell	22 days
Basil Hall	16 days
Derek Christopher	21 days
Patrick Burgin	23 days
Graham Hughes	28 days
Prue Tully	16 days

George Garfoot on Redbourn Common
Basil Hall

The 1981 hunt ball was held on 28th February at the Whitbread's Brewery Porter Tun Room in Chiswell Street, London, notable because of the the Lord Mayor's coach in a glass case and a tapestry *'Overlord'* which depicted scenes from World War Two in the style of the Bayeaux Tapestry. Music was provided by the *Dark Blues*. Tickets were £12.50. The move from the Public Hall in Harpenden after being well satisfied there for over twenty years was a difficult decision for the committee, but the regulations became restrictive and a move was inevitable. The Porter Tun Room became the home of the Aldenham hunt balls from then on so it must have been a popular move. Later they were to move to the Pavilion at Hemel Hempstead and later still to Whipsnade Wild Animal Park.

At the end of the 1980/81 season Basil Hall dropped out of the Joint Mastership leaving Lady Lyell and Pat Burgin to go on alone. He had been a Master for two separate periods adding up to ten years with a gap of eight years between them. Basil was, and is, a man of many parts and has a colourful history.

His father, Bill, was platoon commander of Flamstead Home Guard in the war, to be promoted to company commander at Redbourn in due course. He was succeeded in Flamstead by Alastair Pearse and when Alastair followed the same promotional path he was not replaced and Platoon Sergeant Basil Hall took charge. At twenty three years old he was telling seasoned Great War soldiers what to do. When a Spitfire, still fully loaded with canon shells, made a forced landing at Grove Farm, a 24 hour armed guard had to be put on it until arrangements could be made for it to be moved. The farmer consulted Lady Lyell as to what should be done and she referred him to young Basil for instructions.

Basil Hall and Pat Burgin (mounted) with Elizabeth Burgin and
Peter Wardill (not mounted - right) in 1982
Derek Christopher

Basil has a fund of Home Guard stories that really have no place here, but they ought to be recorded somewhere and perhaps we may permit ourselves the luxury of a couple. There is the one of the time when, doing guard duty, two hours on and two hours off through the night, from the guard post next door to the vicar's garage, somebody emptied the magazine of their Lee Enfield onto the bed, counted the rounds and pulled the trigger to be sure; all regulation stuff, but their counting was suspect, one round had been left 'up the spout', there was an almighty bang and a neat hole appeared in the timber wall. The other side of the timber wall was the vicar's car and everybody was petrified what he might say or do when he found that that his car had been a victim of war next day. To find out how bad it was they went next door and felt all over the car in the dark, but found nothing unusual. Next day, to their relief, they discovered an unsuspected brick wall behind the timber one and embedded in it was the bullet. Shortly after, they were on guard duty in the same way, but this time the magazines had been emptied without incident and Wilf Papworth was lying peacefully asleep on the bed. On the opposite side from the vicar's car was a store where the props for the annual village fête were kept and rummaging inside somebody discovered the Aunt Sally. They took her out, prised Wilf's arms apart, inserted Aunt Sally and then woke him up. In the blackout he was convinced he had been to bed with one of the village maidens!

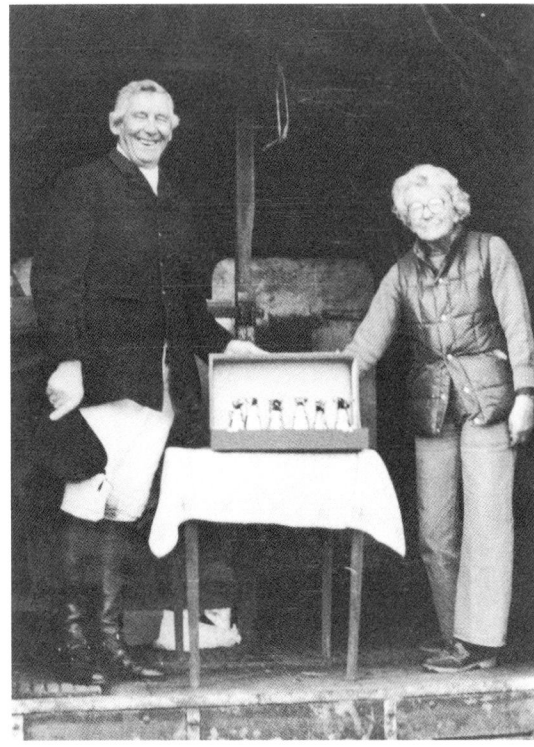

Basil Hall (Joint MH 1963-1967 & 1975-1981) with Lady Lyell at Basil's retirement in 1982
Rita Huxley

In the natural order of things, Basil wooed and won Audrey England, whose father owned three motor cycle shops. Basil showed an interest in the business and was invited to help himself to spare parts to build his first machine, an exercise which was to lead, eventually, to the 'Dash' at Dunstable, and involvement with the BSA development team.

Later on he took to Motocross; motor cycle riding on dirt circuits with obstacles. Brands Hatch was one such before they put the tarmac down. At his peak he would be backwards and forwards across the channel all season starting in Switzerland on 11th March and ending at Algiers on 4th December. To start with he rode for Associated Motor Cycles, but later changed to BSA. His career lasted fourteen years, of which he regards twelve as serious. He was European Champion in 1949 and came fourth in 1950. He was often on radio and TV and of course in newspapers and magazines. *Paris Soir* said of him *"probably Great*

Britain's greatest sporting ambassador". He was invited to run the British Motocross team, but declined. A huge photograph of him adorns the entrance of the National Motor Cycle Museum at Coventry. He also had two years at Speedway with Wembley Lions.

As a result of this frenzied activity he broke a leg four times, fractured ribs and ruptured a kidney, gratefully accepting treatment at Swedish, Belgian and Italian, as well as British, hospitals at various times. After all that, hunting must have seemed a bit tame, but once Basil had given up competitive motor cycling he never looked back and has been loyal to hunting for fifty years.

It was in 1981 that Terry Sturmey, kennel-man and 2nd whip at the Cattistock, was appointed 1st whip to the Aldenham. His wife, Wendy, was taken on as Lady Lyell's groom at the same time and they moved into the cottage next door to huntsman, Graham Hughes at Puddephats. They were to serve Lady Lyell for the rest of her life. Terry was to whip-in from 1981 to 1983 and he was thus engaged one day at Hill Farm, Ayot, when the field had lost hounds. Derek Christopher was Field Master and sent Tony Roberts off to locate them. Coming to a quiet corner of the field he startled 1st Whip Terry and kennel huntsman Graham relieving themselves in the hedge while things were quiet, with hounds milling around them.

Pat Burgin and Peter Wardill
Derek Christopher

Peter Wardill was a keen Aldenham Harriers man and a staunch supporter of all things hunting. He was a bachelor who lived at Stoneheaps in Kimpton and had a dental practice in Luton, but he also found time to be High Sheriff of Bedfordshire at one time and was a Deputy Lieutenant for the same county. He and others had felt for some time that there was a lot of latent goodwill to the Aldenham Harriers about, not just from subscribers and occasional followers, but others, infrequent and non-riders, foot followers and the like. That possible source of funding and talent ought to be tapped for the good of the Hunt and they resolved to try to do something about it. One day in the late seventies he and Peter Flawn paid a visit to the Oakley, which had an active supporters club, to find out how they went about it. What they found inspired them to return and report to Lady Lyell that the Aldenham should do something similar. She agreed.

At a meeting in Flamstead Village Hall on 2nd July 1981 a supporters club was launched. Peter Flawn became the first chairman, Rachel Meers the secretary and Peter Maslin the treasurer. Now, Peter Maslin was just the sort of person supporters clubs were all about; he seldom missed a meet over a long period in the eighties and he did it all on his bicycle. The reservoir had been tapped.

Leading are Peter Wardill, Peter Flawn and Derek Christopher
Peter Flawn

Peter Flawn was another dentist, but lived in Kensworth with a practice in Harpenden. He started with the Harriers in the seventies, more or less at the same time that Peggy Greig, who lived at Sauncy Wood, gave up. She was another staunch Aldenham Harriers supporter, hunted with them for years, and is remembered with affection for never quite knowing where she was. She talked so much that she lost her concentration. She was often lost and could become disorientated without leaving a field, which drew forth the comment from Tony Roberts *"Must be lovely to be like that - new country all the time"*. Peter remembers her saying to him early on *"If you can't stop, use my horse as a stopping block"*. Her horse, MRS TUESDAY, was a particularly placid creature. Peter has given sterling service to the Harriers for over twenty years, they have had their money's worth as the saying is. Indeed that saying is true of a good many people, some of whom have not found a mention in these pages, which is a pity and perhaps it is appropriate to say here that the Aldenham is grateful to them all. It might well have foundered a number of times without them. Returning to Peter, not only was he instrumental in setting up the supporters club and chairing it for the first three years, but he has returned to chair it subsequently and has remained a sort of anchor-man for those twenty years. Later chairmen (alphabetically not chronologically or in order of merit!) have been Alp Arikoglu, Val Barr, Justin MacGregor, Clare Sheppard and Sally Wade. The club had 120 members by the third year, fully vindicating its conception.

The Aldenham Harriers Supporters Club has a proud record of doing just that - supporting. Mainly it raises funds from the profits of events it organises such as in-hand shows, hunter trials, sponsored rides, country rides, race nights, talks and film shows, clay pigeon shoots, treasure hunts, country sports quizzes (where they took the initiative and started a challenge league), darts matches, farmers suppers. They also hold their own annual dinner quite separate from that of the hunt. The first was held at the Hertfordshire Moat House at Flamstead on Friday 30th April 1982. Peter Flawn proposed the first toast, the Queen, and the second, the Aldenham Harriers coupled with the retiring Master, Basil Hall, and his wife Audrey. Basil replied. The next toast was to 'field sports', proposed by Peter Wardill and replied to by W.A.Jackson, editor of *Shooting Times & Country Magazine*. Guest speakers at subsequent dinners included Michael Clayton, Editor of *Horse and Hound*, and Sir Michael Connell, a High Court Judge and a keen horseman with local connections. There is also a very popular opening meet supper, the origins of which go back to the start of the club. Since 1983 it has been hosted by Peter Flawn at Church End Farmhouse, Kensworth and routinely attracts ninety guests.

All of this adds up to a very considerable social calendar, supporting a remark made earlier that hunting is not just a hobby, but a whole way of life. As to the objects of the exercise, the prime one has to be entertainment, enabling like minded people to meet and enjoy one another's company (though it is not all sweetness and light), but fundraising comes a very close second. Between £4,000 and £6,000 a year was made in the eighties and the figures are similar today. The club has found that the best support comes from members if they know that they are contributing to a specific project of benefit to the hunt rather than making money for the general fund. By following that principle it has been possible, over the years, to provide for Aldenham Harriers two freezer boxes for the kennels, vehicles, horses, a huntsman's jacket and many other things. It has been said that through turbulent times for the hunt the supporters club is the one thing that has remained constant.

Peter Flawn on Redbourn Common in 1981
Elizabeth Ansell

In the early eighties Peter Flawn had been regularly holidaying in the Greek Islands for some years and had become friendly with a Greek Army wrestler who was about four foot six high and about the same wide. Also brother Mark, another dentist, had a patient who was a prominent member of the Luton Wrestling Club. A few other names came to mind and soon there was a move afoot to organise 'protection' for the Boxing Day meets on Redbourn Common, but it all came to nothing because the Masters would not hear of it. Another arm of the 'resist' faction made placards which were well in evidence in 1982 and helped balance the one-sided impression created by television pictures.

What the anti-hunt protesters had intended to be a major rally on Boxing Day 1981 was somewhat spoilt when the hunt was cancelled because of the weather. This had happened about a dozen times in the previous thirty years. Between 300 and 400 protesters turned up and they were more peaceful than on some previous occasions. There were about the same number of spectators and as usual the hounds were brought to the common for their benefit in spite of there being no hunting. Afterwards there was an ominous headline in the *St Albans Review* "*Redbourn is becoming the focus for the fraught national issue of blood sports*". Worse was to come.

TOWARDS THE NEW CENTURY

When Lady Lyell retired from the Mastership in 1983 her Joint Master, Pat Burgin, in a circular letter to subscribers, said of her:

"She has been Master of the Aldenham Harriers for the last twenty five consecutive seasons, a truly remarkable record. Indeed, she was a Master even before that. During much of this time Hounds, which are her personal property, have been kennelled at Puddephats; Hunt horses have been stabled there; Hunt servants have lived in her cottages; she has provided transport for both hounds and horses; she has arranged all our meets; she has allowed us to hunt over land on many occasions when no other farmer would have allowed us near; and above all else she has been the driving force and the leader who has kept the Hunt together. Now in a further act of generosity she is allowing the Hunt to continue to be based at Puddephats for a further two seasons on most reasonable terms."

A few words that concisely demonstrate just how much the Aldenham Harriers had become Lady Lyell's Harriers and lead one to speculate whether it might have been a nice gesture, earlier on, to rename the hunt in that style. It would have had a pleasant ring to it and might, just might, have softened the attitude of the hunt saboteurs who were so troublesome at about this time. Certainly 'Aldenham' had ceased to be relevant long since, though admittedly continuity is an important factor in determining these things.

It was at this point that the assets of the Aldenham Harriers were transferred to trustees, the first of whom were the Hon. Lady Lyell, Basil Hall and Pat Turner. At the same time the masters entered into a formal lease with Lady Lyell for the kennels and huntsman's cottage at Puddephats for a period of two years. Graham Hughes was to continue as huntsman and Terry Sturmey would remain in the employment of Lady Lyell who generously agreed to him continuing to serve as 1st whipper-in. She also agreed to provide him with a suitable mount. Messrs Halsey & Partners agreed that hunt horses could be kept at Upperwood Farm on generous terms. Subscriptions were revised to £225 a year, with reductions for young people across the board, plus £3 a day field money with a 'cap' of £20 a day for visitors. In view of the size of the country it was proposed to limit the number of subscribers and members to fifty on a first come first served basis. At this point there were twenty one and a half couple of hounds as to seven and a half couple of dogs and fourteen couple of bitches.

The trust deed is dated 1st May 1983 with Lady Lyell on the one part and Basil Hall and Pat Turner on the other. It was created as a mechanism to hire and fire Masters and appoint secretaries and treasurers and to own the hounds. In practice the rules are very freely interpreted, it is a fall-back, a long-stop. Naturally enough the trustees change over the years; Peter Flawn became a trustee in 1996, Lady Lyell died in 1998, Pat Turner retired and Lady Aldenham and Derek Christopher were appointed.

Lady Lyell with Pat Burgin at her retirement in 1983
Rita Huxley

Naturally enough, as Lady Lyell approached retirement the pace of the hunt slowed, but conversely when Pat Burgin and Derek Christopher took over from her things started to become more exciting. Both liked to finish early and meets tended to be over by 2.30pm. When Lady Lyell retired there was a mood afoot to move the kennels and various options were considered, amongst them being to move to Mill Farm, Bridens Camp, but Mr Pope, the Environmental Officer, met the parties on site and his stipulations were so tough that everybody backed off.

It is usually the responsibility of the Master to contact the farmer and arrange a meet. Lady Lyell was well known, well liked and well respected in farming circles and she had a head start in the arranging business, but when the time came for her to retire, Joint Masters had neither the time to devote to it, nor her enviable reputation. To overcome the problem they divided the country and appointed area hunt managers, leaving the secretary to control operations and send out the meet cards. The Aldenham Harriers did not invent the idea; it was a system that was commonplace with foxhound packs. Nowadays the Joint Masters do all the 'fixing', but at one time it was quite useful to spread the work around. A more minor problem was that of personalities. Some people do not 'click', grudges for supposed slights can be harboured a long time; some farmers who would not refuse Lady Lyell were quite happy to refuse her successors. Sometimes an indiscreet approach could create an atmosphere and the remedy would have to be to leave negotiations to somebody else the next time. Supposed or imagined wounds can take a long time to heal.

Peter Flawn helped out on this front on a number of occasions. In a way it was another instance of non-financial assistance from the supporters club. His most famous 'opening up' was at Sundon, but there were others, Tilsworth, Totternhoe, Hexton, Hatfield, Ashwell, Overs and Staplow, in fact a tidy proportion of today's regulars. Hexton was the result of another call, this time on the Ashley Cooper family.

Again on the non-monetary assistance front, Peter was instrumental in producing thirty or so jumps around the home territory; he hired a JCB to produce a swathe through Ovens Dell (on the Puddephats side of Stags End) and he borrowed a fork lift truck to position a log in one of Basil Hall's hedgelines. Understandably he did not do all of this by himself. There were always armies of unsung heroes to help, many of whom are very loyal and have quietly assisted over many years. Another instance is that Peter regularly walks the hounds every Friday morning. He finds it exhilarating and enjoyable, but he does not take too kindly to having to get up at six o'clock in the morning to do it.

Derek Christopher
(Joint MH 1983-1996)
Rita Huxley

In 1983 Derek Christopher, being already an outstanding Field Master, consolidated his grip on the hunt by becoming a Joint Master. He was an all-round experienced horseman across country and a successful point-to-point rider, also on many occasions riding second string in the show ring on his wife's show hack. With Joyce he competed successfully at the Royal International Horse Show in the Pair Hack Class (the last time it was held) - Joyce riding side saddle and Derek in 'Park' dress. Bernard Weatherall got him the correct trousers, 'officer's overalls', complete with jodhpurs, boots and screw-in spurs. He must have been a splendid sight! He also competed in hunter trials and on one occasion provoked a judge's comment *"a good try on a difficult horse"*. His horse on that occasion, ROMANY, was inclined to 'pace' when excited, that is to trot laterally as opposed to the normal diagonally. He won the members trophy at the Vale of Aylesbury Point-to-Point outright on three different horses.

Joyce was one of the leading show hack riders in the country at that time (a show hack is a relic, quiet and steady, the ultimate for an upper class lady to be seen on in times past) and her achievements are too numerous to mention. She was at Wembley one year and became a leading show judge. Derek too judged in England and Belgium. It was Reggie Streather, the area representative of the British Show Jumping Association for years, who recruited him and he was to serve for twenty five to thirty years. Quote *"A horse can get wound up when being shown, but hunting unscrambles its brain"*.

Derek Christopher at Preston

At this point Derek had been a Police Officer for thirty years, but had retired to run the Halsey Stud and moved to Upperwood Farm, Gaddesden Row.

He was the son of a Metropolitan Police detective inspector at New Scotland Yard, had his first riding lesson in 1945, and was 'hooked' for life. When he left school he became an assistant trainer at a racing stable and that is where he met his wife, Joyce. She was awarded her 'canary' collar at the same time as Derek became a Joint Master. He did his stint of National Service with the Royal Army Veterinary Corps, qualifying there as a farrier, which has stood him in good stead ever since.

Derek and Joyce started hunting with the Aldenham Harriers in 1950 when they had one horse between them called FRED. A typical situation for the couple at that time was that Derek would hunt in the morning and Joyce would cycle over for a swop at lunch time, so that she could hunt in the afternoon. Hunting has been Derek's life's passion. At one stage he had a spell of night duty with Hertfordshire Police and a normal routine for Wednesdays and Saturdays would be to come off duty at six o'clock in the morning and sleep until nine. Meanwhile Joyce and the girls (staff at her riding stable) would have the horses and horse box ready so that he could drive off for a meet. He would perhaps be back by four o'clock in the afternoon to grab a little sleep before he went on duty at nine in the evening. One day the Chief Superintendent called him in and said *"Christopher, your hounds have got out onto the motorway - see to it!"*; that is the way Chief Superintendents always spoke in those days and it demanded immediate action. In fact the problem had nothing whatever to do with the Aldenham, they were Enfield Chace hounds, but Derek had started his hunting career with Enfield Chace and the matter was quickly resolved.

Derek and Joyce Christopher. Derek is riding MERRY BELLS, a horse that he bought for a Belgian client. It had been a Hunter Class Champion in Dublin and Peterborough and became champion in Belgium. André Vandenbrook, a Brussels restaurateur bought it for Irene Prentice who eventually brought it back to England and loaned it to Derek to hunt. Joyce is on BEAU BRUMMEL, another show champion.
Joyce Christopher

Gordon Beningfield, the wildlife artist from Water End, was a particular friend and Derek has every one of his limited edition prints. When the time came for Derek to celebrate his fortieth birthday Joyce commissioned a painting from Gordon for him. Inevitably it was of a hare. Whilst on the subject of art, Liz Ansell, who with husband Ray ran the saddlery shop at Wheathampstead, has painted some very good hunting scenes.

Joyce Christopher ran Park Stables in Leyton Road, Harpenden in the sixties and at this time Derek could usually depend upon having six or seven really fit horses available to him. Amongst horses at livery at Park Stables at that time was Sir Maurice Lyell's NERO; it was sometimes ridden by the Bishop of St Albans, in his gaiters. The Park Stables girls always hunted and made themselves useful while out; they had a reputation for being well trained and well turned out.

Joyce Christopher
side-saddle on a show horse
Derek Christopher

Joyce regularly hunted side saddle on her various show hacks at this time, which included a black thoroughbred called LE DAUPHIN D'OR when only two weeks out of training with Willie Stevenson, the famous trainer from Royston. Jean Patterson often rode side saddle too, in her fawn habit and brown bowler; she was the daughter of the proprietor of Carter Pattersons, who were prominent general carriers at that time in these parts. Another to adopt this elegant style was Sylvia Opperman; often tormented by Basil Hall who, at quiet moments, would ride by her horse and whisper 'ghik, ghik' in its ear, whereupon it would take off regardless of circumstances.

A meet at Stags End - undated
Derek Christopher

A typical example of what happened after the case of cherry brandy had been drunk at Stags End - rider to remain anonymous
Derek Christopher

Later on, when Derek and Joyce were at Stags End, their associates, Mr and Mrs Russell, were very generous and hospitable to the hunt. On one occasion followers got through a case of cherry brandy before they started and there are a series of action photographs showing various dignitaries being thrown at fences to prove the dangers of drinking and driving. There was one year when Mr & Mrs Russell generously agreed to have the hunt ball on their premises. An awning was erected within the indoor riding school, 400 people attended and they had all been served with their first drink within half an hour. There were twenty bar attendants and the booze delivery had a figure of £4,266 on the invoice.

The hunting social round continued, albeit with minor variations, and in 1983 there was an 'At Home' held at Pat Burgin's house in Park Avenue, Harpenden on Saturday 16th July.

Hounds are often paraded at shows. Here we have Graham Hughes and John Richards with a goodly crowd of spectators.
Derek Christopher

Parading hounds at summer shows has become a regular feature of the hunt calendar. They are usually to be seen on both days of the Herts Show at Friars Wash and sometimes at the Royal Windsor Horse Show, Newmarket Race Day, Ashwell Country Fair, Bedfordshire County Young Farmers Rally, Gaddesden Stud open day and others, but they are not necessarily paraded at the same places every year. One year, Terry Sturmey had Basil Hall's big old chestnut, which was normally well behaved, at the Buckingham County Show, and was bringing hounds back across the car park to their lorry. For some reason the horse took fright and, as Terry fought for control, it managed to scrape two cars and sat on a third. Terry was all right; he managed somehow to stay on board, but it was tough on the car owners.

Then there was the time, nine o'clock at night and in the dark at Royal Windsor Horse Show, when they had six packs of hounds in the ring at once; huntsman and hounds at one end, whips at the other. The idea was that when whips hallooed, hounds would race from one end to the other, but Huntsman Graham Hughes' horse became so excited at these stirring events that it bucked three times and then threw him. He was knocked unconscious and was quickly carried to the first aid tent where they did everything they could to make him comfortable. His distraught wife, Linda, vaulted over the rails to join him, but passed out at the sight of him lying there unconscious in the tent, so they put her in the bed beside him. In all the confusion, getting the six packs of hounds back to their proper transports in the dark was a problem; Derek Christopher managed to catch one hound slinking off in the shadows, but it turned out to be a stranger and was so offended at being mistaken for an Aldenham Harrier that it bit him. The St John's Ambulance Brigade had no anti-tetanus vaccine, so Derek had to put up with some from one of the vets and by this time the Aldenham Harriers had taken up all the space in the first aid tent.

Kennel Huntsman Graham Hughes at the Royal Windsor Horse Show
Derek Christopher

This season (1983) Joint Masters Patrick Burgin and Derek Christopher were joined by Chris Todd from Clay Hall Farm, Kensworth, for one season. He had a particular liking for ornamental frogs, which brands him as an individualist, a tab reinforced by his connections in the worlds of showbusiness, modelling and clubs. Celebrity friends of his would sometimes, at his invitation, ride with the Harriers, but on a more down to earth level, he ran Kensworth Garage. It was his horse, LADY, that Lady Lyell liked to use for dressage. Meets that season were on Wednesdays and Saturdays; 40 were called, 30 days were hunted and there was an average field of 35. Fortunately a record of the numbers and places has been preserved and is given in Appendix VI as an example of a not untypical season:

1983 turned out to be the last year that the traditional Boxing Day meet was held on Redbourn Common. After the usual anti-hunt unpleasantness that had by then become as much of a tradition as the meet itself, Lady Lyell, riding Chris Todd's grey, LADY, had had enough and announced that she was going home, whereupon her groom, Wendy Sturmey, said she thought it would be prudent if she accompanied her, to be told *"don't be stupid"*. Accordingly Lady Lyell rode off on her own under the motorway bridge and on to Heavens Gate where she turned right into Green Lane which was her usual route home. Here she was ambushed by protesters who were foolhardy enough to throw a firecracker under her horse. The result could have been a catastrophe, bearing in mind the isolated location and Lady Lyell's immobility, but LADY did not 'bat an eyelid' and carried on as if nothing had happened.

Lady Lyell on Redbourn Common
Derek Christopher

An equally fraught confrontation came about when the rest of the hunt withdrew for Puddephats in a dignified manner down Church End, which being a dead end meant they had to return and run the gauntlet all over again. The scene became ugly and one young lady, Suzanne May from Hog End Lane, only in her teens and riding her grey mare, WIDGEON, was isolated by the protesters. They caught hold of WIDGEON who reared up and saved the day, because Suzanne fortunately stayed aboard while everybody quickly got out of the way. Finally, when the Aldenham Harriers had said *"enough is enough"*, the Boxing day meet moved to Basil Hall's premises at Valley Bottom, Flamstead and after that, following a plea from Peter Flawn to Roger and Maggie Smith, to Gulvers on Cheverells Green.

Many people in Redbourn were saddened by these events. The Boxing Day meet on Redbourn Common had become part of their Christmas festivities and for weeks beforehand they would enquire from those 'in the know' whether it was expected to take place as usual. They were deprived of a colourful, animated and traditional spectacle in their midst, and of a reason for venturing out after Christmas Day idleness.

For the 1983/84 season subscriptions were increased substantially. There was a meeting at the Cricketers at Redbourn when feelings ran high because subscriptions were up and the number of meets was down. Dawn Blowers and Rita Huxley had done their homework; they had discovered that hunting cost less with the Grafton per hour and they made no bones about it - *"the Grafton is better value for money"*. I hasten to add that there were good counter-arguments.

The following year there was a parade of hounds, mares, foals and stallions at Upperwood Farm Stud on 17th June and these gatherings took place each year while Derek Christopher had the stud. His wife, Joyce, provided the tea and cakes.

There is a nice little story about Derek Christopher when he was Field Master to a children's meet at Upperwood with Bruce Claridge and Tony Roberts in attendance. To give the children confidence Derek said *"now, there is nothing to it, do everything I do and follow me"*, He led them off, tried to jump a ditch and came down in the middle of it. Barry Hampton was not impressed *"Do we have to do that too Sir?"* On another occasion Prue Lyell took the field for a children's meet to be faced with a little girl of about eight whose pony was playing up. *"We will change mounts"* said Prue, whereupon the child mounted Prue's Wembley qualified hunter while Prue taught the pony how to mind its manners.

Rachel Meers took over as secretary from Derek Christopher in 1984 and served with distinction for ten years; the Aldenham Harriers were singularly fortunate with their secretaries. She makes the interesting observation about those days that a secretary is only as good as the Masters allow her to be. Which perhaps is a reflection on Lady Lyell who was something of a hero to her and whom she describes as *"brilliant"*. Rachel was the youngest person to be awarded the hunt button and in her own words *"was chuffed to bits"* when Lady Lyell wrote her to confirm it. She was only 22.

Rachel also has the distinction of having been the first secretary of the Aldenham Harriers Supporters Club. She did a lot of work for their annual Markyate Horse Trials which were held at Hill Farm, Flamstead each September. These were essentially fund raising events for the hunt and the day ended with a barbecue at Hill Farm and dancing to the music of the *'Dark Blues'*. She was one of those who helped cook for the three hundred or so who attended and particularly remembers one embarrassing night when she left twenty pork chops in the AGA and forgot about them. They were there all night and were burnt to a cinder. In spite of that she was forgiven and to prove that they bore her no malice they let her help with the catering at the Summer Hunt Ball at Puddephats.

Rachel was, and is, in the dentistry business, so that as she hunted every

Wednesday and could not see patients on those days, it would have been usual to put a line through Wednesdays in the appointments diary as a matter of routine. Not so in her case; the staff ruled out Wednesdays all right, but knowing what she was about early on wrote 'murder' across the page and it stuck!

Rachel Meers on Elizabeth Burgin's MERRYLEGS for the closing meet at Ogglewood
Rachel Meers

Mike Robinson hunted with the Harriers at this time and had a reputation for being charming, and reliable, and ambitious. He was always there when needed, but his reliability is in question because he had an eccentric side when it came to transporting his horse. He used a trailer which was entirely in order, but he towed it behind a TR5 which, for those not in the know, is a touch 'sporty' for the purpose. One day the axle broke on the trailer and it turned over with the horse inside; the horse was badly un-nerved though otherwise uninjured and understandably refused to enter a trailer ever again. The trailer was wrecked, so he bought a blue horsebox from Helen Pearse's father, Pete Evans of Heath and Reach, who built and dealt in them, as indeed had his father before him. The new blue, somewhat conspicuous, horsebox very soon acquired the nickname *'Mothers Pride'* because it resembled a bread van.

Later on Mike Robinson moved to Somerset and became Master of the Devon & Somerset Staghounds (1976-1987).

To return to Rachel Meers. In her early days with the hunt she rode an Irish chestnut called CAUTION; a real secretary's pony. One of CAUTION'S few failings was that she never wanted to give up. In about 1969, the closing meet of

176

the season was at Puddephats but had to be cancelled at the last minute owing to snow and CAUTION was not best pleased when she had to be re-loaded without hunting. She burst out of *'Mothers Pride'* and was not caught until she was 200 yards short of the A5. A similar thing happened one day at Sharpenhoe and CAUTION ended up at Barton. She was certainly not one of those ponies that lived up to her name, although, perhaps, it depends upon which way you look at it - she was 'a bit of a caution'. When the sad day came for her to be put down CAUTION was aged thirty three. Rachael's next horse was called LAWLEY PERGOLA, or PERGIE for short, nicknamed by the Harriers PERGATORY, and she was just the opposite; never wanted to start; she would side step and go just to get out of it.

Graham Hughes (Kennel Huntsman) and Terry Sturmey (Whipper-in)
exercising the hounds. Perhaps in Friendless Lane, Flamstead in 1983
Derek Christopher

Two of the hounds were entered for the Peterborough Harrier & Beagle Show that took place on Thursday 19th July 1984, competing in 3 of the 13 classes. Four year old sisters LAUGHTER and LADYBIRD were entered in the Bitch Hounds (not to exceed 21 inches) Class 7 (18 entries), and again in the Best Single Bitch Class 9 (15 entries), and again in the Perpetual Challenge Cup Class 12 for the best couple of hounds of any age (13 entries); they did not come away with any prizes, but Joint Master Pat Burgin stressed to kennel huntsman, Graham Hughes, that very useful experience had been gained and the lack of a placing was certainly no disgrace to the pack as the standards had been particularly high that year. Pat Burgin's wish was to keep the pack as near twenty couples as possible. From these early showings the successes of the pack have shown a steady improvement; gradually the whole pack were registered in the stud book and for a time there were showings most years. There are only one or two litters a year, giving a total of about a dozen pups.

The Earl and Countess of Verulam rode with the Harriers on occasion and in 1984 the Joint Masters were delighted to be invited by them to draw regularly over the 2,000 acre Gorhambury estate. Rita Huxley considers that some of her best days' hunting were when they first went there and the Countess rode with them. A good day in the field can be reckoned as one when one jumps well, and the Estate saw to it that the jumps were well prepared, with highly satisfactory results.

J.N.P.Watson writing in the *Country Life* issue of 15th November 1984 with a piece nicely titled *Green Coats on London's North Side* reported on the opening meet of that season when he had been a guest of the Aldenham Harriers with Basil Hall as his guide. He makes an interesting comment about the Aldenham's hounds:

> *"There is a liberal element of foxhound blood in the pack, Berkeley, Puckeridge and Whaddon blood, but the strongest influence comes from the Dunston harriers. Graham [Hughes] showed me the progeny of two litters bred by Dunston sires, nice, compact 20in hounds which in a season or two will make the uniform stamp of the Aldenham."*

Most of his piece is the history of the Aldenham Harriers as recorded by Ralph Greaves in his book of thirty years earlier, but J.N.P.Watson also mentions that the meet was at Upperwood Farm, on the Halsey Estate, on 20th October 1984 and amongst those present were *"the intrepid Lady Lyell"*, Patick Burgin (who, with wife Elizabeth, was his weekend host), Derek Christopher (host at Upperwood Farm, with wife Joyce) and the Earl and Countess of Verulam. A *'throng'* of seventy is mentioned, but we are not told whether they were all mounted. There were nineteen and a half couple of hounds. The piece concludes with:

> *"The cavalcade moved off on the early side for harriers, at 11am, and drew first over Mr Basil Hall's rape at Valley Bottom [Flamstead], their cast making quite a picture in the autumn sunlight with green-coated Hughes [Huntsman] and Sturmey [Whipper-in] behind them. That dazzling sun coupled with a strong westerly wind assured us of a fairly inactive day. But it was spent on*

beautiful farmland intersected by just two of Hertfordshire's quietest roads. The Aldenham sport is less demanding (and less expensive) than that of the two foxhunts that overlap its country. It thus gives abundant pleasure to a host of sportsmen, women and children who might otherwise never have ventured to ride to hounds."

With great reluctance it was decided that the traditional Boxing Day meet on Redbourn common would not take place in 1984 for fear that, after the events of the previous year, things would get out of hand. The meet was attracting more and more violent and abusive demonstrators intent upon inflaming the situation to promote their own propaganda in the media, and the threat of violence was becoming unacceptable to all concerned. There were hopes that eventually the pressures would subside and it would be possible for the tradition to be revived. The venue for the alternative Boxing Day meet was kept secret for obvious reasons. It turned out to be on private land owned by Basil Hall at Gill Hill, Flamstead, and, although there was a good turnout, in the event hunting was not possible because of thick fog.

1st Whip Terry Sturmey on Redbourn Common in 1981
Elizabeth Ansell

Joint masters for the 1984/5 season were Pat Burgin and Derek Christopher.

Graham Hughes continued as huntsman and Terry Sturmey continued to act as whipper-in, courtesy of Lady Lyell, whose employee he remained. Hunt horses remained at Upperwood Farm. The leases of the kennels and huntsman's cottage were due to expire at the end of the season and suggestions for alternative arrangements were invited. Forty meets were called, hunting took place on twenty seven days and there were twenty couple of hounds in kennels, including six and a half couple of dog hounds, and two couple of puppies. Within these figures were two litters of pure bred harriers from the previous two seasons and Mrs Gingell, Master of the Cambridgeshire, had drafted in a couple of her puppies. An Aldenham litter sired by her Reserve Champion POACHER was doing extremely well. All of this was the result of the Masters having taken the decision for the future to breed a pack of pure bred harriers.

There had been trouble the previous season when people had left their horse boxes, cars and trailers outside a pub in Lilley when the Aldenham met there. Horses had walked over carefully manicured lawns outside adjacent houses, which was really quite irresponsible of their riders, so for the future there would be a rule that horses must be unloaded at least half a mile from a meet. Thus, as ever, the majority suffer for the thoughtlessness of the few. A note about the rule was appended to the meets cards for fifteen years afterwards.

Anecdotes concerning Prue Lyell and her step mother and their relationships with their staff in the eighties are legion as both could be forceful and they found it difficult to accept incompetence or inadequacy without a waspish comment. On the other hand both could be kindly, understanding and helpful; their moments of irritation were short-lived and they would realise the offence they caused and try to make up for it afterwards.

There was the time when they were eventing at Tidworth and the groom, Wendy Sturmey, forgot the rein stops. There was an almighty row about it, out of all proportion to the sin, because they only cost 50p a pair and could be bought on the site.

On another occasion, when they were going eventing, they knew one of the horses had a shoe loose the previous day and phoned the blacksmith about it who promised to call and put it right. Early morning on the day and everybody was agitated because the job had not been done and the time for leaving was fast approaching. So they all went in to breakfast, and when they reassembled afterwards Prue said *"I suppose I must do everything myself"* and went off to telephone the blacksmith again, to be told that the job had been done while they were breakfasting.

Lady Lyell's horse, ALDWARK, had been plaited and the staff were very proud to see their handiwork displayed when it was taken out hunting, but Lady Lyell complained that ALDWARK had fidgeted and agitated and bucked all day; she strongly suspected that the plaiting was the root of the problem and she had some choice remarks to make about the ineptitude of the people involved with it. Now, groom Gillian often used to ride the hunters for an hour or so to get them settled and on this occasion, whilst so employed, her stock pin had somehow come adrift and got lodged under the saddle so that it was not surprising that

ALDWARK had reacted. Understandably, nobody had the courage to make a clean breast of it to Lady Lyell.

Another unpleasant little scene for all concerned happened one day when the hunt met at Basil Hall's first 'Pantaraxia' (now called Old Hall Farm). Prue, looking out of the kitchen window as they were departing, chanced to see the rear end of LADY and shouted *"What do you mean by taking a horse out with grass stains on its backside"* and that meant all the horses from the Lyell stable being recalled for further grooming before they were considered fit to be seen in public. No fun perhaps, but after all, that is how standards are maintained.

Aldenham hounds were entered in nine classes at the Peterborough Harrier and Beagle Show on Thursday 18th July 1985 and did rather well; CHAPMAN won a reserve rosette in the Dog Hound Class and CHAPMAN & CHAPLIN, who were brothers, obtained a second in the Perpetual Challenge Cup which was for the best couple. The competition was stiff. This was only the second time that the Aldenham had shown after a lapse of a good number of years and the kennel huntsman, Graham Hughes was well pleased.

The policy for choosing names for the hounds has for some years been to use the initial letter of the name of the sire for the initial letter of the offspring's name, if the bitch was sent away, but if covered at home to use the initial of the bitch.

The Lady Aldenham
at Upperwood Farm Stud
Derek Christopher

At this time Mrs Jo Gibbs wrote to the Masters from her house in Aldenham to say that she would like to hunt occasionally. This was an interesting throwback to the previous century when one of her husband's relatives, his great-great-uncle, who later became the 2nd Lord Aldenham, was involved in the formative years of the Aldenham Harriers. She suggested that the hunt might like to try a cross country ride or drag hunt south of the M25 between Watling Street and the M1 near Elstree Aerodrome, which would have been very convenient for her. Nobody knew it, of course, at the time, but this was a momentous letter as things turned out. A cross country ride did indeed take place, but the point is that Mrs Gibbs later became a Joint Master of the Aldenham Harriers with Pat Burgin and Derek Christopher and is today Lady Aldenham and a trustee of the hunt.

The anti-hunting argument took an even more violent and sinister tone during the season when Joint Master, Patrick Burgin's house was vandalised with red paint. The Animal Liberation Front claimed responsibility.

John Daulis became a Joint Master in 1986 and remained so for nine seasons, with a gap between the seventh and eighth.

For the 1986/87 season a new amateur whipper-in was taken on, none other than Ian Pearse about whom more will be said later. This came about when Terry Sturmey relinquished his hunt service after six years with the Harriers and the position changed its status from professional to amateur. Hounds were being exercised at seven o'clock in the morning, six days a week, and there were five and a half couple of young hounds to enter. Aldenham hounds were shown at both Peterborough and Honiton where they did reasonably well; three commendations at Peterborough and a commendation and a third prize at Honiton.

Through the nineties the fields were diminishing, partly because the Harriers were losing land, partly because subscriber numbers were falling, partly because the country was receding. At one point subscriber numbers were down to eight. Pat Burgin paid the bills and the Harriers remained virtually a private pack. However there were those who felt that it ought to expand and it did. There were forty six subscribers by the year 2000 and the increase appears to be continuing. New land was opened up, new subscribers were recruited and the Harriers turned the corner. Into the new millennium Joint Masters, the secretary and others have made a point of opening up new land and that has helped recruitment enormously. Today there are routinely twenty to thirty in the field each Wednesday and forty to fifty each Saturday.

In the early 1990s 'political correctness' reared its ugly head, a thing we had despised in Communist Russia for years. Conscious of the tide of public opinion, the National Trust was trying desperately hard to steer a middle course between the hunting fraternity and the protesters, fearful that if it came down upon the wrong side its subscription income might suffer. So far as the Aldenham Harriers was concerned the effect of all this was the need to acquire a licence to hunt on Trust land at Whipsnade and Sharpenhoe and the application for such became an annual chore for the secretary. There were details of hunt activities to be provided each time, but the licence has never been withheld.

Tony Roberts became a Joint Master in place of John Daulis in 1993 and served for seven years. He has kept his horses in stables off Delmerend Lane, Flamstead for twenty-three years. The site is a little over a mile from kennels and very convenient. He is a shipbroker by profession, but the family business, which he shares with his wife and mother, who started the business forty years ago, manufactures ballet wear. He first subscribed to the Harriers the year George Garfoot died (1980), having been introduced by Wilf Papworth and in turn he introduced Pat Murphy, his vet at the Shenton & Dean, St Albans practice who presided over his horses. For his first venture he took BEN, a splendid animal for the job. They were at Stags End, well orchestrated in a single file, but with Peter Wardill, who had been a Master of beagles, in front, whose horse had a mind of its own and would not tolerate being passed. They came to a fallen tree and Peter's horse stopped dead so Pat Murphy overtook, whereupon Peter's horse, fearful of being overtaken, took off and they collided in mid air. Pat was thrown, but uninjured. Peter stayed on and appeared to be oblivious of the incident, until turning to wait for Pat to remount and join him he remarked *"that's the way to jump a log"*. Pat later went on to hunt with the Berkeley.

Tony's first season was with Lady Lyell and Basil Hall and he remembers a time when one of Lady Lyell's house guests, an American, mounted by her, incurred her disapproval at a post and rail at Valley Bottom to be duly admonished. He commented, *"I can cope with the tongue-lashing, but I have to have dinner with her this evening."* He had misunderstood, as many did, first time, that the episode was forgotten in a flash and Lady Lyell would be charming at dinner. On another occasion the Harriers were hunting at Hexton and Tony was Field Master. As usual all the hares were running uphill on steep grass. Ian Pearse was getting edgy and shouted *"get to the top and try to turn the next one"* He succeeded, but in the process discovered an unsuspected ravine, a hundred foot deep and with a precipitous edge, in the line of pursuit. He flew over to the edge and shouted to everybody to hold hard just as the chase got near. A number of riders got to within twenty feet of the edge where there was an abundance of rabbit holes. It was a near thing.

Pat Burgin jumped a cattle grid at Ayot and so did Tony, at Elstow, when he became distracted while whipping in and was over before he knew it was there. Another time Tony jumped a hedge at Zouches Farm, Caddington, straight onto a harrow concealed the other side. This trick had put paid to poor Reggie Streather some years previously, but Tony was more fortunate and his horse danced through it, whether by luck or judgement we shall never know.

Later on Tony went to Ireland to buy a horse and was shown round a series of stables by a chap called Padraig. They were at a farm in the *'back of beyond'* when a stable door was flung open and there *"in the gloom, steaming fire"* was a big grey stallion. Tony tried it over half a mile across a pole and banks, and a road and was enthralled, 'totally sent' as the saying is. *"I'll take it"* he said; *"thank you sir, that will be £40,000 and I'm cheating myself"* came the reply. That was out of the question, but the next one he was shown he bought. TOM was 17.3hh; he was demonstrated with just a head collar on, no saddle or bridle and he took two oil drums with a pole with ease. TOM was four years old then and is seventeen now and Tony has never regretted buying him.

Not long after there was a meet at Kensworth; Gillian Haworth was out and so was the actor, Gerald Harper in his swallow tails and silk top hat. Now, this was a good place for hedges and Pat Burgin turned to Derek Christopher, who was on a thoroughbred Belgian show jumper and said *"that would be a good one to take"*. It was a hawthorn hedge, with deadly spikes all over, and Derek took it well, as did a few others, but Gerald somehow managed to pancake on top of it and was thrown. Worse, he held on to the reins and as his horse extricated itself was virtually shredded by the thorns. It was not a pretty sight!

Towards the end of his Mastership Tony organised and Field Mastered a meet at Pirton where a hare gave them a good hunt with a three mile point, before being killed in front of the field. He was presented with the mounted mask on his retirement and it has a place of honour on his dining room wall.

Pat Callaghan lived next door to Peter Flawn at Kensworth and was *"one hell of a horseman"*. His two young children, aged about four and five years, of course itched to emulate their illustrious papa and he would take them out hunting, one each side on a leading rein over rough country and jumps. It looked more risky than it was because he could easily have let go of the reins at any point that the situation demanded, and young children know no fear anyway.

Bill Ellis, the actor of *"Just one Cornetto"* fame, rode with the Harriers and kept his horse called OBERON at Puddephats. It is said that he was out one day when somebody bellowed *"Whip on your right"* and he quietly changed his whip over from his left hand to his right. He got a lot of ribbing afterwards, but he took it in good grace.

In 1995 the Master's duties were spread amongst four people:

> Lady Aldenham
>
> Patrick Burgin
>
> Derek Christopher
>
> Tony Roberts.

The huntsman remained Graham Hughes, the amateur whippers-in were John Richards and Michael Halsey and the honorary secretary was Ann Hawkins. All the Aldenham Harriers secretaries were honorary, the point being made here in case the word is omitted elsewhere.

Lady Lyell meanwhile, although well advanced in years by this time, almost house-bound and impaired in her speech, still had a razor sharp mind and took a very keen interest in all matters appertaining to horses. She still ran

Puddephats, which was the most permanent home the Harriers had ever had, and at the stables nearby fourteen horses were housed with two girls to look after them. Here she enjoyed breeding horses, naming the offspring, for a time, after fields on the farm and latterly after things connected with her flying career, hence WARNERS END & FLYING INSTRUCTOR.

1st Whip John Richards at the Royal Windsor Horse Show
Derek Christopher

FLYING INSTRUCTOR is the grey that she raced in the last few years of her life, and she went to a great deal of trouble to be there when it ran. In a wheel chair and with groom, Wendy Sturmey, in attendance, she was driven to Heathrow Airport early one morning to fly to Dublin as FLYING INSTRUCTOR was running at the Punchestown Festival National Hunt Meeting. All went well at this end, but at Dublin the authorities would not let Lady Lyell off the aircraft unless she had a paramedic in attendance. Time was running out for the start of racing, so Wendy offered to carry her off and was told to *"shut up"* , but she did it all the same and they were at the meeting in time to see FLYING INSTRUCTOR come in third. The pair of them were back at Puddephats the same evening, tired but none the worse for the experience and very proud of FLYING INSTRUCTOR.

On another occasion FLYING INSTRUCTOR was racing at Haydock and Wendy allowed three hours to drive Lady Lyell there; M1/M6 practically door to door, but the three obligatory comfort stops on the way wasted a lot of time and it seemed they might miss the start. They did and FLYING INSTRUCTOR was running in the first race, so Wendy left the car in the road outside the course and ran with Lady Lyell in her wheelchair so that she could witness the finish. FLYING INSTRUCTOR was not placed on that occasion, but Lady Lyell's enthusiasm for the animal, and her belief in its abilities, knew no bounds and it no doubt did a great deal to bring interest and enthusiasm and pleasure to her declining years.

One of the Puddephats-bred horses, WARNERS END, was leased to Lady Lyell's niece Philippa and her husband Lt. Col. Eddy Stocker who ran it at Sandown Park, so Wendy drove Lady Lyell down to see it race. When they went up to lunch, Lady Lyell, in her wheelchair, succeeded in getting her leg, the bad one this time, not the one that was broken twice, stuck in the doors of the lift; fortunately it was released uninjured. WARNERS END fell at the fifth. When they were loading up afterwards Lady Lyell somehow or other managed to get her neck tangled up in a rope that had been put round the disableds' car park and could have been throttled, but again escaped uninjured. Wendy had forgotten to put the handbrake on the wheelchair! It was an eventful day and by all accounts there were a goodly number of them, especially in the wheelchair era.

A party from Puddephats were out eventing one day with lorry and car, but the lorry broke down the other side of Guildford on the way home so they had to borrow another and Prue took the car on to London alone. That meant everything and everybody else piling into the lorry, where conditions were so cramped that Wendy did the journey in an awkward corner with her legs in the air and in much too close proximity to Prue's three lurchers. Lady Lyell had been asked three times whether her walking stick was aboard and three times she had assured them that it was and told them not to fuss, but the thing still somehow managed to get itself left behind nevertheless.

Betty Gingell died in about 1995 and shortly after Peter Flawn cold called on her son, Michael, which was to be the start of a very happy relationship. Michael Gingell had run the Cottenham Point-to-Point meetings for some years and in 1996 invited Peter to lunch, with the idea of persuading the Aldenham Harriers to become a partner in them. At that time Peter, though attracted, felt obliged to decline on the grounds that the committee did not feel that they had sufficient manpower. In April 1998 permission was given by the Jockey Club for the formation of the Cambridgeshire Harriers Point-to-Point Hunt Club (CHPHC). The first meeting took place at Cottenham in 1998 and has been an annual attraction ever since. It has acquired the distinction of being the first point-to-point meeting in England of the season. CHPHC needed to fill four slots at the site each season and in 2001 the Aldenham Harriers was able to join them; the result of which is mentioned in more detail later on. An interesting side issue is that CHPHC contributed significantly to Aldenham Harriers funds from 1998 onwards, which was indeed generous.

Lady Lyell died on 19th July 1998 and all of the trials, and care, and concern, that went into her last years are now but a memory. In the past six years the bottom yard at Puddephats has become a DIY livery stable, but apart from that development Nigel Tully has allowed everything to go on very much as before. This is remarkable and shows much forbearance and goodwill on his part because he is not very keen on hunting and tolerates it in memory of Prue and Lady Lyell.

We have heard a great deal about Lady Lyell, indeed more so than of anybody else, but she did, after all, play a particularly important part in the history of the Aldenham Harriers. She had been born Katharine Runciman in Northumberland on 4th December 1909, the third daughter of Walter, 1st Viscount Runciman of Doxford. When she was sixteen she spent half of her summer holidays flying aircraft with her elder brother, who was mad on the sport at the time, but her father refused to sign her application to fly solo and she went to Germany to study the piano for two years. Eventually she had to accept that she was not good enough to become a concert pianist, so went to Girton College to read history, graduating in 1931. Shortly afterwards, on 23rd October 1931, she married Oliver, 4th Lord Farrer and started married life in India where her husband had a P & O assignment. Unfortunately, her husband became ill and they had to return to England after two years. By chance they noticed in a copy of *Country Life* that Puddephats Farm was on the market and bought it in Michaelmas 1936. She was to live there for the rest of her life, sixty two years.

During the Second World War, she hoped to fly for the RAF, but failed the eyesight test and so took a commission with the Air Transport Auxiliary (ATA), becoming Adjutant to Pauline Gower at Hatfield Aerodrome before moving to White Waltham. Her sister, Margaret, did get her pilot's certificate and became a Captain in the ATA. On 4th August 1944, Margaret was piloting an RAF Percival Proctor on a flight from Heston to Speke, with her sister Katharine and a chap from the Ministry of Aircraft Production as passengers. The ground crew had failed to fill the reserve tank on the aircraft and when an attempt was made to change-over tanks over Chester, just a few miles short of the destination, fuel ran out and the inevitable crash followed. Sadly, Margaret was killed. Katharine survived, but received serious injuries to her leg, which put her in hospital for three years. The Ministry chap broke his thumb, but was otherwise unhurt.

At the hunt ball on 4th March 1996 Derek Christopher retired, having completed thirty three years as Field Master, thirty years as hunt secretary and thirteen years as Joint Master. Derek was presented with a cheque and a painting as tokens of appreciation for the sterling service that he had given in the cause of hunting. Nobody had ever achieved this astonishing record before, or come anywhere near it, nor indeed are they ever likely to. Thirty-three years holding one office is commendable enough, but for some of the time he held all three together which is indeed remarkable. His was said to have been the best Field Master since Stanley White and just possibly better even than him, because current farming and road conditions make giving the field a good day and pleasing the paying customers that much more difficult.

In fact two Joint Masters stood down that year; the other one was Pat Burgin who had served with distinction for fifteen seasons, twelve of them with Derek Christopher. He is remembered with affection for the many difficult years that he guided the Harriers through with endless good humour and enthusiasm. At the hunt ball that year his many well-wishers presented him with a painting of himself on a hunter, and a fine spectacle it made. To replace Pat and Derek came John Daulis, back for a second stint, and with him came his neighbour from Kimpton, Mary Arikoglu. Mary came from a hunting family; her parents and grandfather had hunted with the Puckeridge and there was also a great uncle who ended up in a wheelchair through his hunting activities in the 1920s. Mary started her own riding career at the age of two on SALLY the donkey, who arrived one day tied up in the back of an open pick-up. Her hunting career started at the age of eight on SWALLOW, with the Enfield Chace, being led by one of her sisters on foot, and at the age of fourteen she was proudly blooded by Raymond Brooks-Ward. She still has the brush of the same fox. Her hunting career with the Aldenham Harriers began in 1985 on a grey mare called SILVER which she still has, though nowadays she is retired. It was at a time when new baby Alexandra had just arrived and hunting offered light relief from the traumas of motherhood. Mary only hunted once a week at that stage because *"I had to play the mother a bit, some of the time"*. Thankfully Alexandra survived this apparent case of early neglect. One could be forgiven for thinking that playing second fiddle to hunting would have left a lasting antagonism, but not a bit of it; by age eight Alexandra was out with the harriers herself, presumably on the logic of *"if you can't beat 'em, join 'em"*. Later, second daughter Rosanna arrived and now she too rides with the harriers.

Husband Alp completes the family team and competes with the females of the establishment as to who shall ride which of the three available horses when the harriers are out. Although none of them are ready to admit to it, Alp is really the inspiration behind this trio of huntresses; he hunted with the New Forest where he earned the nickname of *'The Mad Turk'* from Sir Newton Rycroft. He was out with the New Forest one day, closely following hounds hot on the scent in a narrow lane, when they suddenly seemed to part immediately ahead; not realising the field were queueing to go through a gate he kicked on the gap and discovered his horse was jumping a cattle grid which, until that moment, he had been completely unaware of. It was he who, when 'shadowing' a fence steward at a Cottenham Point-to-Point meeting in order to learn the job, was told by the steward that all the horses and riders had gone past and that it was safe to stamp in the divots, but there was one more horse to come and he was on the wrong side when he heard it. He threw himself flat on the ground, just in time to be able to stare up into the horse's nostrils as it went over the jump. It was a near thing! Alp was one time chairman of the Aldenham Harriers Supporters Club, standing down in 1996.

Mary has other interesting family hunting connections; her cousin Trevor's uncle was the great Stanley White (the Aldenham Harriers Joint Master 1947-1952) and Audrey Chambers (the Aldenham Harriers Honorary Joint Secretary 1958-1966) was her brother-in-law's mother.

At one meet of the 1997/8 season hounds were at Ivinghoe Aston running on a strong scent when Ian Pearse's horse refused at a narrow fence through a hedge. To quote Richard III in the heat of the chase is really expecting too much of a Master, but Ian managed *"Will no one give me a horse"*, whereupon Alexandra Arikoglu generously offered her MISCHIEF (14.2hh.) which he gratefully accepted. MISCHIEF 'did him proud' and he was reluctant to swop back.

Mary Arikoglu sees a bright future for the Aldenham Harriers, making the point that people are fed up with being told what to do and will rebel. However, she does think that the Aldenham Harriers country is becoming increasingly difficult with encroaching housing, industry and roads, and with changes in farming practices. She feels that the only way to counter-balance these developments will be to take on new country.

The Aldenham Harriers Puppy Show at the kennels at Puddephats was held for the first time in the summer of 1999 and was such a success that it became an annual event thereafter.

In December 1997 the Editor of *Horse & Hound* sent David Edelstein out to find out what the Aldenham Harriers were about and report back. They met at Ayot St Lawrence and the Harriers were anxious to make a good impression, but young hound, ACORN, had her own ideas about what would impress. She dived into a hedge in front of everybody and produced a partly decomposed pheasant which she repeatedly tossed into the air, scattering feathers far and wide. Fortunately *Horse & Hound* had sent a kindly and discreet man who forbore mentioning the unfortunate incident in his piece, but it was a big embarrassment at the time. He did, however, comment upon the smallness of the hounds, with the remark *"The true harrier is a tiny, winning creature, highly active, into everything"*. He obviously had ACORN in mind when he wrote it. He mentions her by name later on in his piece, but not, thankfully, with any reference to feathers. Joint Master Mary Arikoglu was little better; she sliced the top off her finger the previous day and is prominent in the photographs wearing a brilliant yellow rubber glove. To his credit the visitor gallantly overlooked it. It was the pace of the chase that impressed him most and after all that is as it should be. He had been mounted by the Honorary Hunt Treasurer, Martyn Bishop, on his grey mare, WILLOW, and had a good day's sport, *"full of excitement and surprises"*.

Elizabeth Ansell's connection with the Aldenham Harriers goes back to 1949 when she was sixteen. She had moved to St Albans, and started at St Albans School of Art. She had hunted once or twice with the Oakley which gave her the appetite for it, so she put an advert in the local newspaper for a horse. A Mr Beale, who hunted with either the Hertfordshire or the Harriers, responded and she accepted his offer. He had two horses and a trailer; Elizabeth was allowed to hunt one of the horses and to use the trailer.

Later she obtained a horse of her own which she kept at Hall Place Gardens. From 1954 to 1959 she had the old Express Dairy Stables, called

Kingsbury Farm, off Branch Road in St Michael's, St Albans and thirty acres of meadow behind them. Here she ran a riding school with, on average, ten horses, including a couple of point-to-pointers qualified with both the Aldenham Harriers and the Hertfordshire Hunt and kept in training to run at Friars Wash. One of them, MURRAY'S LODGE, won races and the other, PHILOMEL IV, was placed. Her jockeys included Eric Shelley and Harold Bowley. Elizabeth met her husband, Ray, when he came to the riding school. Ray was a printing compositor, but he took a course in saddlery at the Cordwainers and Rural Industries establishment in Yeovil and set up a saddlery business, Centaurs Saddlery, at their house at the top of The Hill, Wheathampstead. He had many Aldenham Harriers customers including present Joint Master Val Barr, who remembers being taken there by her mother to buy her first pair of jodhpur boots.

Elizabeth Ansell on Redbourn Common in 1981
Elizabeth Ansell

Elizabeth Ansell on NUWAYS LODGE with Peggy Greig and her husband (nearest adults behind) 1954/55
Valerie Dickinson

However, Elizabeth eventually became an accomplished artist and set up an enterprise of her own which still thrives today. She specialised in sketches, line drawings and paintings of hunting, equestrian events, countryside, horse racing, dogs and other animal subjects. Her works are in strong demand and she has generously allowed some of them to be reproduced in this book.

Of her time with the harriers, she particularly remembers the good jumps at Cross Farm and Hammonds End, the lawn meets at De Havillands and hunting around Jersey Farm and Oaklands at St Albans, all of which she hacked to.

In later years Elizabeth moved away from the harriers and rode with the Oakley. She was invited to keep her horse up there and stayed with them for ten seasons, 1973 to 1983. Even in the friendliest of hunts there is a hierarchy, a 'pecking order', and it takes a while to work from the bottom to the top, even when you work hard at it and have been reliably introduced.

Then came a new interest. She started carriage driving and after a while she gave up hunting. She taught David Combes to ride and he taught her to drive. For the purpose she bought a three year old hunter, KEOGH, from Ireland, a big black cob, 16.00hh. It was no problem to break to harness and when they were competing round the usual oil drums with poles across she was always fearful that KEOGH might try to jump them, but she never did. Elizabeth made a point of always having a Dalmatian running under the axle, where it is supposed to be, and is remembered for it. KEOGH hunted all winter, both with the Oakley and the Harriers, and was often ridden by her son Richard. She competed at major shows including the Horse of the Year Show in 1977. Elizabeth makes the point that she never had a bad fall from a horse, but she has turned carriages over and had some nasty smashes.

The Aldenham Harriers Joint Master Val Barr on Helen
Pearse's WHIZZY at Holwell Manor, Dorset, on 4th December 1999
Val Barr

In 1999 Val Barr replaced Lady Aldenham as a Joint Master. Val's family did not ride, so her addiction to horses and hunting cannot be blamed on them; it is a self-inflicted wound. At the tender age of two apparently, someone with malice aforethought *"Plonked me on a horse which happened to be parked at a nearby farrier's and I was lost forever"*. Her father, no doubt under considerable daughterly pressure, was entirely supportive. By the time she was eight, she was riding a skewbald gelding called TOMMY at Mrs Greig's Pipers Riding School at Gustard Wood. Rachel Meers, who is a couple of years older, was already there riding her CAUTION. Both would stay with Mrs Greig overnight if they were to be out hunting early next day. Later Val kept her own horse at Pipers, but did not have transport, so had to hack to meets. She has always ridden with the harriers. She was not closely involved with the pony club, but hunted as a pony club member.

Later on she bought a pure thoroughbred (by NETHER KELLY) from Peter Robeson, to show. It had been broken to saddle and bridle and backed a bit, but was only four years old when she first took it hunting with the harriers at Lilley. At the start of that first meet they went down the side of a field that had a horse in it and POLLY (registered name NACUNDA) became excited. Then they turned down a muddy track and Val, desperately trying to calm her excited thoroughbred and at the same time endeavouring not to overtake the Field Master, ran into a bush *"Came out the side door in a sea of mud, held on, and was dragged through it"*. By her own admission she was a disgusting mess when she managed to get to her feet again, but worse, John Richards called loudly *"Did you start out clean?"* It was difficult to forgive. She remounted, however, and carried on while the mud dried and caked, and she ended up having a good day's hunting.

The opening meet of 1999 at Kintyre, Trowley Bottom. Graham Hughes is at the back on WINSTON, then (left to right at the front) Joint Masters Mary Arikoglu on MAGNUM, Val Barr on KATE, Tony Roberts on Roy Smith's FELLAR and Ian Pearse on SCOOTER
Val Barr

Then came marriage and the arrival of son, Giles in 1982 and daughter Zoë in 1985. She rode when she could, but it was Mick Halsey who happened to mention that the Harriers were meeting at Gorhambury one day when Giles was little and it was there that she got back to hunting again. Giles did not take to riding, but Zoë was put on a horse at four years old and has never looked back, hunting whenever she can.

Val's husband, Bill, farms Dane End Farm, St Albans. He had a pony as a boy, just for fun, but with the enthusiasms of the ladies of the establishment, has been encouraged back to it. It was Val who suggested he should go to a farmers' meet at Hill & Coles Farm in the 1998/9 season to get himself started. He rode daughter Zoë's New Forest pony, CONKER, (14.0hh.) at first, but a whisky stop worked wonders for his confidence and he swopped horses with Val. On her grey cob, BERTIE, (15.3hh) he jumped a little log and 'on a high' threw off his 'L' plates and was 'hooked'.

There is a story about BERTIE; he developed a habit of rummaging and munching in the hedge at quiet moments and Val, knowing it to be undesirable, nevertheless let him get away with it. One day they were at a meet at Ayot St Lawrence when John Daulis was Field Master and came upon a shoot, so had to stop and wait while hounds were picked up. BERTIE was up to his old tricks in a hedge when suddenly he started and behaved as if he had been stung, but when they moved off he seemed to get over it, responded well to the bit, and remained only slightly troubled. However, Val took him home where he swelled up, dribbled constantly, and although he was eating normally the vet was called and prescribed an anti-inflammatory drug. In January, three months later, a lump appeared at the back of BERTIE'S jaw and the vet was called again. This time it was antibiotics and a visit by a mobile X-ray, which disclosed a piece of barbed wire, about two and a half inches long, embedded in the jaw. The vet pulled it out with tweezers and BERTIE never complained, although the pain must have been considerable. He was as 'honest' a horse as you would ever have.

Val too tends to be confident about the Aldenham Harrier's future. She makes the point though that times change, people's views and aspirations change, and everything has to move forward. The Aldenham Harriers has been lucky because through all its traumas it seems to have been able to produce the man, or woman, for the hour. Quote *"The horse is a great leveller"*.

To qualify for point-to-point, riders must have hunted seven times in the season and never to have left the field before 1.30pm. No one qualified in the 1998/1999 season and only one qualified in 1999/2000, but six qualified in 2000/2001; highly significant when the Aldenham Harriers, hopefully, are at the dawn of a new golden age of their own point-to-point meetings, as will become apparent later on.

A tradition in recent years has been for the opening meet of the season to be at Rita Huxley's bungalow at Trowley Bottom. Rita no longer rides to hounds, but nowadays follows on foot. She has a splendid record for bringing home injured hounds and a happy knack of being there just at the right time to open and shut gates to let the hunt through.

Kennel Huntsman Graham Hughes at Puddephats
Rita Huxley

At the beginning of the new millennium, Graham Hughes remains the kennel huntsman although he is about to retire after twenty years' praiseworthy service. He is a popular figure and has become an institution over the years. The kennels remain at Puddephats, where hounds have been quartered for over forty years, and Graham lives in the adjacent cottage which is let to the hunt by Nigel Tully.

Graham's day starts at seven o'clock in the morning when he walks the hounds for an hour, a whipper-in or himself in front or behind. After that he hoses down the yard, does the beds and feeds the hounds. He lets the shy feeders in first to give them a fair chance before the gluttons get going. He recognises each one by name and knows their characters. After that comes breakfast for himself at half past nine and then it is time to deal with the flesh. Sometimes collections to be arranged or sometimes farmers deliver. Either way it has to be dealt with promptly. In the afternoon hounds are exercised again, either on another walk or in the grass run. The hounds are not usually washed; they can be relied upon to lick themselves and each other clean; they are very good at it.

Food for the pack comes from fallen stock which the kennel huntsman brings in, skins, and butchers, himself. He is often required to put down animals when they are old or sick or injured. Domestic pets are occasionally brought in and on one memorable Sunday morning a man arrived clutching in his arms his pet cat which had lost control of its bowels. The job has its moments!

In the past such large quantities of fallen stock have been available at times that it has been necessary to call a halt, but times are changing; there is much new regulation and fewer local farms have livestock. In providing this service the hunt benefits as well as the farming community, but disposal of unusable material is becoming more and more regulated and costly and, reluctantly, the Aldenham Harriers have recently decided that they must make a charge for disposing of fallen stock. Rates are £100 for a horse and £5 for a sheep, but, even now, no charge is made for a cow or calf. There are still professional knackers about, but their charges are greater. Hides are still collected by a dealer, but this may not go on much longer. Graham does not usually feed pig meat to hounds, though it can be done, and he is careful over quantities of horse meat because it makes hounds very thirsty.

Graham is very good with fallen stock, and although the knackering side of his job has declined by 80% in twenty years nevertheless the telephone might ring at any time of the day or night and he is expected to respond cheerfully and efficiently. When it comes to putting down a horse that has been a family friend for perhaps fifteen or twenty years and carting away the carcass for dog food, it calls for a special kind of tact and understanding and Graham has it. The hunt bought a new custom-built flesh wagon in 2000, funded by the supporters club, which has a built-in winch and capacity for two or three beasts. Everything is skinned and jointed and used to be stored in the flesh house until needed, but nowadays there is a walk-in freezer and a walk-in fridge to keep the meat fresh and they have made a tremendous difference in warm weather. The skins are salted and saved pending collection by the hide man. The income from them is reckoned to be a kennelman's perk. There is no incinerator at Puddephats; the cost would be prohibitive, so bones and entrails and that sort of thing have to go into a five ton skip for controlled disposal as 'Specified Risk Material' by Prosper Demolder. In summer this can generate a lively aroma. There was trouble one year when a combination of overfilled skip and a brake-happy driver led to little deliveries of unpleasentnesses being made at various places along the way to the disposal point, but particularly at Trowley Bottom where they have especially refined noses. They were not amused and they let the world know it.

Although Graham is kennel huntsman, in practice Ian Pearse hunts the hounds. That poses the question: does Ian do any of the feeding or use any other initiatives to establish his 'leadership of the pack'? There have, after all, been well known and embarrassing cases of failure in this respect elsewhere. The answer is that Ian has a natural affinity with the hounds and has never had to make any special effort over it.

In 2000 there were twenty five and a half couple of hounds in kennels, eighteen couple of them bitches, which is about the usual proportion. The sexes are normally kept apart except when out hunting. The bitches are the faster, but the dogs are steadier and more hard working. When making selections for breeding, an ability to work hard comes first, but a good voice has to be considered. Only three bitches will be selected in 2001. The health of the pack is generally good. Graham worms them regularly and gives each hound one injection for combined distemper and hard pad.

As sometimes happens, there was an occasion, at Cromer Hyde, when contact with the pack was temporarily lost. They all came back eventually except old CARRIE who went off on her own, to be picked up some hours later by Hatfield & Welwyn Council on the roundabout by Tesco's at Hatfield. The council charged £45 to return her and repercussions were feared, but Pat Burgin said *"If there is any trouble, put them on to me"* and nothing ever came of it.

To an outsider it would seem to be an obvious thing that the pack would have a lead hound and the kennelman would have a favourite, but Graham is adamant that although CARVER, one of the Dunstan hounds, is reliable, there is no obvious leader at the moment and he has no favourites. He looks upon them all as the tools of his trade.

Andrew Love was elected Chairman of the Hunt Committee in 1999 and Chairman of the Point-to-Point Committee in 2000. He was a fairly new face on the scene and had 'risen in the ranks' rapidly, only becoming a full member of the Aldenham in 1997, having a couple of years earlier moved to Whitwell. He was born in 1941 and had his first pony when he was five, but went on to boarding school and hardly rode again until he was eighteen when he followed the Enfield Chace under Raymond Brooks-Ward's Mastership. He then moved from the country to London where he devoted his surplus energies to playing soccer for the Corinthian Casuals and cricket for the MCC Schools XI. In 1984 he acquired a flat in Bamburgh Castle and with wife, Amanda, kept two horses in livery, hunting with the College Valley and North Northumberland Hunt. A keen charity worker for Cancer BACUP and the Outward Bound Trust, Andrew still finds time to be Chief Executive of the Ritz Club in London.

Ian Pearse from Hill & Coles Farm, Flamstead who farms in partnership with his parents and wife, has been Joint Master and huntsman for the last three seasons. He does not come from a hunting background, but claims that he has hunted since he was six having started off with the Aldenham Harriers, moved to the Vale of Aylesbury when Jim Bennett was huntsman and then changed to the Whaddon Chase when Albert Buckle, a particular friend of his wife's family, was hunting hounds. He has now come full circle and is regarded as a very good huntsman, often hunting three times a week, one of them following the Vale of Aylesbury. Somehow or other he has managed to wangle two ladies to be Joint Masters with him, a thing never before achieved with the Aldenham and there have been low mutterings about how he contrived it. The ladies in question are Mary Arikoglu who effectively replaced Derek Christopher in 1996 and is thus in her fifth season as a Joint Master, and Val Barr from Dane End Farm, St Albans, who effectively replaced Lady Aldenham in 1999. The usual practice at the moment is for Ian's wife, Helen, to Field Master for him and for Mary and Val to Field Master for the meets they organise. The size of the field is now of the order of fifty to sixty.

Ian is an enthusiastic horseman of considerable ability, but his great abiding interest lies in the hounds. He now has thirty two couple of them which must be somewhere near the record for the Aldenham Harriers, but one senses is by no means the extent of his ambition. He exercises them himself three or four times a week and, as mentioned before, also hunts them. It is said that he has a natural affinity with them, but he insists that although the kennelman feeds them every day of the year, the object of a hound's love and respect will always be the person who hunts it and there is no more to it than that.

He has no plans for showing hounds, his breeding plan aims no further than a 20/21" hound that will hunt. The Aldenham Harriers are stud book hounds and Ian is experimenting with crossing them with West Country harriers which are very biddable and less highly strung. The cross, if successful, will be capable of being registered after the third generation.

One day recently he went to Holkham Hall in Norfolk, talked to huntsman, Boyce Keeling, and came away with a present of six couple of his North Norfolk Harriers which have swelled the ranks considerably.

The Aldenham Harriers Joint Master Ian Pearse on his EDWARD
leaving Holwell Manor for the first draw on 4th December 1999
Val Barr

It was a particular pleasure to the hunt when Lady Aldenham issued an invitation to them to pay her a visit at her home at Holwell Manor, near Sherborne in Dorset. They went, twenty one riders and fourteen and a half couple of hounds, in November 1999. It was the first time that the Harriers had left their country in living memory.

At the invitation of Blackmoor & Sparkford & Vale, they hunted their country. Their Field Master for the day was Peter Wade and twenty five of their hunt and a lot of foot followers joined in. Before starting, the visitors were told that hares were seldom seen in those parts and they were unlikely to find any, but the harriers found one in the first field they drew and within fifty yards of coming into the field behind, the horses put up another and they had two and a half hours of superb hunting. It was a wonderful country for hedges and ditches. Peter Wade was somewhat frustrated - he had been determined to 'bury' the Aldenham. A sad aspect of an otherwise joyous day was when Kevin Shepherd jumped through a hedge, where quite a few had jumped before, but his horse landed on a metal spike and was badly injured. It was taken to the veterinary college in Bristol, but did not survive.

There were some near misses too. At one hedge jump everything appeared to be straightforward and it was only when you were in mid air that you became aware that a strand of barbed wire, two foot out from it on the landing side, was passing underneath. You could only hope that you had missed it. At another place the Field Master jumped what appeared to be patch of brambles, but it was in fact a large deep ditch with a light bramble camouflage. His wife, Mrs Wade, followed him but her horse slipped on the edge and fell in sideways. Then everything had to stop while it composed itself sufficiently to be able to jump out.

A strange thing happened after lunch; an unattended pack of beagles, six couple of them, joined the harriers and hunted with them all afternoon. It transpired later that they were from the Purbeck and Bovingdon Beagles. There was a two mile hack back in the evening and with only six horses left, the huntsman blew for home, whereupon the six couple of beagles abruptly departed. When the harriers got back to base it was discovered that they had a couple missing. Normally a hound that is lost will make for the site of the meet, so Ian Pearse went back there, but there was no sign of them, so he went to where he had last seen them, sat down on a water tank in the dark and blew the horn. Two couple of beagles emerged from the shadows, but would not come to him and there was still no sign of the missing harriers. Still worrying about them, he went back to the manor where a drinks gathering for the farmers had been arranged for seven o'clock and five minutes before one hound returned. The other came in five minutes after the party. One is tempted to speculate upon how they managed to find their way back in a strange country. Perhaps they homed in on familiar raised voices from the party on the night air; more likely they just followed the scent of their comrades. That evening the Aldenham had their meal at a local pub, the Poacher's Inn at Piddletrenthyde, and afterwards some of them enjoyed the hospitality of Lord and Lady Aldenham for the night while others were accommodated by local farmers.

The hounds were paraded at the South of England Show *'Pageant of*

Hounds' at Ardingley in June 2000. There were thirteen packs of hounds involved, of which only one was of harriers. Each pack came into the ring, one at a time, by way of introduction, and was paraded round once to take up a set position together with their huntsman and whippers-in. Once all thirteen packs were in position, one of the huntsmen went to the centre, blew his horn, and all 140 couple of hounds went to him and followed him out of the ring. The other huntsmen and whippers-in followed on behind. It was an awesome sight and there were people in the audience who wept openly at the drama of it. Outside, the mixed, very mixed, 280 hounds had to be sorted out. Surprisingly, it all went remarkably smoothly except for Aldenham Harriers' bitch CARELESS who had been given to the Aldenham by Duston Harriers' Master, Robert Bothway, and had a reputation for living up to her name. She had gone off on an enterprise of her own to investigate the premises and took a deal of finding.

Later on the hounds were paraded at the Countryside Alliance Countryside Race Day at Newmarket. Hounds had to be taken to the end of the July course, by the seven furlong marker, after which horsemen were supposed to gallop flat out with them up the course past the New Millennium Grandstand. They made a spectacular sight and everybody cheered and made a great noise, but Ian Pearse's horse, BETTY, was not amused. She jumped several times sideways and tried to throw him, while he somehow stayed on by the skin of his teeth. The crowd thought it was part of the act and cheered louder than ever which did nothing for Ian's predicament, but he won through. It would have been a terrible embarrassment if he had been thrown when so much in the public eye. Parading the hounds usually appears to be a calm, controlled, peaceful sort of exercise, but sometimes it can be quite stressful. Matthew Higgs paraded the neighbouring pack, South Herts Beagles, there the same day.

Ian Pearse at the Cottenham Point-to-Point on 11th February 2001
Ian Pearse

As mentioned the Aldenham Harriers became by degrees not just a hunt, but a whole way of life, offering not only action and comradeship in the field, but a full social life to boot.

Joint Master and huntsman, Ian Pearse, is optimistic about the future of the Aldenham Harriers and makes the point that it is stronger now than it has been for fifty years. There have never been so many subscribers; the finances are sound, but even so charges for a day's hunting come to no more than £5 or £6. Hounds are out more often; in the 2000/01 season there were forty four days hunting. Also a lot of country has been opened and in some cases reopened.

To add to this happy state of affairs, on Sunday 11th February 2001, thirty five year old Ian Pearse won the Members Race at Cottenham at the first the Aldenham Harriers point-to-point meeting for thirty seven years. That was indeed a splendid thing, but it was not his crowning achievement of the occasion; to his great credit he had lost over a stone to make the weight, and that represents a tidy number of breakfast sausages, about a hundredweight by my estimation. So much dedication and denial from one so young!. He was riding Mick Stevens' (the Aldenham's amateur whipper-in) LONESOME TRAVELLER. The going was good, but there had been record rainfalls for weeks before the event and it was touch and go as to whether the meeting would be called off; however, there was much at stake, great enthusiasm and determination, and that is what won through. John Papworth had found LONESOME TRAVELLER and bought him for Mick Stevens. Later he was sent back to John for his early preparation.

On the other hand February 2001 had a darker side; it was notable for another reason; it saw the start of a farmer's nightmare, one of those things that a livestock man dreads, something that he has at the back of his mind all the time and prays will never happen again - an outbreak of foot and mouth disease. This one was particularly severe and the Aldenham Harriers were unable to hunt for the rest of the season after the meet on 21st February. We are indeed fortunate that Ian Pearse has kept a diary note of that last day:

> *"On 21st February 2001 fourteen and a half couple were out and one and a half brace of hare were killed bringing the season's total to twenty nine brace. The scent was excellent and six brace of hares were found. I rode WHIZZY and Helen* [Mrs Pearse] *rode FRANKIE. There was a field of twenty out including Fred Dickinson and Alexandra Bishop, both only seven years old. The weather was fine and clear with no rain for a change!* [it had been a particularly wet winter - a record one] *We met at Medbury Farm, Elstow and our host was Sam Clark.*
> *Graham* [Hughes, the kennel huntsman] *is still ill, so I did kennels again today. We were a bit pushed for time by the time I had done the kennels and fed the cattle and I was slightly late leaving with the hound-van. Helen followed in the lorry with Zoë Barr with the*

horses. Unfortunately the hound-van engine blew up shortly after leaving home and I had to complete the journey with only three cylinders and a maximum speed of 30mph. 'Phoned forward to warn everyone that I would be late and when I arrived at 11.15am the field had enjoyed the hospitality of Sam Clark in the house and some of them were well oiled. This was a bad start to the day as hounds should never be late to the meet.

Mike Stevens was whipping in today as Graham is ill and Joy Lewin was Field Master.

Found our first hare behind the farm, but hounds almost immediately put up another hare and the whole pack, except QUEENBERRY who carried on with the hunted hare, changed and hunted the second hare on a circular route towards the landfill site at Elstow where Mick and I stopped them because of the main road nearby, meanwhile QUEENBERRY, who had been hunting the first hare on his own for nearly twenty minutes, brought her round to the cover behind New Medbury where I laid the rest of the pack on and we hunted her in fine fashion in and out of the cover and again towards the landfill site. With Sue now obviously tiring we dodged in and out of the thick hedgerows flanked by some quite fearsome ditches before eventually pulling her down in the open, a short, but furious hunt of thirty five minutes, approximately two miles as hounds ran, although QUEENBERRY was on his own for half of that. Awarded a pad to Fred Dickinson as it was his first proper day's hunting off the leading rein.

We then had a steady hunt with a brace of very unenterprising hares that kept going in very small circles on some very wet, heavy, ploughed land that made it very difficult for the horses to get about. Eventually got one of these hares away and had a sharp forty five minutes hunting in a wide circle around the farm and across the airstrip before Sam, who was following on his motorbike, stopped hounds on the side of the A6, which was a shame because they were getting up to their hare by then and scent was good.

Our next was truly a remarkable hunt. Finding our hare behind Cardington Aerodrome, we took her to Wilstead on a pretty straight line and then round and back to the airstrip and on to the farm yard where she beat us for a while on sheep foil, but they worked it out well and went on towards Elstow where she doubled back on herself and went back on down the airstrip again. I changed horses with Helen at this point as the ditches were starting to look wider! The pace slowed down now as Sue started to jink and twist with hounds really working hard to stay with her on the heavy plough, she then took to the grass fields behind Wilstead and the pace quickened again although we could only watch from a distance as we were *wired in. She skirted the village of Wilstead and ran parallel to the A6 for half a mile. When they got up to her on some very heavy corn ground with hounds deserving their reward. A hunt of one and three quarter hours or five miles as hounds ran with a point of just over one and a half miles.*

The field had dwindled by now, no doubt the thought of Mr & Mrs Clark's very inviting tea had something to do with it, so home was blown at 4.30pm after a very busy day."

POSTSCRIPT

When the Aldenham Harriers chronology was brought to an end at the beginning of 2001 in the previous chapter, it seemed to be a neat and natural climax to the story. Ian had had his first point-to-point win at Cottenham in the first Aldenham Harriers point-to-point meeting for thirty seven years; he had provided a detailed report of a twenty first century meet, the Mastership and the finances had consolidated and the future looked bright, or as bright as it could be with the ever present threat of political action to bring about its demise. It seemed the ideal point to 'chop' and publish.

However, the road to publication was a stony one for a variety of reasons, not least that the interviews, collection of photographs and researches had taken longer than expected and were still going on apace; a publisher had to be found and the funds had to be raised for a partnership arrangement.

So it was that another year went by. If it had been an ordinary, humdrum, run-of-the-mill sort of a year, with nothing much going on, adding a few extra comments to bring the story up-to-date would not have spoiled a neat finish, but, as it turned out, it was no ordinary year and the opportunity for a second 'rounding off' has had to be taken. For a start, the Meet recorded at the end of the last chapter, entirely by accident, proved to be the last Meet for almost a twelvemonth. In general terms two half-seasons were lost and this, of course, had a disastrous effect on all aspects of the Aldenham Harriers' activities.

Then, towards the turn of the year, came the death of another of the Aldenham Harriers' impressive band of leaders, a man who had, over the years, given unstinting support and assistance with endless enthusiasm and good humour to keep the hunt going; Pat Burgin had been ill for some time and died in December 2001. The Aldenham Harriers had lost another of its stalwarts, another who had steered it through some difficult years. The funeral was a private affair, but there was a well attended Memorial Service at St George's School Chapel in Harpenden on 8th February 2002 conducted by the school chaplain, Rev. John Green who is now the Priest-in-Charge of St Leonard's, Flamstead. Pat had been educated at St George's, as indeed had his four sisters. He had started there when aged eight in 1927 and eventually became head boy. He never forgot his old school and both he and his father before him were benefactors. Pat became a Governor in 1967 and remained so for thirty five years, being Chairman of the Board of Governors for twenty nine of them. A testimony to the effectiveness of his leadership and enthusiasm is the magnificent Burgin Technology Centre.

As the season progressed there were further unexpected developments. Ian Pearse, who a year earlier had seemed set for a long and innovative Mastership, announced that he was giving up farming in Flamstead and would move to the West Country to take up an appointment as Master of the South Devon Hunt. Val Barr announced that she would be relinquishing her Joint Mastership at the end of the season too. Both have done great work for the Aldenham Harriers and will be sorely missed. Here was a big gap in the leadership needing to be filled and it was feared that much continuity and expertise would be lost especially as Graham Hughes, the kennel huntsman, had left at the end of the previous season. However, all was not lost; Mary Arikoglu, already with six years experience as a joint master under her belt, agreed to carry on, while Jeremy Quin, a Past Master of the South Herts Beagles, and Andrew Love, Chairman of the Hunt Committee, agreed to join her and were duly appointed by the trustees. We heard of Andrew earlier, but Jeremy is new to the Aldenham scene and needs an introduction. Much of his background has been in beagling; his family connection with hunting hare going back over a hundred years to the Berkhamsted Foot Beagles. He became Joint Master of the South Herts Beagles in 1994, a post from which his father had retired five years earlier. Jeremy retired last year, latterly combining Saturday beagling and mid-week mounted hunting with the Bicester Hunt and the Whaddon Chase. Having at one time been President of the Oxford Union he nurtures a smouldering political ambition, fighting the Snowdonia constituency in the 1997 General Election (unsuccessfully). The kennel huntsman vacancy was advertised and filled, temporarily, by a locum. After a number of applicants had been interviewed Adrian Robinson, who last season was 1st whipper-in to the Thurlow and before that served for six years as huntsman to the Airedale Beagles, was taken on to succeed Graham Hughes from 1st May 2002. All of these changes, hopefully, to be achieved 'without any sign of the join' so that the enviable reputation of the Aldenham Harriers can remain constant.

As if all of that were not enough, there remained throughout this addendum period the threat of a ban on hunting with dogs. The Labour Government was committed to a bill and when it was eventually presented to Parliament early in 2002 it was passed, on a free vote, by an overwhelming majority. By the natural order of things it was duly presented to the Upper House who, as expected, threw it out. So hunting is still legal, but the Government is determined to have its bill and it is feared that it will invoke the Parliament Act and overrule the House of Lords. This procedure is, however, regarded by all sides as an extreme measure which should be reserved for major issues and there are those who feel that further reform of the House of Lords itself would be preferable, so that a replacement assembly would favour the bill. Arguments for and against this procedure continue and some think that a compromise may yet be possible. Indeed some think that to declare the hare an endangered species would be a greater threat. In any case, the redoubtable Bill Corby who fights a running campaign on behalf of country pursuits from deepest Little Gaddesden, thinks that he detects a 'softening' in the attitude of the ranks of the Labour Party who fear that they may be alienating a sizeable portion of the electorate and are starting to think about the next general election, so all may yet not be lost.

Indeed it is fair to say that there is not really an air of despondency within the followers of the Aldenham Harriers, rather the opposite; there is an air of optimism, a feeling that all will be well in the end. They have good reason to be optimistic. They have come through 124 years of continuous hunting, many of them difficult years and although they have never before had to face the full force of the Government of the day, there is a feeling that somehow they will win through. I for one wish them luck. I have seen and heard nothing in my time interviewing and researching this narrative that leads me to suppose that it would be right to persecute them. They are honourable ordinary people with a deep love of animals and the countryside and my considered, and I hope unbiased opinion, in spite of anything that might be read into what I have said before, is that they should be left alone.

ACKNOWLEDGEMENTS

This book was not initiated on my own inspiration; it was the brainchild of the Aldenham Harriers Committee and it was they, or rather Ian Pearse on their behalf, who contacted me in January 2000 and invited me to take the project on. I accepted, without needing any persuading, which surprised one or two who had been expecting a long and tedious search to find somebody prepared to take it on. On the other hand this is in no way an official history; I have had a completely free hand in how I approached the subject. Then comes the clever bit; the committee elected Val Barr to act as liaison officer to facilitate the collection of material from the membership and others. This proved to be a very happy arrangement and I would like firstly to put on record my sincere debt of gratitude to Val for her enthusiasm to see the project through and for her efforts as a go-between. The ploy was for Val to make the arrangements for an interview and during it to keep the conversation going with provocative questions while I made my notes. It worked splendidly and most of those interviewed enjoyed participating in the project. It brought to the fore recollections of hunting experiences that they did not realise they had tucked away in their memories. The prime object of this book is as a vehicle for putting on record the mass of new material that these talks produced. I am also indebted to Val for being one of the proof readers.

Another 'prime mover' has been Derek Christopher, a man full of enthusiasm for anything to do with horses and hunting, a retired Master with a lifetime of memories of joyous days in the field which he gladly passed to me, being keen to see them recorded. He has also allowed access to his very considerable archive, accumulated during his long years as secretary. His wife, Joyce, has also helped by mentioning a number of things Derek had forgotten (the ladies are good at that sort of thing). Lord Aldenham has provided Gibbs family detail and corrected some of the secondary source detail relating to the dawn of the Aldenham Harriers. Julian Watson, whose grandfather was William Walker from High Canons, provided photographs and other material from the early days.

As mentioned elsewhere, Elizabeth Ansell is a talented artist and I must express particular thanks to her for allowing the use of a number of examples of her work here. The very 'atmospheric' dust jacket is hers and so are the pen and ink sketches.

Val Barr, Ian Pearse and Graham Hughes provided much of the up-to-the-minute information about the hunt, and hounds, and kennels, as only they could and Mary Arikoglu, in addition to providing her own memories, produced three of Stanley White's photograph albums kindly lent by Stanley's nephew, Trevor White, which were a great help.

As might be expected, a good number of other people were extremely helpful in providing memories, detail, photographs and press cuttings etc. I hesitate to mention individuals for fear of giving offence by leaving others out, but I would like to express particular thanks in this respect to Mary Allen, who does a very good lunch at her farm at Chipping Norton, to Elizabeth Ansell, Joan Cunningham, Valerie Dickinson, Peter Flawn, Basil Hall, Gillian Haworth, Rita Huxley, Fiona Kinlock, Rachel Meers, Tony Roberts, Wendy Sturmey and Pat Turner. It is quite remarkable how, between us, we have managed to make so much out of the relatively short history of a local pack of hounds.

Extensive reference has been made over the past two years to the treasures housed in the British Library Newspaper Library at Colindale and the Hertfordshire Archives and Local Studies Department at Hertford. The staff at both have, as ever, been helpful and welcoming and I would like to place on record my gratitude for their assistance.

Finally I must mention my good friend Arthur Addington who, in spite of having absolutely no interest in the subject matter, has listened to me going on about it over endless pints of beer (not all at once!) over the past three years, and has helped plan and criticised, researched, chauffered and proof read to a greater extent than it would have been reasonable to ask. Thank you.

APPENDIX I

MASTERS OF HOUNDS

1878-1881	G.L.M.Gibbs
1881-1885	H.C.Gibbs
1885-1890	L.E.Rickards
1890-1897	Hon. C.R.G.W.Bampfylde
1897-1899	Hon.C.R.G.W.Bampfylde & H.Bailey
1899-1901	H.Bailey
1901-1906	H.S.Bailey
1906-1907	F.C.Swindell
1907-1910	K.Walker
1910-1912	B.Ravenscroft
1912-1922	W.Walker
1922-1928	A committee
1928-1934	C.E.Stevenson
1934-1938	C.E.Stevenson & Mrs E.Hall
1938-1940	Major Sir Jocelyn Lucas
1940-1941	Major Sir Jocelyn Lucas & Miss A.Handley Page
1941-1942	Major Sir Jocelyn Lucas & E.J.M.Jones
1942-1943	E.J.M.Jones
1943-1946	E.J.M.Jones & E.W.Taylor (Stanley?)
1946-1947	A committee
1947-1952	G.H.Hartop & S.White
1952-1956	G.H.Hartop & Lady Farrer
1956-1958	G.H.Hartop
1958-1962	Hon. Mrs Lyell & Mr Lyell
1962-1963	Lady Lyell & Sir Maurice Lyell
1963-1967	Lady Lyell, Sir Maurice Lyell & B.Hall

1967-1975	Lady Lyell & Sir Maurice Lyell
1975-1980	Lady Lyell & B.Hall
1980-1981	Lady Lyell, P.Burgin & B.Hall
1981-1983	Lady Lyell & P.Burgin
1983-1984	P.Burgin, D.J.Christopher & C.Todd
1984-1986	P.Burgin & D.J.Christopher
1986-1992	P.Burgin, D.J.Christopher & J.P.Daulis
1992-1993	P.Burgin, D.J.Christopher, J.P.Daulis & Lady Aldenham
1993-1996	P.Burgin, D.J.Christopher, Lady Aldenham & A.Roberts
1996-1998	Lady Aldenham, A.Roberts, Mrs A.Arikoglu & J.P.Daulis
1998-1999	Lady Aldenham, A.Roberts, Mrs A.Arikoglu & I.Pearse.
1999-2000	Mrs A.Arikoglu, A.Roberts, I.Pearse & Mrs W.Barr
2000-2002	Mrs A.Arikoglu, I Pearse & Mrs W.Barr

APPENDIX II

KENNEL HUNTSMEN

1890-1897	….. Webb
1901-1905	Will Turk
1910-1912	David Sheppard
1912-1914	H.F.Reynolds
1914-1947	Patrick James (Rick) Fenn
1947-1958	Ben Wilkinson
1958-1965	Harry Smith
1966-1980	George Garfoot
1980-2001	Graham Hughes

APPENDIX III

SECRETARIES

1920-1921	H.S.Bailey
1922-1930	Mr Whitehead
1930-1938	Stovin Bradford
1938-1945	Mrs Duncan
1945-1952	John Hodgson
1952-1958	Reggie Streather
1958-1965	Reggie Streather & Audrey Chambers
1965-1966	Derek Christopher & Audrey Chambers
1966-1984	Derek Christopher
1984-1994	Rachel Meers
1994-1999	Anne Hawkins
1999-	Amanda Bishop

APPENDIX IV

RECENT HARE SURVEY STATISTICS

1999

15Sep	Kennels	Flamstead	Arable	10 seen	0 killed	Early morning
18Sep	Kennels	Flamstead	Arable	6	2	Early morning
22Sep	Valley Bottom	Markyate	Arable/grass	15	1	Early morning
25Sep	Bridens Camp	Gaddesden Row	Arable	22	2	Early morning
6Oct	West End	Wheathampstead	Arable	30	2	Early morning
1 Oct	Corner Farm	Kensworth	Arable/grass	12	2	Early morning
20Oct	Jockey End	Studham	Arable	20	1	Early morning
30Oct	Trowley Bottom	Flamstead	Arable/grass	12	1	
3Nov	Brocket Arms	Ayot StLawrence	Arable	17	3	
6Nov	Ashley Green	Berkhamsted	Arable/grass	18	2	
10Nov	Highdown Farm	Pirton	Arable	8	2	
13Nov	West End Farm	Harpenden	Arable	10	2	
17Nov	Offley Grange	Offley	Arable	18	3	
20Nov	Flamstead House	Flamstead	Arable	18	2	Granta Harriers ovisited
24Nov		Aldbury	Arable/grass	12	2	National Trust licence
28Nov		Bramfield	Arable	20	2	
1Dec		Sundon	Arable	0	0	Luton walkers disturbed hares
4Dec	Holwell Manor	Sherborne	Grass	10	0	Visiting BS Vale
8Dec	Lilley Manor	Lilley	Arable	18	3	
11Dec		Chesterford	Arable	15	4	Joint with Granta

Date	Place	Location	Type	Seen	Killed	Notes
15Dec	Kennels	Flamstead	Arable	11 seen	2 killed	
18Nov	Brocket Arms	Ayot St Lawrence	Arable	16	3	
22Dec	Church End Farm	Kensworth	Arable	12	3	
27Dec	Cheverells Green	Markyate	Arable/grass	14	2	
30Dec	Bury Farm	Tilsworth Arable		7	0	

2000

Date	Place	Location	Type	Seen	Killed	Notes
1Jan	The Chequers	Gaddesden Row	Arable	16	2	
5Jan	Wards Hurst Farm	Ringshall	Arable/grass	12	3	National Trust licence
8Jan	Puddephats	Flamstead	Arable	9	0	
12Jan	Porters End	Harpenden	Arable	16	0	
15Jan	Ivinghoe Aston Farm	Ivinghoe Aston	Arable/grass	12	0	
19Jan	Bendish Farm	Bendish	Arable	70?	3	Too many to count
22Jan	Staploe	Huntingdon	Arable	12	0	Visiting country
26Jan	Highdown Farm	Pirton	Arable	7	3	
29Jan	Grove Farm	Flamstead	Arable	10	0	
2Feb	New Medbury Farm	Elstow	Arable	20	2	
5Feb	The Raven	Hexton	Arable	15	2	
9Feb	Home Farm	Beechwood	Arable	20	3	
12Feb	Stagenhoe Bottom	Whitwell	Arable	18	0	
14Feb	Blue Gates Farm	Ashwell	Arable	13	0	
16Feb	Dane End Farm	St Albans	Arable	40	2	
19Feb	Hill Farm	Hatfield	Arable	12	2	
23Feb		Longworthe	Arable/grass	20	0	
26Feb	Red Lion	Preston	Arable/grass	25	1	
28Feb	Bright Star	Peters Green	Arable	25	3	
1Mar		Cotton End	Arable	15	3	
4Mar	Lordship Farm	Bennington	Arable	23	1	
8Mar	The Hoo	Whitwell	Arable/grass	28	2	
11Mar	Holtsmere End	Redbourn	Arable	16	1	
18Mar	Brook Farm	Ravensden	Arable/grass	22	1	
13Sep	Kennels	Flamstead	Arable	9	1	
16Sep	Wood End Farm	Flamstead	Arable	8	0	

20Sep	Dane End Farm	St Albans	Arable	6 seen	0 killed	
23Sep	Bibbs Hall Farm	Gustard Wood	Arable	10	2	
28Sep	Hatches Farm	Jockey End	Arable	18	5	
29Sep	Bibbs Hall Farm	Gustard Wood	Arable	15	5	Early morning
30Sep	Bridens Camp	Gaddesden Row	Arable	18	2	
4Oct	Kimpton Hoo	Kimpton	Arable	14	2	
7Oct	Valley Bottom	Flamstead	Arable	4	2	Very wet
11Oct	Hill Farm	Ayot St Lawrence	Arable	12	3	
14Oct	Corner Farm, The Lynch	Kensworth	Arable	8	0	
16Oct	Highdown Farm	Pirton	Arable	8	0	Early morning
18Oct	Highdown Cottages	Pirton	Arable	4	3	
21Oct	Greenhall Farm	Bramfield	Arable	11	8	Very cold
22Oct		Sundon	Arable	0	0	Early morning
23 Oct		Tilsworth	Arable	6	0	Early morning
23Oct	Prae Farm	Gorhambury	Arable	30	2	
27Oct	Gorhambury	St Albans	Arable	25	2	Early morning
28Oct	Trowley Bottom	Flamstead	Arable	12	3	
8Nov		Sundon	Arable	0	0	
15Nov	Offley Grange	Hitchin	Arable	10	2	
18Nov	Grove Farm	Ivinghoe Aston	Arable/grass	5	0	
22Nov	Beaumont Hall	St Albans	Arable	6	1	
25Nov	West End Farm	Wheathampstead	Arable	4	0	
29Nov		Aldbury	Arable/grass	9	0	
2Dec	Defrindle Farm	Haddenham	Arable	5	0	Visiting Granta Harriers
6Dec	Lilley Manor	Lilley	Arable	21	2	
9Dec	Flamstead House	Flamstead	Arable	4	0	
14Dec	Porters End	Wheathampstead	Arable	6	0	
16Dec	Brocket Arms	Ayot St Lawrence	Arable	10	1	Granta Harriers visiting
19Dec	Highdon Cottages	Pirton	Arable	5	1	
23Dec	Church End	Kensworth	Arable	7	1	
26Dec	Cheverells Green	Markyate	Arable	6	0	
30Dec	Bury Farm	Tilsworth	Arable	16	0	On foot - snow/ frost

2001

Date	Place	Location	Type	Seen	Killed
6Jan	Puddephats	Flamstead	Arable	4 seen	0 killed
10Jan	Bendish Farm	Bendish	Arable	24	3
13Jan	Aldersfoot Farm	Aley Green	Arable	9	1
24Jan	Saccombe Hill Farm		Arable	16	2
27Jan	Blue Gates Farm	Ashwell	Arable	40	3
31Jan	Grove Farm	Flamstead	Arable	8	0
3Feb	The Raven	Hexton	Arable	10	2
14Feb	Bennington Park Farm	Bennington	Arable	24	2
17Feb	Hatfield House	Hatfield	Arable	32	2
21Feb	New Medbury Farm	Elstow	Arable	12	3

Activities curtailed for the season because of the severe outbreak of foot and mouth disease.

NOTE: *Gaps appear where there is no record of the detail*

APPENDIX V

RECENT FIELD STATISTICS

		1996/7	1997/8	1998/9	1999/00	2000/1
Oct	Opening meet	43	45	43	52	41
Nov	Wed 1	9	27		20	C-wet
	Sat 1	21	25	ec	15	C-wet
	Wed 2	22	32	11	16	10
	Sat 2	14	24	25	32	C-wet
	Wed 3	23	32	C	15	27
	Sat 3	28	C	38	40	27
	Wed 4	C	9		29	18
	Sat 4	19	36	11	16	20
	Wed 5	C	25	11	8	20
Dec	Sat 1	C	26	4	29	9
	Wed 1	16	C	14	17	18
	Sat 2	27	17		11	40
	Wed 2	21	C	25	13	13
	Sat 3	C	27	20	28	19+9Granta
	Wed 3	14			12	16
	Boxing Day	32	C	35	44	33
	Sat 4	14	C	5	14	25
Jan	Wed 1	C	C	8	6	C-wet
	Sat 1	14	C	4	41	42
	Wed 2	C	C	29	12	20
	Sat 2		15	C	28	20
	Wed 3	15	C	19	C	
	Sat 3	22	C	7	25	C-frost
	Wed 4	12	35	12	18	14

	Sat 4	30	19		17	13
	Wed 5	C	17	17	14	33
Feb	Sat 1	22	12	8	20	17
	Wed 1	19	42		24	C-wet
	Sat 2		25	19	23	C-wet
	Wed 2	20	C	17	27	10
	Sat 3	30	28	20	25	32
	Wed 3	24		22	18	20
	Sat 4	27	25	24	22	
	Wed 4		21	15	16	F&M
Mar	Sat 1	C	22	14	16	F&M
	Wed 1	C	17	13	28	F&M
	Sat 2	42	35	28	26	F&M
	Wed 2		25		34	F&M
	Sat 3				18	F&M
Average		23	26	18	22	23

APPENDIX VI

A REPRESENTATIVE SELECTION OF SEASON'S MEETS

1953/4

31 Oct	Redbourn	Field:	40
4 Nov	Shenley		20
7 Nov	Redbourn		30
12 Nov	Pulmer Water		18
18 Nov	Bowmans Green		15
21 Nov	Oak Farm, St Albans		18
26 Nov	Ivinghoe		18
2 Dec	Potters Crouch		20
5 Dec	Porters End		40
10 Dec	Aldenham		20
16 Dec	Long Acre, Pipers Lane		18
19 Dec	Hatching Green		36
23 Dec	Black Lion, Shenley		24
26 Dec	Redbourn		55
28 Dec	Potten End		28
31 Dec	Puddephats		50
6 Jan	Knebworth		60
9 Jan	Delaport		Lost-frost
14 Jan	Chipperfield		20
20 Jan	Nicholls Farm, Redbourn		24
23 Jan	Coleman Green		24
28 Jan	Ivinghoe		Lost-frost
3 Feb	Delaport		Lost-frost

6 Feb	Redbourn	Field:	Lost-frost
11 Feb	Lilley		Lost-frost
17 Feb	Hatching Green		20
20 Feb	Potten End		40
25 Feb	Delaport		Lost-foot & mouth
3 Mar	Black Lion, Shenley		Lost-flood
6 Mar	Redbourn		Lost-foot & mouth
11 Mar	Pirton		3
17 Mar	Nomansland		30
24 Mar	The Grove, Ivinghoe Aston		30

29 Oct	Trowley Bottom	Field:	48
3 Nov	Redbourn		11
9 Nov	Kensworth		15
2 Nov	Harpenden		50
16 Nov	Ayot St Lawrence		15
19 Nov	Gaddesden Row		26
23 Nov	Caddington		11
30 Nov	Streatley		13
7 Dec	Cross Farm, Harpenden		20
10 Dec	Trowley Bottom		20
14 Dec	Ayot St Lawrence		16
17 Dec	Aldbury		30
22 Dec	Studham		29
31 Dec	Puddephats		83
14 Jan	Haynes		22
21 Jan	Caddington		14
23 Jan	Gaddesden Row		23
25 Jan	Streatley		13
1 Feb	Lilley		13
4 Feb	Ayot St Lawrence		27
6 Feb	Long Acre		41
11 Feb	Redbourn		33
18 Feb	Sharpenhoe		15
22 Feb	Kensworth		19
25 Feb	Puddephats		35
1 Mar	Praewood Farm		15
4 Mar	Harpenden Common		38
8 Mar	Caddington		9
11 Mar	Puddephats		39

29 Oct	Puddephats	Field:	48
2 Nov	Ayot St Lawrence		25
5 Nov	Kensworth Grange		35
9 Nov	Coleman Green		19
12 Nov	Pirton		32
15 Nov	Caddington		6
19 Nov	Kimpton Hall		36
26 Nov	Studham		30
30 Nov	Nomansland		20
3 Dec	Lilley		25
7 Dec	Gaddesden Row		Cancelled-frost
10 Dec	The Hoo, Kimpton		Cancelled-wet
14 Dec	Gaddesden Row		28
17 Dec	Kensworth		32
21 Dec	Cross Farm, Harpenden		17
24 Dec	Zouches Farm, Caddington		20
26 Dec	Redbourn Common		28
30 Dec	The Hoo, Kimpton		29
4 Jan	Puddephats		80
7 Jan	Pirton		19
11 Jan	No meet		
14 Jan	No meet		
8 Jan	Gaddesden Row		22
21 Jan	Gilvers		Cancelled-frost
25 Jan	Zouches Fram, Caddington		Cancelled-snow
28 Jan	Studham		Cancelled-wet
1 Feb	Holwell		19
4 Feb	Coleman Green		25
8 Feb	Bendish		Cancelled-wet
11 Feb	Ayot St Lawrence		52
15 Feb	Offley Grange		Cancelled - wet/fog/ice

18 Feb	Gilvers	Field:	28
22 Feb	King's Walden		21
25 Feb	Studham		Cancelled-wet
29 Feb	Gorhambury		24
3 Mar	Whitehouse		14
7 Mar	Stagenhoe		18
10 Mar	Offley Grange		23
14 Mar	Bendish		21
17 Mar	Upperwood Farm		48

SOURCES

Berry, Michael F.: *The History of the Puckeridge Hunt* (Country Life Ltd 1950)

Billett, Michael: *The History of English Country Sports* (Robert Hale 1994)

Black, J.B.: *The Reign of Elizabeth 1558-1603* (Oxford University Press 1959)

Boswell, Joyce: *The Book of Shenley* (Barracuda Books Ltd 1984)

Brander, Michael: *Portrait of a Hunt - The History of the Puckeridge &*

Newmarket & Thurlow Combined Hunts (Hutchinson Benham 1976)

Cameron, L.C.R: *The Hunting Horn - What to Blow and How to Blow it* (Kohler & Son 1950)

Clingain, Ben: *Hunting Tales* (Maverick 1994)

Country Life

The Daily Telegraph

Edwards, Eric: *Friars Wash Point-to-Point Races* (Flamstead Society 1996)

        "   *A New History of Flamstead* (Flamstead Society 1999)

Fairfax-Blakeborough, J Ed.: *Thirty Years a Hunt Servant - Being the Memories of Jack Molyneux* (Hutchinson & Co 1935)

The Farmer & Stockbreeder

The Field

Gaskell, Ernest: *Hertfordshire Leaders Social & Political* (Queenhithe Printing & Publishing Co Ltd. c1907)

Greaves, Ralph: *A Short History of the Aldenham Harriers* (Reid-Hamilton c1948)

Hands, Rachel: *English Hawking & Hunting in the Boke of St Albans 1486* (Oxford University Press 1975)

Harvey, Tony: *If St Peter Has Hounds - A day with every mounted British pack* (Paul Rackham Ltd 1998)

Hemel Hempstead Gazette

Herts Advertiser

Horse & Hound

Lawrence, Andrew: *The Aldenham House Garden: A Brief History of the School Grounds* (The Haberdashers' Aske's School 1988)

Lucas, Captain Jocelyn MC: *Hunt and Working Terriers* (Chapman & Hall Ltd 1931)

The National Trust Magazine

Page, Robin: *The Hunting Gene* (Bird's Farm Books 2000)

Shooting Times & Country Magazine

Smith, J.T.: *Hertfordshire Houses : Selective Inventory* (Royal Commission on the Historical Monuments of England 1993)

The Spectator

Sport & Country

Stone, Lawrence & Jeanne F.C.: *An Open Elite? England 1540-1880* (Oxford University Press 1984)

The Tatler & Bystander

Walsh, E.G.: *The Poacher's Companion* (The Boydell Press 1984)

Williams, Michael: *The Continuing Story of Point-To-Point Racing* (Pelham Books Ltd 1970)

Woolner, Lionel R.: *The Hunting of the Hare* (J.A.Allen & Co 1971)

INDEX

(illustrations indicated in **bold** type)

Robinson, Adrian, 204
    Mike, 176
Rochetts, Brentwood, 37
Rose & Crown, Tring, The, 155
Roundwood, 111
Rowley Farm, 56
Royal Agricultural Benevolent Institution,
    51
Royal International Horse Show, 168
Royal Observer Corps Post, Brent Pelham,
    87
Royal Windsor Horse Show, 172, **173**, 185
Royston, 47
Runciman, Walter 1ST Viscount Doxford,
    187
Runley Wood, 43
Russell, Mr & Mrs, 171
    W.E, 147
Rycroft, Sir Newton, 188
Ryder, S, 47
Rye Field Farm, 86

St Albans City Hospital, 109, 118
St Albans Town Hall, 23, 60, 68, 73, 77, 82,
    84, 86
St Bartholomew's Priory, 54
St George's School, Harpenden, 156, 203
St John's Ambulance Brigade, 173
St Leonard's Church, Flamstead, 108, 157,
    203
St Paul's Walden, 141
St Paul's Walden Park, 112
St Peter's, St Albans, 46
St Peter's Street, St Albans, 52
St Stephen's Parish Council, 46
Salisbury, Frank, 47
    Lady, 47
Sandown Park, 186
Sandridge, 85, 133
    School, 85
Sandridgebury, 52
    Livery Stables, 152
Saunders, Jill, 134
Scatterdells, 43
Schreiber, Mrs, 39
Scott, Mrs, 51
Seabrook, Mrs
Sealyham, 75, 76, 79
Sebright, Sir John, 47
Sellar, Miss K, 109
Sewell, Harry (Little Harry), **125**, 133, 136,
    151

Shafford, 69
Shand-Kydd, Bill, 123
Sharpenhoe, 127, 132, 177, 182
Shelley, Eric, 109, 131, 133, 140, 145, 190
    Mrs Monica, 29, 109, 117, 125, 127, 131,
        134, 139, 140, 147, **153**
Shendish, 42
Shenley Hill, 72
Shepherd, Kevin, 198
    Mr, 31, 32
Sheppard, Clare, 163
    David, 50
Sherriff, A.J, 89
    Geoffrey, 111, 127
Shillington, 143
Sibley, Charles, 42, 45
    C.F, 38, 47
    J, 51
    Miss, 38
Simons, R.E, 116
Skimpot, 44
Slapton Mill, 87
Slater, T, 47
Slaughter of Animals Act 1933, 115
Slimmon, W, 51
Smith, D, 51
    Dolphin, 38, 45
    Elizabeth Rachel, 57
    Harry (Big Harry), 113-115, 119, 119,
        120, 128
Smith, H.T, 50, 51
    Major, 123
    R, 50
    Robert, **88**
    Roger & Maggie, 174
    Roy, 192
    T, 51
    Terry, 114
    Walter, 57
    Will, 38, 45
Snaith, Mr, 39
Snape, Jim, 139
Social events, 135, 136, 147, 151, 157, 163,
    172, 175, 200
South Hill, Hemel Hempstead, 57
South of England Show, The, 198
Sparrow, G, 75
    L.G, 82, 89, 102
    Mrs, 89
Sporting Lucas Terrier, 76
Sportsmen's Hall, St Albans, 57
Spragg, Mike & Jill, 145
Stags End, **120**, 145, 147, **171**, 183

NB. A number of people have MH or MFH added to their names when, at the time of publication, they were no longer Masters of Hounds and so, strictly speaking, were not entitled to be so distinguished. The reason is that at some stage during this narrative they were Masters and indeed may have been so at the time the reference applies to. It would have been unreasonable either to leave the letters out through uncertainty or to attempt to be correct in all cases - damned if you do and damned if you don't!

Books Published by THE BOOK CASTLE

COUNTRYSIDE CYCLING IN BEDFORDSHIRE, BUCKINGHAMSHIRE AND HERTFORDSHIRE: Mick Payne. Twenty rides on and off-road for all the family.

PUB WALKS FROM COUNTRY STATIONS: Bedfordshire and Hertfordshire: Clive Higgs. Fourteen circular country rambles, each starting and finishing at a railway station and incorporating a pub stop at a mid way point.

PUB WALKS FROM COUNTRY STATIONS: Buckinghamshire and Oxfordshire: Clive Higgs. Circular rambles incorporating pub-stops.

LOCAL WALKS: South Bedfordshire and North Chilterns: Vaughan Basham. Twenty-seven thematic circular walks.

LOCAL WALKS: North and Mid Bedfordshire: Vaughan Basham. Twenty-five thematic circular walks.

FAMILY WALKS: Chilterns South: Nick Moon. Thirty 3 to 5 mile circular walks.

FAMILY WALKS: Chilterns North: Nick Moon. Thirty shorter circular walks.

CHILTERN WALKS: Hertfordshire, Bedfordshire and North Bucks: Nick Moon.

CHILTERN WALKS: Buckinghamshire: Nick Moon.

CHILTERN WALKS: Oxfordshire and West Buckinghamshire: Nick Moon. A trilogy of circular walks, in association with the Chiltern Society. Each volume contains 30 circular walks.

OXFORDSHIRE WALKS: Oxford, the Cotswolds and the Cherwell Valley: Nick Moon.

OXFORDSHIRE WALKS: Oxford, the Downs and the Thames Valley: Nick Moon. Two volumes that complement Chiltern Walks: Oxfordshire, and complete coverage of the county, in association with the Oxford Fieldpaths Society. Thirty circular walks in each.

UNEXPLAINED OXFORD & OXFORDSHIRE: Marilyn Yurdan. The unexplained in all its guises in one of the country's most historic towns and the villages of the rest of the county.

THE D'ARCY DALTON WAY: Nick Moon. Long-distance footpath across the Oxfordshire Cotswolds and Thames Valley, with various circular walk suggestions.

THE CHILTERN WAY: Nick Moon. A guide to the new 133 mile circular Long-Distance Path through Bedfordshire, Buckinghamshire, Hertfordshire and Oxfordshire, as planned by the Chiltern Society.

CHANGES IN OUR LANDSCAPE: Aspects of Bedfordshire, Buckinghamshire and the Chilterns 1947-1992: Eric Meadows. Over 350 photographs from the author's collection spanning nearly 50 years.

JOURNEYS INTO BEDFORDSHIRE: Anthony Mackay. Foreword by The Marquess of Tavistock, Woburn Abbey. A lavish book of over 150 evocative ink drawings.

COCKNEY KID & COUNTRYMEN: Ted Enever. The Second World War remembered by the children of Woburn Sands and Aspley Guise. A six year old boy is evacuated from London's East End to start life in a Buckinghamshire village.

CHANGING FACES, CHANGING PLACES: Post war Bletchley and Woburn Sands 1945-1970: Ted Enever. Evocative memoirs of post-war life on the Beds/Bucks borders, up to the coming of Milton Keynes new town.

BUCKINGHAM AT WAR: Pip Brimson. Stories of courage, humour and pathos as Buckingham people adapt to war.

WINGS OVER WING: The Story of a World War II Bomber Training Unit: Mike Warth. The activities of RAF Wing in Buckinghamshire.

JOURNEYS INTO BUCKINGHAMSHIRE: Anthony Mackay. Superb line drawings plus background text: large format landscape gift book.

BUCKINGHAMSHIRE MURDERS: Len Woodley. Nearly two centuries of nasty crimes.

WINGRAVE: A Rothschild Village in the Vale: Margaret and Ken Morley. Thoroughly researched and copiously illustrated survey of the last 200 years in this lovely village between Aylesbury and Leighton Buzzard.

HISTORIC FIGURES IN THE BUCKINGHAMSHIRE LANDSCAPE: John Houghton. Major personalities and events that have shaped the county's past, including Bletchley Park.

TWICE UPON A TIME: John Houghton. North Bucks short stories loosely based on fact.

SANCTITY AND SCANDAL IN BEDS AND BUCKS: John Houghton. A miscellany of unholy people and events.

MANORS and MAYHEM, PAUPERS and PARSONS: Tales from Four Shires: Beds., Bucks., Herts. and Northants: John Houghton. Little known historical snippets and stories.

THE LAST PATROL: Policemen killed on duty while serving the Thames Valley: Len Woodley.

FOLK: Characters and Events in the History of Bedfordshire and Northamptonshire: Vivienne Evans. Anthology of people of yesteryear - arranged alphabetically by village or town.

JOHN BUNYAN: His Life and Times: Vivienne Evans. Highly praised and readable account.

THE RAILWAY AGE IN BEDFORDSHIRE: Fred Cockman. Classic, illustrated account of early railway history.

A LASTING IMPRESSION: Michael Dundrow. A boyhood evacuee recalls his years in the Chiltern village of Totternhoe near Dunstable.

ELEPHANTS I'LL NEVER FORGET: A Keeper's Life at Whipsnade and London Zoo: John Weatherhead. Experiences, dramatic and sad, from a lifetime with these well-loved giants.

WHIPSNADE MY AFRICA: Lucy Pendar. The inside story of sixty years of this world-renowned institution. Full of history, anecdotes, stories of animals and people.

GLEANINGS REVISITED: Nostalgic Thoughts of a Bedfordshire Farmer's Boy: E.W. O'Dell. His own sketches and early photographs adorn this lively account of rural Bedfordshire in days gone by.

BEDFORDSHIRE'S YESTERYEARS: The Rural Scene: Brenda Fraser-Newstead. Vivid first-hand accounts of country life two or three generations ago.

BEDFORDSHIRE'S YESTERYEARS: Craftsmen and Tradespeople: Brenda Fraser-Newstead. Fascinating recollections over several generations practising many vanishing crafts and trades.

BEDFORDSHIRE'S YESTERYEARS: War Times and Civil Matters: Brenda Fraser-Newstead. Two World Wars, plus transport, law and order, etc.

DUNNO'S ORIGINALS: A facsimile of the rare pre-Victorian history of Dunstable and surrounding villages. New preface and glossary by John Buckledee, Editor of The Dunstable Gazette.

DUNSTABLE DOWN THE AGES: Joan Schneider and Vivienne Evans. Succinct overview of the town's prehistory and history - suitable for all ages.

HISTORIC INNS OF DUNSTABLE: Vivienne Evans. Illustrated booklet, especially featuring ten pubs in the town centre.

EXPLORING HISTORY ALL AROUND: Vivienne Evans. Planned as seven circular car tours, plus background to places of interest en-route in Bedfordshire and parts of Bucks and Herts.

PROUD HERITAGE: A Brief History of Dunstable, 1000-2000AD: Vivienne Evans. Century by century account of the town's rich tradition and key events, many of national significance.

DUNSTABLE WITH THE PRIORY: 1100-1550: Vivienne Evans. Dramatic growth of Henry I's important new town around a major crossroads.

DUNSTABLE IN TRANSITION: 1550-1700: Vivienne Evans. Wealth of original material as the town evolves without the Priory.

DUNSTABLE DECADE: THE EIGHTIES: A Collection of Photographs: Pat Lovering. A souvenir book of nearly 300 pictures of people and events in the 1980's

STREETS AHEAD: An Illustrated Guide to the Origins of Dunstable's Street Names: Richard Walden. Fascinating text and captions to hundreds of photographs, past and present, throughout the town.

DUNSTABLE IN DETAIL: Nigel Benson. A hundred of the town's buildings and features, plus town trail map.

DUNSTAPLELOGIA: Charles Lamborn. Facsimile of a well-respected mid-Victorian town history, with a number of engravings og local buildings.

DUNSTAPLE: A Tale of The Watling Highway: A.W. Mooring. Dramatic novelisation of Dunstable's legend of Dunne the Robber - reprinted after a century out of print.

25 YEARS OF DUNSTABLE: Bruce Turvey. Reissue of this photographic treasure-trove of the town up to the Queen's Silver Jubilee, 1952-77.

DUNSTABLE SCHOOL: 1888-1971: F.M. Bancroft. Short history of one of the town's most influential institutions.

BOURNE and BRED: A Dunstable Boyhood Between the Wars: Colin Bourne. An elegantly written, well illustrated book capturing the spirit of the town over fifty years ago.

OLD HOUGHTON: Pat Lovering. Pictorial record capturing the changing appearances of Houghton Regis over the past 100 years.

ROYAL HOUGHTON: Pat Lovering. Illustrated history of Houghton Regis from the earliest of times to the present.

WERE YOU BEING SERVED?: Remembering 50 Luton Shops of Yesteryear: Bob Norman. Well-illustrated review of the much loved, specialist outlets of a generation or two ago.

A BRAND NEW BRIGHT TOMORROW... A Hatters Promotion Diary: Caroline Dunn. A fans account of Luton Town Football Club during the 2001-2002 season.

GIRLS IN BLUE: Christine Turner. The activities of the famous Luton Girls Choir properly documented over its 41 year period from 1936 to 1977.

THE STOPSLEY BOOK: James Dyer. Definitive, detailed account of this historic area of Luton. 150 rare photographs.

THE STOPSLEY PICTURE BOOK: James Dyer. New material and photographs make an ideal companion to The Stopsley Book.

COMPLETELY HATTERS: An A-Z of Luton Town: Dean Hayes. Major stars and incidents throughout the good days and not so good in the club's history.

PUBS and PINTS: The Story of Luton's Public Houses and Breweries: Stuart Smith. The background to beer in the town, plus hundreds of photographs, old and new.

LUTON AT WAR - VOLUME ONE: As compiled by the Luton News in 1947, a well illustrated thematic account.

LUTON AT WAR - VOLUME TWO: Second part of the book compiled by The Luton News.

THE CHANGING FACE OF LUTON: An Illustrated History: Stephen Bunker, Robin Holgate and Marian Nichols. Luton's development from earliest times to the present busy industrial town. Illustrated in colour and mono.

WHERE THEY BURNT THE TOWN HALL DOWN: Luton, The First World War and the Peace Day Riots, July 1919: Dave Craddock. Detailed analysis of a notorious incident.

THE MEN WHO WORE STRAW HELMETS: Policing Luton, 1840-1974: Tom Madigan. Fine chronicled history, many rare photographs; the author served in the Luton Police for fifty years.

BETWEEN THE HILLS: The Story of Lilley, a Chiltern Village: Roy Pinnock. A priceless piece of our heritage - the rural beauty remains but the customs and way of life described here have largely disappeared.

KENILWORTH SUNSET: A Luton Town Supporter's Journal: Tim Kingston. Frank and funny account of football's ups and downs.

A HATTER GOES MAD!: Kristina Howells. Luton Town footballers, officials and supporters talk to a female fan.

LEGACIES: Tales and Legends of Luton and the North Chilterns: Vic Lea. Mysteries and stories based on fact, including Luton Town Football Club. Many photographs.

THREADS OF TIME: Shela Porter. The life of a remarkable mother and business-woman, spanning the entire century and based in Hitchin and (mainly) Bedford.

HARLINGTON - HEYDAYS & HIGHLIGHTS: Edna L. Wisher. One of Bedfordshire's most historic villages, Harlington's yesteryears are seen through the eyes of one of its most empathetic residents.

FLITWICK: A DAILY TONIC: Keith Virgin. Written as a "Book of Days" containing extracts from the Flitwick Parish Magazine and local newspapers of around 100 years ago.

FARM OF MY CHILDHOOD, 1925-1947: Mary Roberts. An almost vanished lifestyle on a remote farm near Flitwick.

STICKS AND STONES: The Life and Times of a Journeyman Printer in Hertford, Dunstable, Cheltenham and Wolverton: Harry Edwards.

CRIME IN HERTFORDSHIRE Volume 1 Law and Disorder: Simon Walker. Authoritative, detailed survey of the changing legal process over many centuries.

THE LILLEY PICTURE BOOK: Betty Shaw. A picture book depicting village activities during the late nineteenth century and mainly the twentieth century.

JOURNEYS INTO HERTFORDSHIRE: Anthony Mackay. A foreword by The Marquis of Salisbury, Hatfield House. Introducing nearly 200 superbly detailed line drawings.

HAUNTED HERTFORDSHIRE: Nicholas Connell. Ghosts and other mysterious occurrences throughout the county's market towns and countryside.

LEAFING THROUGH LITERATURE: Writers' Lives in Herts and Beds: David Carroll. Illustrated short biographies of many famous authors and their connections with these counties.

A PILGRIMAGE IN HERTFORDSHIRE: H.M. Alderman. Classic, between-the-wars tour round the county, embellished with line drawings.

THE VALE OF THE NIGHTINGALE: Molly Andrews. Several generations of a family, lived against a Harpenden backdrop.

SUGAR MICE AND STICKLEBACKS: Childhood Memories of a Hertfordshire Lad: Harry Edwards. Vivid evocation of gentle pre-war in an archetypal village, Hertingfordbury.

SWANS IN MY KITCHEN: Lis Dorer. Story of a Swan Sanctuary near Hemel Hempstead.

MYSTERIOUS RUINS: The Story of Sopwell, St. Albans: Donald Pelletier. Still one of the town's most atmospheric sites. Sopwell's history is full of fluctuations and interest, mainly as a nunnery associated with St. Albans Abbey.

THE HILL OF THE MARTYR: An Architectural History of St. Albans Abbey: Eileen Roberts. Scholarly and readable chronological narrative history of Hertfordshire and Bedfordshire's famous cathedral. Fully illustrated with photographs and plans.

THE TALL HITCHIN INSPECTOR'S CASEBOOK: A Victorian Crime Novel Based on Fact: Edgar Newman. Worthies of the time encounter more archetypal villains.

HARE & HOUNDS: The Aldenham Harriers: Eric Edwards. Detailed highly illustrated history of a countryside institution.

SPECIALLY FOR CHILDREN

VILLA BELOW THE KNOLLS: A Story of Roman Britain: Michael Dundrow. An exciting adventure for young John in Totternhoe and Dunstable two thousand years ago.

THE RAVENS: One Boy Against the Might of Rome: James Dyer. On the Barton Hills and in the south-east of England as the men of the great fort of Ravensburgh (near Hexton) confront the invaders.

TITLES ACQUIRED BY THE BOOK CASTLE

BEDFORDSHIRE WILDLIFE: B.S. Nau, C.R. Boon, J.P. Knowles for the Bedfordshire Natural History Society. Over 200 illustrations, maps, photographs and tables survey the plants and animals of this varied habitat.

BIRDS OF BEDFORDSHIRE: Paul Trodd and David Kramer. Environments, breeding maps and details of 267 species, with dozens of photographs, illustrations and diagrams.

A BEDFORDSHIRE QUIZ BOOK: Eric G. Meadows. Wide ranging quizzes and picture puzzles on the history, people, places and bygones of the county.

CURIOSITIES OF BEDFORDSHIRE: A County Guide to the Unusual: Pieter and Rita Boogaart. Quirky, well-illustrated survey of little-known features throughout the county.

THE BIRDS OF HERTFORDSHIRE: Tom Gladwin and Bryan Sage. Essays, maps and records for all 297 species, plus illustrations, photographs and other plates.

BUTTERFLIES OF HERTFORDSHIRE: Brian Sawford. History and ecological guide, with colour photographs and maps for nearly 50 species.

WELWYN RAILWAYS: Tom Gladwin, Peter Neville, Douglas White. A history of the Great Northern line from 1850 to 1986, as epitomised by the five mile stretch between Welwyn Garden City and Woolmer Green. Profusely illustrated in colour and black and white - landscape format.

LIFE AND TIMES OF THE GREAT EASTERN RAILWAY (1839-1922): Harry Paar and Adrian Gray. Personalities, accidents, traffic and tales, plus contemporary photographs and old o.s. maps of this charming railway that transformed East Anglia and Hertfordshire between 1839 and 1922.

THE QUACK: Edgar Newman. Imaginative faction featuring characters in a nineteenth-century painting of a busy Hitchin market scene - especially quack doctor William Mansell.

D-DAY TO ARNHEIM - with Hertfordshire's Gunners: Major Robert Kiln. Vivid, personal accounts of the D-Day preparations and drama, and the subsequent Normandy battles, plus photographs and detailed campaign maps.

THE BOOK CASTLE
12 Church Street, Dunstable
Bedfordshire LU5 4RU
Tel: (01582) 605670 Fax (01582) 662431
Email: bc@book-castle.co.uk
Website: www.book-castle.co.uk

HAUNTED HERTFORDSHIRE

by Nicholas Connell and Ruth Stratton

The most extensive collection of the county's ghosts ever written, with over 300 stories. Many are little-known and previously unpublished, having been hidden away in the vaults of Hertfordshire Archives and Local Studies. Others are up to the moment accounts of modern hauntings in the words of those who have experienced them. All supported by dozens of rare and evocative pictures, an outline of the latest theories and diary dates of regular apparition appearances.

Stories feature a feast of phantoms, including grey ladies, dashing cavaliers, spectral transport, headless horsemen and a gallery of Kings and Queens.

Locations include Bishops Stortford, Datchworth, Harpenden, Hertford, Hitchin, Hoddesden, St. Albans, Ware and Watford.

The Book Castle

CRIME IN HERTFORDSHIRE
Volume One
LAW AND DISORDER

by Simon Walker

This volume covers the history of law and order in Hertfordshire from the Anglo Saxon period to the middle of the twentieth century. Criminal law, the courts, the punishments and the means of enforcement have changed over the course of more than a thousand years, and the author traces those changes, illustrated with examples drawn from throughout Hertfordshire. He has included the unusual and the commonplace; from murder to highway robbery and petty the theft. How did claiming of sanctuary actually work? What is the truth about trial by ordeal? What happened to John Doggett who swore, "By God, he shot your dogs" in the 1600's? Take a tour round the prisons and places of confinement in the county; what were conditions like in the dungeons at Bishop's Stortford castle? Meet the "resurrection men", or bodysnatchers, the murderers, thieves, poachers and vagabonds. How was law and order enforced in the past, and how did the police forces of today originate? This book will appeal to students of both the history of crime and punishment and those interested in the history of Hertfordshire as a whole.

JOURNEYS INTO HERTFORDSHIRE

by Anthony Mackay

This collection of nearly 200 ink drawings depicts buildings and landscape of the still predominantly rural county of Hertfordshire. After four years of searching, the author presents his personal choice of memorable images, capturing the delights of a hitherto relatively unfeted part of England.

The area is rich in subtle contrasts - from the steep, wooded slopes of the Chilterns to the wide-open spaces of the north-east and the urban fringes of London in the south. Ancient market towns, an impressive cathedral city and countless small villages are surrounded by an intimate landscape of rolling farmland.

The drawings range widely over all manner of dwellings from stately home to simple cottage and over ecclesiastical buildings from cathedral to parish church. They portray bridges, mills and farmsteads, chalk downs and watery river valleys, busy street scenes and secluded village byways.

The accompanying notes are deliberately concise but serve to entice readers to make their own journeys around this charming county.

CHANGES IN OUR LANDSCAPE
Aspects of Bedfordshire, Buckinghamshire
and the Chilterns 1947-1992

by Eric Meadows

In the post-War years, this once quiet rural backwater between Oxford and Cambridge has undergone growth and change - and the expert camera of Eric Meadows has captured it all...

An enormous variety of landscape, natural and man-made, from yesteryear and today - open downs and rolling farmland, woods and commons, ancient earthworks, lakes and moats, vanished elms. Quarries, nature reserves and landscape gardens. Many building styles - churches of all periods, stately homes and town dwellings, rural pubs, gatehouses and bridges. Secluded villages contrast their timeless lifestyle with the bustle of modern developing towns and their industries.

Distilled from a huge collection of 25,000 photographs, this book offers the author's personal selection of over 350 that best display the area's most attractive features and its notable changes over 50 years. The author's detailed captions and noted complete a valuable local history.